GIFTS AND COMMODITIES

MATERIAL CULTURES
Interdisciplinary studies in the material construction of social worlds

Series Editors:
Daniel Miller, Dept of Anthropology, University College London;
Michael Rowlands, Dept of Anthropology, University College London;
Christopher Tilley, Institute of Archaeology, University College London

MATERIAL CULTURE AND TEXT
The Art of Ambiguity
Christopher Tilley

ARCHAEOLOGICAL THEORY IN EUROPE
The Last Three Decades
Edited by Ian Hodder

EXPERIENCING THE PAST
On the Character of Archaeology
Michael Shanks

THEORY AND PRACTICE IN ARCHAEOLOGY
Ian Hodder

TECHNOLOGICAL CHOICES
Transformation in Material Cultures since the Neolithic
Edited by Pierre Lemonnier

ARCHITECTURE AND ORDER
Approaches to Social Space
Edited by Michael Parker Pearson and Colin Richards

THE SWASTIKA
Constructing the Symbol
Malcolm Quinn

GIFTS AND COMMODITIES

Exchange and Western Capitalism since 1700

James G. Carrier

London and New York

First published 1995
by Routledge
11 New Fetter Lane, London EC4P 4EE

Simultaneously published in the USA and Canada
by Routledge
29 West 35th Street, New York, NY 10001

Typeset in Garamond by
Ponting–Green Publishing Services, Chesham, Bucks
Printed and bound in Great Britain by
TJ Press (Padstow) Ltd, Padstow, Cornwall

British Library Cataloguing in Publication Data
A catalogue record for this book is available from
the British Library

Library of Congress Cataloging in Publication Data
James G. Carrier
Gifts and commmodities: exchange and Western capitalism
since 1700 / James G. Carrier
p.   cm. – (Material cultures)
Includes bibliographical references and index.
1. United States–Commerce–Social aspects–History.
2. Great Britain–Commerce–Social aspects–History.
3. Shopping–Social aspects–United States–History.
4. Shopping–Social aspects–Great Britain–History.
5. Gifts–United States–History.   6. Gifts–Great Britain–
History.   7. Materialism–United States–History.
8. Materialism–Great Britain–History.   I. Title.   II. Series.
HF3021.C32   1995   94–8920
306.3—dc20

ISBN 0–415–11752–6

CONTENTS

PREFACE

In this book I work through an intellectual problem that arose when, in 1987, I returned to the United States after four years in England, followed by eight years in Papua New Guinea.

With the perspective granted by long absence, I was struck by the vast number of *things* Americans had and by the extraordinary amount of time, energy, space and money they devoted to them. Certainly, Americans are not the only people who value objects, but they seemed to do so much more and in different ways than the people in the places where I had lived for almost a third of my life. This is not just another rediscovery of American materialism. It is true that Americans seemed intensely interested in acquiring objects, especially in shopping; but equally I was struck by the interest in giving objects and the almost bizarre mixture of commercialism and sentimentality that went with that giving. This mixture was most striking in Christmas shopping, which was starting earlier and more garishly than I had remembered. I noticed it as well, however, in the more mundane, fabricated ceremonies like Secretary's Day.

Although I did not know it at the time, and certainly did not intend it, my experiences in England and Papua New Guinea made me more sensitive to these aspects of American life. However, and equally fortuitously, my academic work was providing me with the ideas that would help bring the problem into focus. That work was the anthropological study of Ponam Island, a small Papua New Guinea society where I lived in 1979 and which I visited repeatedly over the following seven years when I was teaching at the University of Papua New Guinea. What intrigued me was the way that villagers were involved both with the urban, monetized world of wage labor and commodities, and with the rural round of kinship and ceremonial exchange, as well as the ways that these two parts of their lives affected each other.

This research interest led me to ideas then being developed among anthropologists of Melanesia, of which Papua New Guinea is a part, that drew on the work of the French anthropologist Marcel Mauss. Mauss was especially attractive to Melanesianists for two reasons. He was interested in forms of exchange, a central aspect of Melanesian social life and long a central topic in Melanesian ethnography. Also, Mauss analyzed material from Melanesia itself, especially Bronislaw Malinowski's description, in *Argonauts of the Western Pacific* (1922), of the *kula* system of exchange in what is now the Milne Bay Province of Papua New Guinea. The most important exponent of this new Maussian approach was a political economist, C. A. Gregory, and the most complete statement of his work is his *Gifts and Commodities* (1982). I have borrowed his title for my own book, because it identifies issues I address here, as it identifies the intellectual debt I owe him. Gregory, and others like him, drew heavily on *The Gift*, which Mauss finished in 1925; but what they wrote was not simply a recapitulation of what Mauss had said about social organization and exchange in pre-capitalist societies. Instead, they extended Mauss with a strong mix of Marx, and while I will draw on Mauss and refer to a "Maussian model" in this book, it is important to remember that this is a Marx-ized Mauss.

Although the bulk of *The Gift* analyzes forms of circulation in societies outside of the modern West, Mauss used these analyses to address briefly the same question that concerned Marx, as it concerned so many of the founders of modern social science: how do we identify and understand the features that distinguish modern capitalist society from what went before and what goes on elsewhere? This question has become more subtle as scholars have unpacked the unitary concept of "The West" to reveal its complexities and the ways that it does not differ from other times and places as strikingly as might appear at first glance. Indeed, I pursue that tactic in this book, as I have done elsewhere (e.g. Carrier 1992c). None the less, all these unpackings do not do away with the fact that life in Chicago differs from life in Melanesia or Georgian England. The question of that difference remains intriguing and important.

Those anthropologists who have extended Mauss's model have attempted to address this question by elaborating the truncated part of *The Gift*, the consideration of circulation in industrial capitalist societies and how it differs from circulation elsewhere. The intellectual atmosphere of Paris in the first half of the twentieth century was permeated with Marxian ideas, and Mauss obviously absorbed them, as have those who have elaborated Mauss's basic formulation to produce the Maussian model to which I refer; but while this model parallels Marx in many ways, it is distinct from it as well.

Perhaps the best way to identify the distinction is to say that the Maussian model does not share what Colin Campbell (1987: 7) calls a "productionist bias", a privileging of the sphere of production as the analytical core of social life. As Daniel Miller (1987: 48) notes, for Marx, consumption, distribution and production should form a unified whole, but in practice consumption "becomes merely the logical outcome of the sphere of production, that moment which completes the production cycle", by reproducing labor. For Mauss, on the other hand, the privileged sphere is circulation. To address circulation does not entail just addressing the physical movement of object from person to person. (Though I write of objects here and elsewhere in this book, it is important to remember that other things can circulate as well, such as labor and ideas.) Instead, to address circulation entails addressing the nature of the relationship that links those who transact the object and the nature of the relationship between person and object. Seen in this broad sense, circulation pervades production in a way that production does not pervade circulation, for when production takes place in groups it necessarily involves the transaction of objects and labor among group members.

In addition, the focus on circulation allows us to broaden our conception of capitalism, a term I use throughout this book elliptically, to refer to American and British capitalism. To the degree that we are the heirs of political economy, we will root capitalism in a particular form of production and its social relations. However, as John Kelly (1992: 116) argues in his analysis of firms in Fiji, profit need not be "a surplus value extracted from a process producing new value" in production using wage labor, as modern analysts usually conceive of it. Alternatively, profit may arise, as capitalism may spring, from "a circulation system". Thus, to focus on circulation allows us to see more clearly how there may not be just "capitalism", but varieties of capitalism that people conceive of and enact in their own ways. The capitalist firm, the core of modern Western economy, does not exist independently of the understandings and social arrangements of modern Western society.

Cast broadly, the Maussian model is an over-arching framework that allows us to interrogate and interpret social and cultural practices and beliefs in a range of times and places. While such frames are, from time to time, in bad academic odor, they are necessary both to motivate people to ask scholarly questions and to enable them to construct answers to those questions in the evidence available to them. With the apparent fall from favor of the Marxian framework, the Maussian may be the alternative that is most attractive to those who continue to be interested in economic forms and understandings and who continue to search for a powerful critique of economic life and thought in the West and elsewhere.

Many of the anthropologists concerned with Mauss's model have followed his lead and characterized entire societies in terms of distinctive forms of circulation: societies of the gift and societies of the commodity. However, in my analysis of Ponam society in Papua New Guinea I decided that this was not very revealing. Instead, it seemed to me that the model could be used more fruitfully to consider different parts of a single society and different aspects of people's lives. In other words, like "The West", societies like Ponam need to be unpacked and the different areas of life within them need to be distinguished. In the case of Britain and the United States, this meant distinguishing home life and economic life. However, the more I worked on this book, the more I saw that I misunderstood the complexity and subtlety of this distinction between areas of people's daily round that are more separate in terms of popular conception and analytic framework than they are in practice.

As I explored this Maussian perspective, shopping, Christmas, sentimentality and a high concern with objects began to appear as parts of a single set of issues and relationships closely linked to the capitalist nature of British and American society, issues and relationships that have developed over the past few centuries as capitalism itself emerged and developed. But while these aspects of life were linked to capitalism, they could not be reduced to it. Instead, I could make sense of them only if I saw society as containing a capitalist sphere, a sphere of Maussian commodity exchange, existing together with a non-capitalist sphere, a sphere of Maussian gift exchange, though as I will show, this dichotomy is a simplification of a muddier reality.

This book is the result of my efforts to develop this perspective, to see how useful this dichotomy is, to see how much the basic distinction between gifts and commodities can be applied to British and American society and, by implication, to industrial capitalist societies more generally.

Consequently, I do not advance a novel theory in this book. Mauss's ideas are standard anthropological fare, though perhaps less familiar to sociologists, historians and economists. However, because those ideas are commonly applied to village societies rather than the West, I will be extending and using them in unusual ways. Equally, I do not attempt to test the Maussian model rigorously by the detailed analysis of one or another area of social life. Instead, I use it to sketch a number of divergent areas of life and the connections between them. In the different chapters of this book I touch on the emergence of Christmas and Thanksgiving, the spread of self-service stores, the idea that gifts are voluntary expressions of sentiment, the rise of factory production, the appearance of pre-processed foods, the nature of shopping in supermarkets and much more. Partly this is self-indulgence, the exhilaration that comes with exploring a model to see how many interesting places it leads. However, this strategy also is appropriate. The Maussian model I present appeals to me in large part because of its scope, its ability to point out the significance of and the connections among areas of life that more established models and approaches, and more detailed cultural analyses, often treat as relatively insignificant or unconnected.

In seeing where the Maussian model leads, I have necessarily pursued some issues and ignored others. Selection is obligatory if I am to sketch the main outline and attractions of the model without making even longer a book that is already too long. Two of the things I omit deserve mention.

Perhaps the most glaring is the fact that Britain and the United States have large populations consisting of or descended from migrants from beyond the West. There is no reason to assume that what such people think about objects, people and social relations conforms to standard Western patterns; and in fact, in many cases they do not, as Pnina Werbner (1990), for example, shows in detail in her description of Pakistanis in Manchester. Were I trying in this book to describe Britain and the United States as present-day geographical and social entities, such an omission would be inexcusable. However, I am concerned rather with these countries as embodiments of that place in the imagination, the modern West. Further, I am concerned as much with their historical development as their modern condition, a development in which non-Western immigration is less important than it is today.

The second main omission are the issues of power and inequality. I inject them from time to time and they are implicit in many of my historical sections, but I make no effort to incorporate them systematically. While this is an obvious absence, I doubt it is very serious, given my goal of sketching the Maussian model. People are not equally able to engage in many of the activities I describe, and those activities and the relationships they entail are channels through which power is expressed. If my basic exposition is clear, readers concerned with power and inequality should have little trouble filling in the sketch for themselves in the pertinent ways. Were I to do so, however, it would make this work longer and more complex than it has any right to be.

Any substantial attempt to apply the Maussian model to Western societies requires drawing on a number of different scholarly disciplines, as it touches on the concerns of even more. I have found this requirement congenial because of my own mixed disciplinary background and interests, though anyone who attempts a project of such scope is sure to stumble clumsily from time to time. This book touches on matters that interest economists, social psychologists and even literary critics. It uses extended historical analysis to investigate the applicability of the model to the West. But the project itself springs from the two disciplines in which I have done the most work, sociology and anthropology.

Conventionally, of course, anthropologists have studied societies outside the modern West, while sociologists have claimed the study of modern Western societies. This distinction does not apply as well as it used to. A growing proportion of anthropologists, constrained by decreases in funding and influenced by changing disciplinary fashion, have chosen to study people in the West. This growing change in where anthropologists do their research appears to be leading to a change in the conception that people, both inside and outside the discipline, have of what anthropology is.

As the old subject-matter is disappearing, so is the old intellectual frame that anthropologists used to approach it. The most obvious casualty is the concern to study social units as wholes, the concern to understand how the various aspects of people's lives in a social unit relate to each other. Indeed, the recent concern with the ways that different individuals interpret their lives and worlds has made such a broad, synthetic approach suspect for many

anthropologists. Another casualty is the models and theories that anthropologists had developed to deal with these aspects and their relationships.
Models of kinship, patronage, economics, exchange, religion and the like
formed the discipline's conceptual tool kit, the parts of which seem
increasingly rusty when applied to the modern West. With the abandoning
of these elements anthropology is undergoing a sort of methodological
reduction, as it is stripped down to what one commentator calls the
"anthropological imagination" (Sanders 1993), the method of participant
observation and the concern with local meaning. The thick description of
Clifford Geertz comes to make more sense than the structural-functionalism
of Radcliffe-Brown.

However, while the Geertzian project may be attractive and revealing,
it is limited, and needs to be complemented by the kind of approach I take
in this book. Pierre Bourdieu's strictures about an earlier academic form
of the privileging of local meanings, phenomenology, applies as well to the
more recent variants. Bourdieu argues that the concern with representation
and understanding (or "accounts") is misleading to the degree that analysts
assume that these representations are coterminous with the social world.
He says:

> One is entitled to undertake to give an "account of accounts", so long
> as one does not put forward one's contribution to the science of pre-
> scientific representation of the social world as if it were a science of the
> social world . . . . Only by constructing the objective structures (price
> curves, chances of access to higher education, laws of the matrimonial
> market, etc.) is one able to pose the question of the mechanisms through
> which the relationship is established between the structures and the
> practices or the representations which accompany them, instead of
> treating these "thought objects" as "reasons" or "motives" and making
> them the determining cause of the practices.
>
> (Bourdieu 1977: 21)

An analogous change seems to have happened to sociology. While that
discipline retains the modern West as its subject-matter, it too has experienced
a methodological reduction. If participant observation and a concern with
meaning are becoming the defining features of anthropology, statistical
analysis has become the defining feature of the sociology that is embodied in
many of the core journals. Statistical and computer skills become more and
more central to graduate education and, at least in the United States, the
General Social Survey becomes the source for more and more graduate
research. Partly, I suspect, this is one consequence of the growth of sociology
around the decade of the 1960s. With that growth came fragmentation, and
sociologists increasingly found it difficult to agree on substantive criteria for
evaluating one another's work. All that was left were methodological criteria.
Whatever the cause, the change has meant abandoning sociology's own

holistic approach, the interest in understanding systems as wholes that motivated the functionalism of the 1940s and 1950s and the Marxism of the 1960s and 1970s. It has also meant abandoning the old question that animated social thinkers through the early decades of the twentieth century: what is the nature of the modern West and how did it emerge?

This book, then, bridges the disciplines of anthropology and sociology, but not in their reduced forms. From both disciplines I take a holistic approach, for I am interested in the relationships that pervade a number of areas in people's lives, as I am interested in the general nature of a social system. From anthropology I take a substantive topic, the nature of the circulation of things in society, and I take a theoretical model, that of Marcel Mauss. Like a sociologist, I investigate modern Western society, and from sociology I draw the old question about the nature of the modern West. This mixture has a practical consequence. I write assuming that some readers will have little knowledge of anthropology and that others will have little knowledge of sociology. The result is that different parts of this book may be tediously familiar to those knowledgeable about either discipline. Feel free to skim the offending bits.

As well as bridging sociology and anthropology, this book makes use of a third discipline that is increasingly popular in both, history. The result is an interplay among anthropology, the modern West and its history. The anthropological model of gifts and commodities bestows significance on forms of exchange and on people's understandings of objects in their lives. In this book I try to trace changes in those forms and understandings in British and American history since the beginning of the eighteenth century, and before. My purpose is not, however, just to use anthropology to define interesting areas of history and, I hope, tell an interesting historical tale. In addition, that tale has a use of its own, one that resembles the anthropologist's fieldwork in exotic places. It allows us to see how things have been different, and so allows us to begin to see the significance of practices and beliefs that, for natives of the modern West, are likely to be seen as trivially self-evident.

Furthermore, the changes that this history reveals and the questions that emerge from it allow us to reconsider the anthropology that I invoke. Although the Maussian model, and anthropological models of exchange more generally, have been applied primarily to small societies outside the West, they are shaped by tacit assumptions about the West, to which those small societies are opposed. Primary among these assumptions is the common rendering of the West as a land of economic rationality and autonomous individuals, the world of the commodity relationship. By a demonstration of the limitations of this common rendering, it is possible to begin to discern its effects on anthropologists, and so begin to construct better anthropological models of both the West and non-Western societies.

History, anthropology and sociology are bound together in this book, the goal of which is to help us understand better how people in the West live their economic lives – not the lives defined by formal economics or dominant public rhetoric, but the lives that people constitute through exchange.

Editorial note: Because I take punctuation marks literally, I prefer not to insert punctuation at the end of a quotation (in the American style) if it is not there in the original. Equally, I avoid beginning a quote with a capital letter if it is not there in the original.

ACKNOWLEDGMENTS

In writing this book about social relations and obligations I have accumulated many debts and a compulsion to acknowledge them. My main inspiration came from my research and residence of eight years in Papua New Guinea, where things, giving and getting mean something different from what they do where I live now. My understanding of Papua New Guinean societies was made much easier because of the help of my wife, Achsah Carrier, whose own doctoral research in anthropology led us to Papua New Guinea in the first place and touched on many of the issues addressed in this book. Her continual personal and professional interest have helped to ensure that this book is better than it otherwise would have been. I also owe familial thanks to Stephan Carrier, my brother, who brought his experience of a career in business, as well as a continuing interest in my varying intellectual foibles, to bear with encouragement, many helpful comments and a close, critical reading of this work.

When I was mulling over the ideas that underlie this book Murray Milner, the head of the sociology department at the University of Virginia, encouraged me to mount a course dealing with this topic. Teaching it obliged me to try to present systematically and coherently what had previously been a mush of notions. The students who took that course tolerated my efforts and my peculiar fascination with history with good grace, for which I thank them. I thank them as well for their unknowing encouragement when they told of their own attempts to cope with the distinction between commodities and gifts.

Earlier versions of portions of this book benefited from the sympathy and encouragement of a number of other people. Chris Crocker, Deborah Gewertz, Burke Grandjean, Harriet Guest, Rosemary Harris, Eric Hirsch, Gianfranco Poggi and Viviana Zelizer read different parts of this book over the years that I was working on it, and I want to thank them for their helpful comments.

There are others who deserve special thanks for their special help. David Cheal not only gave me access to some of his unpublished work, he also obliged me to consider anew an issue that is central to this book, the degree to which one can apply the classic anthropological conception of gifts to modern industrial society. Russell Belk read the manuscript closely and provided many interesting and useful suggestions. To my delight, C. A. Gregory was enthusiastic about the theme of this work and very politely critical of the mistakes I made in describing his own work and that of Marcel Mauss, about which he knows far more than I. Jonathan Parry, another Maussian scholar whose influence pervades this book, listened to me try, at length, to explain the arguments I develop in the second half of this book and obliged me to think more carefully about what I wanted to say. He also read and commented on papers that form the core of Chapters 2 and 3. Tim Ingold read and commented on papers that form the core of Chapters 2 and 6. Daniel Miller helped this project in two ways. First, he encouraged me to write the paper that became Chapter 8, and so set off the final push to finish the manuscript. Second, he read and commented on the entire manuscript, which he had encouraged me to submit to the series he edits, and in which it appears.

Like many, this book is the result of an intellectual project. Not all projects succeed, and they are particularly fragile in their early stages. When they are new, even minor expressions of interest and encouragement have a disproportionate effect, for without them doubt can set in and the project die. Because they took this fledgling project seriously at its most incoherent but fragile stage, I owe a debt of gratitude to Theodore Caplow, Thomas Guterbock, Paul Kingston and Steve Nock. They did not make this book, but with their encouragement to a new and uncertain colleague they helped it to grow.

Portions of this book contain material I have written that has been published elsewhere. Chapter 1 contains material from "Gifts, Commodities and Social Relations: A Maussian View of Exchange", *Sociological Forum* 6 (1991): 119–36, copyright by Plenum Publishing Co. Ltd.; Chapter 2 contains material from "Emerging Alienation in Production: A Maussian History", *Man* 27 (1992): 539–58, copyright by the Royal Anthropological Institute; Chapter 3 contains material from "Alienating Objects: The Emergence of Alienation in Retail Trade", *Man* 29 (1994): 359–80, copyright by the Royal Anthropological Institute; Chapter 5, particularly the section "Appropriation in Shopping", contains material from "Reconciling Commodities and Personal Relations in Industrial Society", *Theory and Society* 19 (1990): 579–98, copyright by Kluwer Academic Publishers; Chapter 6 contains material from "The Symbolism of Possession in Commodity Advertising", *Man* 25 (1990): 190–207, copyright by the Royal Anthropological Institute; Chapter 7 contains material from "Gifts in a World of Commodities: The Ideology of the Perfect Gift in American Society", *Social Analysis* 29 (1990): 19–37, copyright by the Department of Anthropology of the University of Adelaide; and Chapter 8 contains material from "The Rituals of Christmas Giving", pp. 55–74 in Daniel Miller (ed.), *Unwrapping Christmas* (1993), published by Oxford University Press, copyright by James G. Carrier.

I acknowledge permission granted by the copyright holders to reproduce this material, and I note that this permission does not extend to permission to reprint these passages elsewhere.

INTRODUCTION
Approaching Objects

How are we to approach the relationship between people and objects in industrial societies? Only those with a *naïveté* bordering on the perverse would argue that the relationship is just one of utility, just one of satisfying the material needs of human beings. Humans do have material needs, and objects can satisfy them; but to reduce what we do with objects to no more than this means that we would be unable to distinguish the gourmet's dinner from "solitary feeding, where the person wolfs or bolts his food, probably standing by his refrigerator in his overcoat" (Douglas and Isherwood 1978: 66–7).

Clearly there is much more in our relationship to objects than sheer utility, as is made plain by the tremendous attention and resources that people individually and societies collectively devote to objects in the West. However, for a long time sociologists have attended to objects really only as an aspect of production. They have lost interest once the production process is complete, once things leave the factory and enter the warehouse or store. Part of the reason for this may be that sociologists share with many Westerners a cultural tendency to see certain areas of life rather than others as being serious, significant, worthy of attention. These are the areas that our culture defines as public and male: government, industry, science. The devalued areas of life, the areas not worthy of serious attention, are private and female (see, e.g., Anderson, M. L. 1988: 16–21). Objects, and particularly consumer goods, begin to enter more private and female realms once they are produced. They enter stores. People shop for them. People take them to what may be the most private and female realm there is, home.

This lack of interest in people's relationship with objects has not been absolute. Instead, there has been a growing interest in the study of what is called "consumption" in the social sciences. While "consumption" is a handy term, it is applied to a broad, heterogeneous range of activities and relations with objects, which rarely have to do with consumption in the normal sense, including looking at advertisements, shopping, displaying objects in social settings, transacting them with other people and even disposing of them (this breadth is illustrated in Orlove and Rutz 1989 and Warde 1990; Silverstone,

1

Hirsch and Morley 1992 provide a useful unpacking of the term). The result is that the term carries little more than a negative definition, "not production". Consumption would seem to be a relatively private or domestic matter, at least compared to production. However, the vast majority of the work on consumption reflects the common sociological concern with the more public and serious side of life, for it looks at consumption in terms of public structures. This is apparent in the two main sociological approaches to objects: as markers in a status hierarchy and as elements in a semiological system.[1] I want to describe these two approaches, spending more time on the latter, as it is the more recent, the more active and the less well known of the two.

OBJECTS AND STATUS

The idea that objects mark status is not new. For example, Max Weber invoked it when he said that "differentiation by status goes hand in hand with a monopolisation of ideal and material goods or opportunities", so that "'status groups' are stratified according to the principles of their consumption of goods as represented by special 'styles of life'" (Weber, M. 1946: 190, 193). From Weber's perspective, then, different objects are associated with different status groups. The corollary is that objects signify status identity and so constitute a claim to status-group membership on the part of those who have them.

Thorstein Veblen's notion of conspicuous consumption is probably the most familiar example of treating objects as status markers. He asserts that the use of objects to signify social rank is basic, so basic that it underlies the very institution of ownership.

> Ownership began and grew into a human institution on grounds unrelated to the subsistence minimum. The dominant incentive was from the outset the invidious distinction attaching to wealth, and . . . no other motive has usurped the primacy at any later stage of development.
> (Veblen 1927: 26)

Thus, we cannot understand how people think about objects unless we attend to the ways that having an object bestows distinction upon the owner. Here Veblen and Weber differ on the link between wealth and status. Veblen (1927: 87) stresses the link, the importance for status of the "unremitting demonstration of the ability to pay". In contrast, Weber (1946: 187) distinguishes wealth and status identity. He says status "normally stands in sharp distinction to the pretensions of sheer property", though in the long run status and class tend to march together.

Veblen also differs from Weber when he introduces a distinctly historical, if somewhat conjectural, dimension to the relationship between people and objects. He argues that objects are more important as status markers in mass societies than in smaller ones. In smaller societies people are more likely to know of each other. Consequently, those who are able to distinguish themselves by their conspicuous leisure can do so, confident that they will become known and esteemed accordingly. However, in more anonymous societies, conspicuous leisure is not so good a way to proclaim one's status. This is because

> [t]he means of communication and the mobility of the population now expose the individual to the observation of many persons who have no other means of judging of his reputability than the display of goods . . . which he is able to make while he is under their direct observation.
>
> (Veblen 1927: 86)

It is with the growth of mass society, then, that objects come into their own as status markers. Veblen's point is illustrated by Michael Young and Peter Willmott in their study of people moving from Bethnal Green, an established working-class area in East London, to a new suburban area, Greenleigh, around 1960. They observed that those who made the move ended up being more concerned with each other's material possessions than those who stayed behind. Though they do not invoke Veblen by name, they echo him:

> When nearly everyone is a stranger, there is no means of uncovering personality. People cannot be judged by their personal characteristics . . . . Judgment must therefore rest on the trappings of the man himself. If people have nothing else to go by, they judge from his appearance.
>
> (Young and Willmott 1986: 134)

Veblen's idea that objects are claims, are status markers, has been applied to an historical study of consumer behavior in England during the Industrial Revolution by the economic historian Neil McKendrick. McKendrick argues that the Industrial Revolution was caused in part by a consumer boom, and while he describes a number of causes and conditions necessary for that boom, some fit Veblen's view of objects. He says that the strata that existed in English society were not radically distinct from each other, a lack of distinction that Veblen said was likely in mass societies. In the widely quoted words of an economist of the time, "[i]n England the several ranks of men slide into each other almost imperceptibly" (McKendrick, Brewer and Plumb 1982: 11). This made it easier to emulate those of a higher rank and so insinuate oneself among them. McKendrick describes not only the widespread desire to emulate one's betters, but also the widespread fear that those from the ranks below were threatening to move up, at least in their level of consumption. This fear led superiors to increase their own levels of consumption to maintain their distinction from their inferiors. This was a time of regular complaint that servants aped their masters, that their masters aped the gentry and that the gentry aped the nobility (McKendrick, Brewer and Plumb 1982: ch. 2).

McKendrick's study illustrates the argument that people think of objects as status markers. For him, as for Veblen and Weber, objects are important because of their social identity, because they are associated with different sets of people in society. Further, for McKendrick and Veblen, though less so for Weber (see Weber, M. 1946: 189), these sets of people are arrayed in a relatively uniform hierarchy defined by wealth. In having objects with certain sorts of identity, people define and proclaim their position in society, a fact that was recognized formally in the English sumptuary legislation that restricted certain sorts of objects, especially clothing, to different ranks of people (Baldwin, F. 1926; Hooper 1915).

OBJECTS AS SIGNS

As it has been developed and used, the idea that objects are status markers refers to a gross social phenomenon: there are identifiable social groups and objects associated with them, and people select objects that are appropriate to their social position or aspirations. Other writers have used a somewhat different approach to the same issue, concerning themselves with the way that objects are part of a more complex set of meanings and are implicated in a more complex process of self-identification in a universe of signs. Discussions of this are found in somewhat different forms and with somewhat different moral evaluations in the work of Hegel, Marx and Simmel (see Miller, D. 1987). What is of concern here is the ways that people identify themselves in terms of the objects around them and the ways that these objects bear cultural meanings that are more varied than what Weber and Veblen describe.

Most of the modern work using this approach is concerned with those cultural meanings and reflects, in one way or another, the semiological model presented in Roland Barthes's *Mythologies*. Although Barthes's model is a general one, it is appropriate to illustrate it here by advertising. Most advertisements are not neutral descriptions of a product. Instead, they juxtapose the product and an object, event or person that carries a particular cultural meaning, such as sexuality, athletic prowess, domesticity, wealth or whatever (this is described and illustrated in Leiss, Kline and Jhally 1986). The person who views the advertisement is likely to endow the product with the meaning of that with which it is associated. The product then becomes a metaphor for the cultural meaning. In semiological terms, the signifier (the product) takes on the meaning of the signified (the attributes represented by the object, event or person) and so becomes a sign (the meaningful product). In this way the advertised commodity becomes a commodity-sign. (It should be clear that objects have some sign properties for Weber and Veblen as well.)

Jean Baudrillard has extended this semiological approach in *For a Critique of the Political Economy of the Sign* (1981) by combining it with elements of Marx, Veblen and Lévi-Strauss's (1969b) model of totemism. He argues that one key way people think of objects is in terms of what he calls "sign value".

This meaning of the object-as-sign springs from the way that it stands in relation to other signs in a system of differentiated and opposed signs. In other words, objects exist primarily as elements in relations between objects. As Baudrillard (1981: 75) puts it, their meaning "is to be found . . . in difference, systematizable in terms of a code". But sign value cannot be understood only in terms of the scheme of relations between objects. A second scheme is involved as well, that of social positions and differences between social positions. Objects acquire a social meaning, then, based on their position in a public code that relates objects and differences between objects to social positions and differences between social positions. Thus, in having objects, people assert distinctions between themselves and other people, people who own and display other objects, so that objects are to be seen as part of "the social tactic of individuals and groups, and the living element of their aspirations" (1981: 36, emphasis omitted).

Baudrillard thus describes a relationship between the structure of the meaning of objects and the structure of society. Pierre Bourdieu (1984) investigates this relationship at length. His concern is "taste" – broadly, the way people interpret and evaluate the range of human productions, which is to say the meanings that things have for people. What he argues is that taste varies markedly in association with a range of social characteristics, especially family background, education and occupation. The structure of meaning reflects the structure of society. To return to the example of advertising, this means that different social groups will create different signs out of the same juxtaposition of signifier and signified; that the same advertisement, for example, will attract some and repel others. This is illustrated by Kathy Myers's report (in Gardner and Sheppard 1989: 52) of a Chanel No. 5 perfume campaign in the early 1970s in Britain. The symbols that the advertisement associated with the perfume – jazz and the avant-garde in the form of "an icily beautiful couple spinning on a blanched dance floor to the accompaniment of electronic twangs" – were reasonably pleasing to higher-strata audiences. However, they were selected in order to repel people in the lower white-collar and upper blue-collar strata, whose growing use of the product was threatening its exclusive aura.

Just as Veblen saw a link between conspicuous consumption and mass society, so many writers see a link between a growth in the perception of objects as signs and the emergence of capitalism. Rosalind Williams's description of changes in retail practices in Paris in the nineteenth century is illustrative. The new ways of selling helped to redefine objects as sign values, not simply as signs of status. Though shop displays did resonate with the status concerns of the Parisian bourgeoisie, they contained a strong element of fantasy and escape. Fantasy features particularly in Williams's discussion of the Bon Marché and the Louvre, department stores that opened in 1852 and 1855. For example, she says (1982: 70–1) the décor used in these stores was intended "to lure people into the store in the first place and then imbue the store's merchandise with glamor, romance, and, therefore, consumer appeal" (the darker side of this allure is described in Katz 1988: ch. 2). To anticipate a point I will develop in later chapters, this display of glamor and romance meant that just walking through the store, alone or in company and without even the intention of buying, was a pleasurable activity. Shopping could be an agreeable leisure pursuit. Williams's explanation of this change in the understanding of objects extends beyond retail practices to encompass production as well. Through the later nineteenth century the mechanization of production meant that the origin of objects became more opaque, and objects themselves became divorced from comprehensible production processes and human activity. They became fetishistically endowed with an independent existence of their own (Williams, R. 1982: esp. 205–7).

Williams's themes of fantasy and evasion recur among those who study modern orientations toward objects. For example, Janice Winship (1983) illustrates these themes clearly in the presentation of commodities in a modern British women's magazine. Stuart Ewen (1976) argues that the fantasy of consumption in the early part of the twentieth century served the important function of diverting the American working class from efforts to unite and exercise control over their work lives. Instead, they were seduced by the essentially individualistic glamor of consumption.

Those who see objects as status markers differ in important ways from those who see objects as signs. However, they have one important thing in common. They use a thoroughly structural orientation, and they identify objects and people only as locations in common public structures of power, meaning and identity.

Because of this orientation, the object exists only as an abstract element of a class of objects of comparable sign or status value. Baudrillard (1981: 132) puts it this way: "Every object is translatable into the general abstract code of equivalence, which is . . . its meaning". Furthermore, it is not just the object that exists only as a type. The person with whom it is associated exists only as a type as well, the type of person who has that type of object. Speaking specifically of advertising, Michael Schudson calls this structural typification "Capitalist Realism". He says that

> the people pictured in magazine ads or television commercials are abstract people . . . . The actor or model does not play a particular person but a social type or demographic category. A television actress, for instance, will be asked to audition for commercials that call for a "twenty-six to thirty-five-year-old P&G housewife." She is not supposed to represent a twenty-six-year-old or a thirty-year-old or a thirty-five-year-old but a "twenty-six–thirty-five-year-old" housewife, the sort likely to buy Procter & Gamble products. The age range . . .

corresponds ... to a presumed social type with predictable consumer patterns. It is a demographic grouping used for market research.

(Schudson 1984: 211–12)

Consequently, the purchasers of such public signs create for themselves a sort of identikit personality, a self constituted of impersonal, prefabricated elements.

While this structural approach helps to make sense of what people buy and how they use objects, it has shortcomings. Objects are not things that spring into existence unbidden or, manna-like, fall out of the sky for us to pick up and parade up and down with in front of some anonymous mass, or even contemplate in isolation. Instead, objects exist concretely in practical relations with concrete individuals. We make objects in the workplace, buy them in the shop and take them home to our families (a similar point is made in Rochberg-Halton 1986: 57–60). The workplace, shop and household, like the people and objects within them, exist in public structures but are not reducible to those structures. These concrete settings and our experiences and personal relationships within them affect our experiences with objects and the ways we understand them. As John Davis (1992: 78) says, those who study meaning "have paid little attention to private or restricted meanings and have concentrated on public ones".

My point is that these studies generally are too abstract to give an adequate picture of people's relationships with objects. They focus too much on types of objects and types of people and fail to relate objects to the distinct and concrete social relationships in which people experience them and the institutions in which those relationships exist. In most cases this is because writers treat objects as bearers of public meaning and private desire, as objects that people have, contemplate and display as they seek to define or comment on themselves and their place in society. These writers do not see objects as really made, bought, given or even used. It is these neglected issues that I address in this book, as I try to situate objects in terms of interpersonal, private structures of social relationship.

In making these points I do not mean that one can neatly distinguish these private and public meanings and experiences. Instead, as I note from time to time in this book, they twine about and shape each other. The ways that people think of and deal with objects in their private lives are shaped by public structures of meaning. This is most obvious in terms of a core public meaning that is rarely addressed explicitly by those concerned with the symbolism of objects, cost. (For a rare treatment of cost in this context, see Dittmar 1992.) Generally, to give an expensive present is to indicate a desire for a close personal relationship, and to accept it is to acquiesce to that desire (see, e.g., Belk and Coon 1993). As John Davis (1992: 6) shows with a simple example, a "gift has meanings which involve class, social mobility, matrimony, patronage, employment, manufacturing processes, issues of style, and of changing rituals or conventions of gift-giving". In their turn, these public structures are regenerated, modified and subverted in part by what people do in their private lives. Moreover, the social worlds of relationship and identity that people create through their private transactions can be public, from the point of view of those involved.

In spite of the difficulty of distinguishing the private and the public realms in this way, however, it is worth while making the effort to do so. This is not just because this distinction is embedded in the thought of many in the modern West. Making the distinction is worth while also in order to counter the predominant scholarly concern with abstract public codes and structures of meaning and identity. It is only after we have paid more attention to mundane, private practices that we will be able to understand the nature and limitations of the public realm, and it is only then that we will be able to understand the nature and degree of integration of the public and the private uses and meanings of objects.

OBJECTS IN PRIVATE STRUCTURES

The use of objects to mediate between individuals differs from the more public use. First, typically the object does not mediate because a person owns or displays it, but because a person transacts or shares it. Second, the significance of the object does not spring from its position in public structures of meaning and identity, but from its existence in a private relationship. This second view of objects has attracted less attention than the first, doubtless because it focuses on private rather than public spheres of life, and most who use this approach are anthropologists concerned with societies outside the modern West rather than sociologists studying the modern West.

The sociological work that comes closest to this second view of objects is research on social exchange (Emerson, R. M. 1976). However, writers in this area commonly take a structural approach. They are concerned with how people exchange primarily in order to describe the structure of the networks that link people with each other and the ways that individuals get different sorts of support through different relationships within their networks (e.g. Granovetter 1973; Wellman and Wortley 1990). On the other hand, the approach to objects that situates them in private structures is concerned not so much with structure as with meaning: how people understand their links to the objects that they transact and how they understand their relationship to the people with whom they transact.

The idea that underlies this approach is simple. When people share or transact objects, their understanding of the object interacts with their understanding of the relationship, strengthening or weakening it, modifying or reproducing people's understandings of each other in their relationship and of the objects involved. The object transacted in the relationship, in other words, takes on a special meaning for the people involved that is over and above, and may even contradict, its meaning as a commodity-sign or even its utility.

This is illustrated in Eric Hirsch's (1992) study of how English families incorporate consumer goods: what they buy, how they use it, what they keep and discard. He shows that people assess the items they buy not simply as commodity-signs, but as things that affect and reflect family relations. The item that, as used, threatens those relations falls into disuse or disrepair, or is discarded. The object that meshes with and facilitates those relations is looked-after and valued, allowed to continue to express, influence and regenerate those relations. Likewise, the sociologist Viviana Zelizer (1989) studied the link between private relations and money, the object commonly thought to have the most corrosive effect on social relations (but see Bloch and Parry 1989). She shows that in the United States in the decades around 1900, both law and opinion shaped the social meaning of money in a way that reduced its effect on household relations. Money was defined as the province of the male head of household; women's access to money was restricted legally and morally. As a result of this distinct identity within the household, money had little corrosive effect on the content of domestic structure. Both Hirsch and Zelizer illustrate what it means to see objects as mediating relations in private structures, for they show how the nature of the relationships and people's understanding of the objects involved interact with each other.

Much of the work on objects in private structures draws on Marcel Mauss's (1990) classic essay, *The Gift*. Mauss deals primarily with exchange practices in what he called "archaic" societies of Melanesia, Polynesia and the Pacific Northwest, as well as India, ancient Rome and Germany. However, his concern was broader than just exchange. Like his teacher and uncle Emile Durkheim, Mauss was interested in the distinction between Western indus-trial societies and pre-industrial societies, which he (1990: 47) saw as stages "in social evolution". Further, Mauss's interest was not restricted to exchange practices and how people understood them, for he saw that these can be understood only when they are related to the corresponding perceptions of people and things.

At one end of Mauss's social scale are societies where transactions are motivated by a mixture of need and social obligation. Here people are indistinct from the groups that define and contain them, just as objects are indistinct from the groups that possess them. Here the object is not a neutral thing but a part of the group itself, carrying and defining the group's being or substance. In such societies, those who transact objects are not independent individuals motivated by autonomous will, but representatives or even embodiments of groups. Likewise, the object transacted is not an entity independent from those who give it. Instead, it bears the identity of the giver, and after it is given it bears as well the identity of the recipient and of the relationship between recipient and giver. At the other end of the scale are societies where transactions are bifurcated into those motivated by need and those motivated by social obligation. Here people and things are individuated and even impersonal. That is, people are seen as having an identity that is distinct from and even opposed to the identity of the groups of which they are a part, and objects are seen as having no substantial relationship with those who own them. Thus, people, objects and society increasingly have come to be seen as independent of each other.

The sequence of forms of exchange that Mauss describes – from archaic societies, through ancient German and Roman society, to modern Western societies – traces the emergence of distinct market transactions and relations. In other words, Mauss describes how "economic relations become increasingly differentiated from other types of social relationship" (Parry 1986: 466). This differentiation does not appear only in the changing ways that people transact. It appears as well in the emergence of divergent cultural understandings of economic and social transactions and relations. People come to see economic transactions as impersonal and rational; they come to see social transactions as personal and affective.

ORGANIZATION OF THE BOOK

In this book, then, I will investigate the ways that objects are implicated in personal relationships, rather than seeing them in terms of mass structures of meaning and identity. I will do so by describing historical changes in people's relationships with objects, as well as the modern state of those relationships. I will pursue this investigation by using the model of people, objects and social relations that springs from the work of Marcel Mauss, a model that has been developed and elaborated by anthropologists concerned primarily with pre-capitalist societies. One of my purposes in this book is to bring out the ways that the Maussian model can be applied to industrial societies.

Mauss's concern was with the different ways that people think of themselves and the objects that they transact with each other in different sorts of social relations. Two key concepts in the Maussian model are "identity" and "alienation" (Chapter 1 is a thorough presentation of this model). A person who is in a relationship of identity with an object or other person shares substance or being with it. With alienation there is no such sharing. (Though I treat these here as exclusive alternatives, in fact they define a continuum of possibilities.) Other key concepts are "possession", "commodity" and "appropriation". "Possession" refers to a relationship of identity between person and object. It refers as well to the object in such a relationship. The opposite of a possession is a commodity, which is alienated, seen as separated from the people associated with it. "Appropriation" refers to the process by which a person establishes a relationship of identity with an object, makes it a possession.[2] People who are in a relationship of identity with each other are in a gift relationship or personal relationship. People who interact with each other but are not in a relationship of identity are in a commodity relationship or impersonal relationship.

In the first chapter, "Gifts and Commodities, People and Things", I lay out the Maussian model that I will apply and illustrate in subsequent chapters. This chapter investigates the distinction between gift relations and commodity relations in terms of three linked variables. The first is the degree to which the transactors are obligated to transact with each other. From the Maussian perspective, and in contrast to much popular and scholarly belief, gift transactions are obligatory: the parties are obligated to give, receive and repay. On the other hand, commodity transactions are voluntary, for relations in the marketplace are free: we may buy and sell as we like and where we like. The second variable is the degree to which the object is linked with the transactors. In gift transactions, the object is linked to the giver, the recipient and the relationship that binds and defines them. In commodity transactions, the object is not linked in any significant, personal way to the transactors: it is an alienable and impersonal property. The third variable is the degree to which transactors are linked and obligated to each other. In gift relations the parties are personally linked and bound to each other. In industrial societies the most obvious form this takes is kinship: parents and children or siblings are inevitably linked to each other in fundamental and enduring ways, and as part of that linkage are obligated to each other in ways that are equally fundamental and enduring. In commodity relations the parties are not linked to each other in any enduring or personal ways. They are linked temporarily in the transaction at hand, but are independent before the transaction and resume their independence afterwards. Consequently, they are under no obligations to each other except while the transaction is in progress, and even then their obligations are restricted to the transaction and do not pervade other areas of their lives.

Although my purpose is to apply the Maussian model to contemporary industrial capitalist societies, my method is largely historical. The historical issue that concerns me is the movement of much production and circulation into distinct realms characterized by commodity relations, and how this has affected the ways that people conceive of, and transact in, gift relations. The core of my historical argument, laid out at length in this book, is that the spread of industrial and commercial capitalism has meant the spread of alienated relations and objects. This spread, however, has not done away with people's need to have their objects be possessions, nor has it abolished the need to transact possessions in personal relationships. Rather, in some ways it has made that need more urgent. At the same time, however, the spread of capitalism has made it more difficult to fulfill that need, for one of its consequences has been that most of the objects people confront are commodities, inappropriate for transactions in personal relations. Thus, people have the need to appropriate objects, to convert them into possessions, more intensely than they did in earlier forms of society.

11

In Western capitalist societies people generally understand the objects that surround them as commodities that bear no personal identity. While this is a cultural understanding, it reflects people's common experience of the production of objects in manufacturing and the circulation of objects in retail trade. The next three chapters describe the historical appearance of the modern form of production and circulation in Britain and the United States. These chapters, then, trace a set of common changes in people's practical experience of objects in two important areas of life that are themselves oriented toward objects. In doing so, these chapters provide the background for the final four chapters, which describe some of the ways that people have been affected by these changes, how they have interpreted these changes and the constraints they impose, and how people have responded to them.

Chapter 2, "Changing Production Relations", describes the development of capitalist forms of production over the past three centuries. In it I show how people's experience of the productive realm has been one of growing alienation of the things produced from the people who produce them. The description focuses on two dimensions or sorts of alienation. The first is the degree to which the productive process is governed by the producers, as distinct from being beyond their control. The second is the degree to which the social relationships between producers are durable, personal and pervasive, as distinct from being transient, impersonal and limited to the sphere of production itself. The chapter looks at four general stages of production.

The first of these is cottage industry, in which production for the market is carried out within the household by its members cooperatively, producing objects that are the property of the household and using its own tools, equipment and raw materials. The second is the putting-out system, in which production occurs within the household, but does so at the direction of a merchant capitalist who determines what is to be produced and who owns the raw materials and finished product. The third stage is early factory production, in which production moves to a central factory under the direction of an employer, but still makes use of family relations among producers to provide and coordinate labor. The final stage is modern factory production, in which production comes more fully under the control of the employing capitalist, and in which family relationships disappear. Thus, the chapter shows that as the organization of production has changed over the past three centuries, workers have been increasingly likely to be alienated from production. Increasingly, they have found themselves producing in settings and using processes over which they have no control; increasingly, they have found themselves producing in cooperation with others who are linked to them in no enduring, pervasive ways. As a result of these practical changes, people are increasingly likely to see manufactured objects as alienated commodities.

Because the history of production relations has attracted so much attention from historians and social scientists, it is likely to be fairly familiar and so not require extensive treatment. However, the history of circulation relations – what is now retail trade – has attracted much less attention. Although trade has been slighted by sociologists and historians, it is important for understanding people's experience of objects. One consequence of the emergence of industrial capitalism has been that more and more people have acquired more and more objects through retail trade. As a result, the way people experience and think about those objects will be affected by the changing social relations of that trade. Because it is important and likely to be unfamiliar, it is appropriate to treat the history of circulation relations at greater length. I do so in Chapters 3 and 4.

Chapter 3 is "Changing Circulation Relations: The Emergence of the Market". In it I trace the emergence of "the market", by which I mean the idea that people who buy are an impersonal mass of individuals alienated from the seller. This is a key element of modern retail trade that became pronounced first in England around 1800. By way of background, I begin by describing first the main forms of circulation that existed earlier, particularly local market trade. This trade was organized and conceptualized in terms of transaction between people linked and obligated to each other in numerous ways that derived from their common membership in the local community. I then describe the changes that marked the emergence of the impersonal market. These changes were conceptual: the notion that trade was between people known and linked to each other in relatively enduring ways was being displaced by the belief that trader and customer came together only fleetingly for the purpose of the transaction at hand. These changes also were practical: retail traders began to act in ways intended to attract casual customers. Shop design and pricing policies changed; advertisements and shop window displays appeared. Together, these changes marked the beginning of alienation in retail trade.

Chapter 3 describes only the beginning of the transformation of retail trade; in Chapter 4, "Changing Circulation Relations: Institutionalizing Alienation", I trace the continuation of these changes. I do so by describing the extensive reorganization of retail trade that occurred around 1900 in Britain and the United States. Unlike the earlier changes I describe in Chapter 3, these affected just about all branches of trade. While many of the sociologists who have studied retail trade in the period around 1900 have focused on the department store, in this chapter I focus on trade that catered to the growing working-class demand, for it is there that the institutionalization of impersonality is most pronounced. In this chapter I examine five core, common changes in retail trade. The first of these is the growing scope, and hence impersonality, of retail firms, as stores got bigger and chain stores (in the U.S.) and multiples (in the U.K.) became more common. Second is changes in the nature of credit, which severed an important link between storekeeper and customer. Third is changes in labor relations in stores, which alienated the sellers from the store and from their work. Fourth is the shift to passive distribution. Sellers were less and less actively involved in selecting and transforming their wares, and so were more likely to be alienated from what they sold. Fifth is a related phenomenon, the appearance of national brands and advertising by manufacturers. This alienated the shopkeeper from the goods being circulated and from the customer who bought them.

These three historical chapters describe people's experience with objects in production and circulation over the last few centuries, and show that the emergence of industrial and commercial capitalism has meant a growing alienation. As producers, people have become increasingly alienated from the objects that they produce; as purchasers, people have become increasingly alienated from the objects that they buy. These chapters, then, present a familiar tale of modernity and its discontents, one that has been written and rewritten numerous times before. But I do not mean this book to be just another story of death by alienation, another chronicle of the world we have lost, for people have not merely suffered passively this growing alienation. Instead, and hardly surprising, the historical process I describe has been generative as well as destructive. In the second half of this book I turn to this generation, as I describe some of the different ways that people understood these changes and built upon them.

The growing impersonal alienation of the realm of the economy that I describe in my three historical chapters is not simply an historical event. In addition, that alienation and its distinction from the personal and social realm of the family is part of British and American culture (and indeed Western culture more generally). Because this cultural differentiation of economy and society informs the social and cultural beliefs and practices that concern me in the second half of this book, I deal with it in the beginning of Chapter 5. There I describe how people construct a marked opposition between two key spheres in their lives, personal and affective home, and impersonal and utilitarian work. This opposition reflects and shapes people's experience and understanding of the objects that they have and that they transact with each other. Consequently, this opposition underlies and helps make sense of the generation and spread of novel features of the way people deal with objects.

Briefly put, the bleak sphere of work colors the things that are produced there, endows them culturally with an impersonality that means that they are not suitable for use in the personal sphere of home. In the second half of this book I am concerned with the beliefs and practices that people developed and adopted that enable them to deal with and even transcend this stark cultural opposition that they have in part constructed themselves. In particular, I describe the ways that people appropriate commodities for use in family relationships and the ways that they understand and give gifts on formal occasions. In other words, these chapters are concerned with shopping and presents.

In Chapter 5, "The Work of Appropriation", I pay particular attention to appropriation in shopping. Shopping is an area of life that has attracted little interest from sociologists, even though it is a necessary part of people's lives. But as I show, shopping is not simply the mechanical process by which people purchase the things they need to have in order to survive. In addition, where people shop and the ways they shop can be important for changing those things from impersonal commodities to possessions that embody the shopper's identity and location in a web of personal relationships. The chapter describes different forms of shopping, but attends especially to shopping for food and the ways that different styles of food shopping bring about appropriation in different ways.

The discussion in Chapter 5 focuses on the shopper in the store. However, the need to appropriate purchased commodities and the ways that people appropriate them can be affected as well by the ways commodities are presented in advertisements. As I have described in this Introduction, advertising has attracted sociological attention, but primarily as a means of discerning the way that objects are situated in public structures of meaning. In Chapter 6, "Presenting Commodities in Catalogues", I look at advertising in mail-order catalogues. My purpose is to investigate how some catalogues cloak commodities with the symbolism of possession and so, in effect, do part of the work of appropriation in advance. The first way that I describe bestows upon the commodities the personality and identity of specific people who are said to be instrumental in their design or manufacture. The second of these ways bestows upon the commodities the personality and identity of the people who sell them, so that the customer is presented as buying from specific people in a relationship that mimics gift exchange. The third of the ways bestows upon the commodities the personality of the people who have them, who take pleasure in them and who give them to others, so that the customer is presented with objects that have already shown themselves to be possessions and gifts. While these modes of presentation differ, they all involve making objects more attractive by removing them from the status of commodities produced by anonymous people and purchased from anonymous people by anonymous users. They all, in other words, seek to cross the divide between commodity and possession.

The next two chapters look at presents, another topic ignored by most of those concerned with modern societies. From a Maussian perspective presents warrant attention for two reasons. First, the growing importance of commodity relations means that people are likely to see as more fragile the sorts of relationships that presents celebrate and recreate. Second, in the giving of presents people confront in the most immediate form the contradiction between the ubiquity of commodities and the need to give a possession.

In Chapter 7, "The Ideology of the Gift", I describe an ideology of the perfect gift between intimates. This ideology stresses two things. First, the gift should be a pure possession: it should bear intensely the identity of the giver. Second, the gift should be purely disinterested: it should express only affection and carry no taint of obligation or expectation of return. In this chapter I show that this ideology reflects two important elements of modern society. One element is that the gift needs to be a possession, while the only objects that most people have to give are commodities. The ideology accommodates this contradiction by disembodying the object given, by asserting that the sentiment that the gift carries is important while the object itself, the vehicle, is insignificant. While people in all societies see formal presents as something more than their material embodiment, the modern ideology is a result of an historical circumstance, the growing separation of economic necessity from personal relationships. That separation is both an empirical fact, as a growing proportion of production has moved out of the family sphere, and a cultural understanding, as people increasingly see their families as purely social units with no significant economic dimension. The other important element of Western society contained in the ideology of the perfect gift is the belief that people in gift relations are free and independent of each other. Like the disembodied gift, this belief also reflects historical circumstance. In this chapter I describe the spread of the idea that people are autonomous and show how this belief is associated with the spread of impersonal commercial capitalism around the end of the eighteenth century.

Christmas is the premier occasion on which Britons and Americans give presents to each other, which makes it a fitting illustration and summation of the themes I develop in this book. In Chapter 8, "Christmas and the Ceremony of the Gift", I describe the ways that Christmas embodies the Maussian model of gift relations in the context of a capitalist society. The core of Christmas is Christmas giving, and the giving that is most intense and conforms most closely to the Maussian model is giving within the family, the setting that people see as most distinct from the impersonal economic sphere of life. Equally, Christmas giving illustrates in heightened form the contradiction between gifts and commodities, and in this chapter I describe how people cope with this contradiction through ritualized acts of appropriation. One of these is Christmas shopping. While many see shopping as a sign of a distasteful commercialism that has been imposed on the genuine, familial core of the season, I argue that the shopping and the distaste are central parts of Christmas. They express and strengthen people's sense of the distinction between the family and commercial world. Further, they transcend that distinction by allowing people to demonstrate that they can take recalcitrant commodities at this most social time of the year, transform them and use them to recreate enduring personal relations.

Like much of what I describe in the second half of this book, modern Christmas is a consequence of the growth of Western capitalism. In this chapter I demonstrate this link in two ways. First, and briefly, I describe the giving of presents in Japan, where relations in the world of work are not distinguished from personal relations in the way they are in the United States and Great Britain. While the Japanese give large numbers of presents, they do so in ways very different from Westerners. Second, and at greater length,

I describe the history of modern Christmas. That celebration is no ancient ritual, but emerged in the middle third of the nineteenth century, a period marked by the intense growth of commercial and industrial capitalism.

In the second half of this book I describe some of the ways that people perceive and cope with the changes I describe in the first half, changes that have led to a greater impersonality in the production and circulation of objects in manufacturing and retail trade. Those changes have been real and profound, but they have not been absolute. As I note in those earlier chapters, those changes have not meant the disappearance of personal relationships in the economic sphere. However, much of both scholarly and public understanding takes these changes to be absolute: for most economists, sociologists and anthropologists, as for many ordinary people, the economic realm is populated by autonomous, calculating and self-serving individuals. While this view contains truth, it also contains error.

In the Conclusion, "Oppositions of Gifts and Commodities", I address directly this common, idealized conception of ourselves as, alternatively, autonomous rational actors in the market and affective family members at home. That cultural conception is not an adequate reflection of the world that people experience. Instead, it is an authoritative construction that ignores the fact that the household is no more purely social than the world of work is purely economic, just as it assumes that all people in the West are likely to see themselves and their world in the cultural way I have described. In this last chapter I describe just how inaccurate this simplification is, and why such a distortion can exert such an attraction in both scholarly and popular opinion. I suggest that it attracts because it reflects the high value placed on a distinct way of life in Western society, just as it reflects the high value placed on the modern West itself. In other words, this cultural construction is as much normative as it is descriptive. It tells us what people ought to do and be if they are to live up to, and so maintain, the genius of the modern West as embodied in dominant elements of Western society. In doing so, this cultural construction does not look just to the different realms of people's lives. It looks as well to a broader order, one dominated by people, relations and societies of particular sorts, and the construction draws its legitimacy from that domination, as it gives legitimacy to that domination in turn.

1

GIFTS AND COMMODITIES, PEOPLE AND THINGS

In this chapter I present my interpretation of the model that springs from Marcel Mauss's *The Gift*. As I described in the Preface, a number of anthropologists have elaborated the model, to the extent that it is better to speak of a "Maussian" model, rather than "Mauss's" model. Put most simply, the Maussian model identifies two polar types of social relations: commodity relations and gift relations. At the risk of over-simplifying, commodity relations are transient and impersonal, though certainly not necessarily unpleasant or cold, for they can be cheerful and gracious (e.g. Hochschild 1983). Equally, gift relations are durable and personal, though certainly not necessarily pleasant or warm, for they can involve conflict (Schwartz 1967: 5–7), even the exchange of blows rather than gifts (Schiltz 1987). In commodity relations objects are impersonal bundles of use value and exchange value that are bought and sold. In gift relations objects are personal possessions that are given and received.

Before turning to a discussion of these two sorts of objects and social relations, I need to explain what "gift" means and what can be a gift, for I do not use the word in its everyday sense.

"Gift" is likely to call up images of presents wrapped and tied with a bow, or more broadly of objects given from one person to another consciously and with some degree of ceremony as "a present". This is the usage followed by David Cheal in *The Gift Economy*, his analysis of the giving and receiving of formal presents in Winnipeg, Canada. While almost all presents are gifts in the Maussian sense, "gift" is much broader, for it includes all things transacted as part of social, as distinct from more purely monetary, relations, and it includes labor and immaterial things like names and ideas as well as physical objects. In fact, the common restriction of "gift" to objects strengthens the distinction between thing and labor, and hence between thing and laborer. On reflection, however, this distinction appears suspect. Most people in industrial societies have things only as a result of labor. The wage worker sells labor for a wage, so that the things those wages buy are the result of that labor. Not only does the gift embody the labor of the wage, it also embodies the effort of selection and preparation. Westerners readily make the distinction between object and labor, but it can be dangerous to adopt it uncritically in an analysis of the social meaning of objects.

A few examples will illustrate the breadth of "gift". If I invite friends to my house for a meal, I am giving them a gift of food and drink. I do not put the meal in a box, wrap it and tie it with a ribbon, but it is a gift none the less. If friends go out together, they may go in one car, in which case the person who owns and drives is giving transport to the others. If a pair of office-mates stops for a drink after work and if one of them buys a round of drinks for both, then that one is giving a gift to the other. Within the household giving gifts is even more ubiquitous and automatic. When I prepare dinner for my family I give my wife and children the effort involved in preparing the meal. However, when my wife buys the ingredients that I cook, she gives the effort of shopping. The point of these examples is to show that it is not the form and ceremony of the giving and getting that make a transaction a gift. Instead, it is the relationship that exists between the transactors and the relationship between them and what is transacted.

THE REALMS OF GIFTS AND COMMODITIES

The distinction between gift and commodity can be more than just the distinction between different relationships between transactors. For many anthropologists who work in the Maussian tradition the distinction between them marks the distinction between different types of social life and social organization. Here, however, I will apply the distinction to realms of life within a single society, and I will do so in ideal terms. In real social life, there are very few objects, transactions or relations that conform to the pure descriptions of gift and commodity that I present.

C. A. Gregory says that commodity exchange is oriented to the system of the material production of objects, and thus "must be explained with reference to the social conditions of the reproduction of *things*", which means ultimately "class structure and the principles governing factory organization" (Gregory 1980: 641). His use of "reproduction" highlights an important point. Commodity exchange is not simply oriented to the *physical* production of objects, for such production is important in all societies. Instead, commodity exchange is oriented to the *social* production of objects. This includes not just their physical production, but also the creation of their social identity as commodities and the creation of people's unequal relationships with them in the process of production, and consequently elsewhere in society. These unequal relationships include the division of labor, the class structure, the different roles of producer and consumer and the significance of people's positions in these orders.

One consequence of Gregory's account of commodity relations is that they are not in any sense unsocial. Instead, these relations are bound by social rules that can be elaborate and constraining. To say that commodity relations are social, even if impersonal, is also to say that they are not a residual or primary category that naturally reflects some supposed innate desire to exchange utilities. Instead, commodity relations are made by transactors and the society in which they exist. We do not, after all, engage in such transactions with people who are totally unknown to us. We engage in them only with people who have a specific social identity, whether as store clerks, stock brokers or the gentleman who offers to take our order on the telephone. In transacting with these people in the appropriate ways we reaffirm the identities of each of us as a commodity transactor and of our relationship as a commodity relationship.

At their simplest, commodity transactions consist of a transfer of value and a counter-transfer: the transfer of an object or service from A to B and the counter-transfer of money from B to A. In other words, A sells something to B. These two transfers can occur at the same time (cash on the nail) or the counter-transfer can be delayed (buying on credit, for example). Selling your labor power for a wage, buying a loaf of bread in a store, taking out a mortgage to buy a house – all are commodity transactions. It is not the fact that money is involved that makes these commodity transactions, for money is used in gift transactions in many societies. Instead, these are commodity transactions because of the relationship that links the transactors to each other and to the object they transact. Put most simply, in commodity relations the objects are alienated from the transactors: they are not especially associated with each transactor, nor do they speak of any past or future relationships between transactors. Instead, such objects are treated solely as bearers of abstract value or utility.

In contrast to commodity exchange, gift exchange is oriented to the system of social reproduction, and thus "must be explained with reference to the social conditions of the reproduction of *people*", which, for the archaic societies that concerned Mauss, means ultimately "clan structure and the principles governing kinship organization" (Gregory 1980: 641). Just as the concern in commodity systems is with more than the mechanics of producing things, so the concern in gift systems is with more than the mechanics of producing people, physical procreation or even socialization in some abstract sense. Instead, it is with the creation and recreation of people as social identities, defined by their identifiable relationships with other individuals and groups in the society.

Gift transactions resemble commodity transactions in that they consist of a transfer and a counter-transfer. And also like commodity transactions, the counter-transfer can take place at the same time as the transfer or it can be delayed. What makes such a transfer a gift transaction is the relationship that links transactors to each other and to the object they transact. In gift transactions objects are not alienated from the transactors. Instead, the object given continues to be identified with the giver and indeed continues to be identified with the transaction itself (this is presented in social-psychological terms in Belk 1976).

Gift and commodity relations are analytical categories in the Maussian model. Equally, however, they echo the ways that many people in the West understand different parts of their lives. They are likely to think of the household, family, friends and neighbors as defining an area of life characterized by gift relations. Conversely, they are likely to think of the world of work and the store, and economic activities more generally, as defining an area of life characterized by commodity relations. Furthermore, they are likely to understand these two realms in ways that stress and even heighten the differences between them. In this chapter I will describe gifts and commodities as though they were situated in these cultural realms of home and work. However, this is a simplification of a more complex set of experiences and understandings.

I want now to turn to a more systematic consideration of the sorts of transactions that exist in these two realms. The Maussian view is that gift exchange is (1) the obligatory transfer of (2) inalienable objects or services between (3) mutually obligated and related transactors (see Gregory 1980: esp. 640). Accordingly, I will compare gifts and commodities in terms of the key dimensions implicit in this view of gifts: how much and in what way is the transaction obligatory, how much and in what way is what is transacted associated with the transactors, how much and in what way are the transactors linked with and obligated to each other.

OBLIGATORY TRANSFER

Buying and selling are formally voluntary and free. We can buy or not as we like, wherever we like. All that most of us have to sell is our labor, and we can sell it or not as we like, wherever we like. We are restricted only by whether we have the money to buy what we want or whether we have the skills to make our labor attract the wage we want. In contrast to this formal voluntary freedom of commodity transactions, gift transactions are obligatory, albeit in a special way. In Mauss's classic statement (1990: 13), parties to a gift relationship are under "the obligation to reciprocate presents received ... the obligation ... to give presents, and ... to receive them". In other words, people in a gift relationship are obliged to give and take and reciprocate. Anyone who fails to conform to these three obligations effectively is denying that he or she is in a social relationship, and hence is rejecting amity and indicating indifference. Thus, even though these gifts are given freely in the sense that there is no institution monitoring performance and enforcing conformity, yet they are obligatory because they are induced by expectation and belief. We have to give to those close to us, even if it drives us into debt (Davis, J. 1992: ch. 4; Lea, Walker and Webley 1992).

As I will describe in Chapter 7, the Maussian point that gifts are obligatory contradicts an important element of the Western industrial view of the gift, "that (a) it is something voluntarily given, and that (b) there is no expectation of compensation" (Belk 1979: 100). In view of this common stress on voluntarism, it is important to remember that the Maussian assertion that giving is obligatory is a generalization: it does not mean that gifts are never free. Some are, in the sense that the giver is under no obligation to give. This freedom exists primarily when people are creating a new relationship, as when a couple is dating, or modifying an old one, as when a couple is breaking up. The very fact that these gifts are relatively free and the act of giving them relatively self-conscious means that they are more visible than the mundane gifts of established relationships. Those who study or reflect on gifts in American or British society are, thus, prone to fasten on these sorts of gifts and describe them as ways that transactors signal to each other their estimation of and aspirations for their relationship with each other (e.g. Belk and Coon 1993; Camerer 1988).

While these sorts of analyses may be revealing, their conclusions can not be generalized very much because they attend to gifts in just those situations where the links between transactors are problematic. Most gift transactions, on the other hand, occur within stable relationships, in which transacting is obligatory and this sort of self-conscious signalling generally missing. Family and household members are expected to do things willingly for other members and to accept willingly what other members do for them, as Mirra Komarovsky (1987) describes for Glenton and as Michael Young and Peter Willmott (1986) describe for Bethnal Green. Those who are under this obligation are unhappy when they are denied the chance to transact. Thus, one young man reported to Colin Bell (1969: 93): "My father was hurt I think when he knew I went to the bank rather than him for a down payment on a new car".

Those who are related to each other within certain degrees are expected to give to and receive from each other willingly in certain ways in certain situations, as exemplified positively by the strong regularities in the giving of Christmas presents among kin in Middletown (Caplow 1984, discussed in Chapter 8, below) and as exemplified negatively in Rhian Ellis's (1983) description of the marked association between the violent breakdown of marriage on the one hand, and on the other the wife's failure to cook and the husband's failure to accept the meal. Even when there is little affection among close kin, they are obligated to continue to transact with each other, and generally they do so (e.g. Allan 1979: 94–5). As I said, there is no over-arching institution that enforces the obligations that people have in these relationships in the way that the state enforces a contract. We are not bound by law to give; our lives may be sufficiently private and anonymous that our neighbors would not know of our dereliction. But dereliction it would be; and dereliction it appears to those who see the request not made, the favor not reciprocated, the visit not returned, the obligation not fulfilled.

Although gift transactions are obligatory, this is not the kind of obligation that can be discharged by fulfilling it. Instead, fulfilling the obligation recreates it by reaffirming the relationship. If my neighbor helped me move some large stones in my garden, and if later I loan that neighbor a garden tool, I would not simply be discharging my obligation. Instead, I would be transacting in a neighborly way, reaffirming our neighborly relationship, and so reaffirming my (and my neighbor's) obligation to continue to give and receive in this way. (Bulmer 1986, esp. ch. 4, presenting the sociological work of Philip Abrams, describes this sort of neighborliness and its limitations.) This recreation of relationships and obligations in gift transactions is just the opposite of what occurs in commodity relations.

There, transacting as one ought dissolves the obligations that bind the parties to each other. This reflects the cultural understanding that in commodity relations people who are free and independent bind themselves only temporarily when they contract to transact with each other, and that when the transaction is completed the parties resume their former independence. I am obligated to pay the store the money I owe for the shoes that I buy. Once I pay, however, my obligation ends and our relationship is dissolved: I owe them nothing and can go my own way. Indeed, there is the assumption that actors are competent to transact *only if* they are free and independent of each other, for only then will they be able to protect their own interests. But with gift relations this assumption is inverted (or stood on its feet, if you prefer). People are able to transact only if they are *not* independent of each other. The gift transaction affirms and reproduces this mutual dependence, this relationship that links transactors. Their relationship makes them part of each other, and in transacting they express and recreate that relationship, and so recreate their obligation to transact in a similar way again in the future.

Gift transactors, then, are not autonomous individuals. Instead, they are morally obligated to give, receive and repay. Consequently, gift transactions cannot be explained in terms of economic or emotional individualism, though they may have important economic and emotional correlates and consequences. When I prepare a meal for my family it has an emotional dimension: it expresses the fact that I love my wife and children; it has an economic dimension: we can eat better for less at home than in a restaurant. But emotional expression and economic utility are not adequate explanations of why I cook, what each of us thinks of it or the relationships that link us to each other and to the meal.

Doubtless, if one party to a gift relationship feels regularly and unjustly slighted, he or she will consider ending the relationship. But this need not mean that the transactor is calculating debts and credits, emotional or material. Instead, the repeated imbalance itself marks a repeated violation of the obligation to give, receive and repay, and hence marks the end of the relationship as it had been. Openly ending the relationship in such a situation is just an open recognition that the relationship has already ended.

In this section I have described the idea that gift transactions are obligatory. Underlying my discussion is the point that gift transactions are not dictated only by considerations of utility or the desire to express emotion by independent transactors: in some cases these considerations may be relatively insignificant. In addition, these transactions are manifestations of the personal relationship between the transactors, and hence cannot be encompassed by a model that treats transactors as isolated individuals. Alternatively, in commodity relations the transactions are encompassed by such a model, for in extreme form (as I describe later) transactors are not linked in any enduring or personal way. Instead, they are related only temporarily through the impersonal objects that they transact.

INALIENABLE OBJECTS

The second element of the Maussian model of gift relations is that the things transacted are inalienable – that they are in important ways bound to people (Mauss 1990: 14). The gift is inalienably linked to the giver, and therefore it is important for regenerating the relationship between giver and recipient. The Christmas present that my mother gives me continues to bear her identity after I receive it, and so continues to affirm that she and I are linked as mother and son. At a more mundane level, the many everyday objects that my wife and I buy for each other as part of the routine of keeping house continually remind each of us of the other, and so affirm and recreate the relationship that links us.

As these examples indicate, I take "inalienable" simply to mean associated with a person, a possession, "part of the self, somehow attached, assimilated to or set apart for the self" (Beaglehole 1932: 134). For the archaic societies that Mauss described, the association was strong and inalienability was pronounced. However, the degree of association, its bases and consequences, will vary according to situations and societies. For example, in English law since the thirteenth century the gift has been formally alienated from the giver: once made, "the transaction is then irrevocable" (Lowes, Turner and Wills 1968: 220). In other words, saying that the gift is inalienably linked to the giver does not necessarily mean that the giver has the jural right to reclaim the object, that such a right could be exercised in practice, or that the recipient has no right to dispose of the object. The nature of these rights and practices is an empirical question. What is important is the central point that the object continues to bear the identity of the giver and of the relationship between the giver and the recipient.

Where does this relationship between possessor and possession reside? At the very minimum, it can reside in the mind of only one person and be a matter of individual psychology. In practice, of course, it is likely to exist in the minds of several people and so be a social understanding of the object. More broadly yet, social structure and practices will affect the ways that

24

different sorts of people are likely to interact with different sorts of objects, and so affect the ways they are likely to experience those objects and hence think about them.

Although Mauss based his discussion of inalienability on archaic societies, others have described it in industrial societies. Ernest Beaglehole explicitly linked the two:

> Animistic feeling is the hidden thread, strong though invisible, which binds civilized as well as savage to the objects he regards as his own. It is the real core of ownership, the psychological basis of the philosopher's cry: "In making the object my own, I stamped it with the mark of my own person; whoever attacks it attacks me; the blow struck it, strikes me, for I am present in it. Property is but the periphery of my person extended to things".
>
> (Beaglehole 1932: 302, quoting Jhering 1915: 58–9)

William James discusses a similar merging of the self and object. He says (1890: 291) that people see themselves as more than just their body and mind: "Our fame, our children, the work of our hands, may be as dear to us as our bodies." The range of objects that can be linked to the self is broad: a man's "clothes and his house, his wife and children, his ancestors and friends, his reputation and works, his lands and horses, and yacht and bank-account" (James, W. 1890: 291). James elaborates this link between self and object when he says (1890: 293) that the loss of a possession is not just the loss of enjoyment, use or future profit, for "there remains, over and above this, a sense of the shrinkage of our personality, a partial conversion of ourselves to nothingness". Two sociologists, Mihaly Csikszentmihalyi and Eugene Rochberg-Halton (1981: 16), make a similar point, saying that, for most people, objects serve as depositories of personal meaning and identity. Objects are a way that we define who we are to ourselves and to others, so that "[t]he material objects we use . . . constitute the framework of experience that gives order to our otherwise shapeless selves".

Because of the association between person and object, the object has a history and carries the stamp of those who possessed it previously. In possessing the object, then, we possess as well that object's past. According to Annette Weiner, this is the case with *taonga*, a type of Maori valuable heirloom. These objects carry the power and identity of those who possessed them in the past and confer power and identity on those who possess them in the present. These objects are so bound up with the people associated with them that to acquire another's *taonga* "is to acquire another's rank, name, and history" (Weiner 1992: 64). An extreme form of possession closer to home is the relationship of Lois Roget and her ancestral property, described by Grant McCracken. Lois Roget lives in her family's farmhouse in Canada, a house that is "crowded with the objects that have descended from her family and from the family of her husband" (McCracken 1988: 44). Chairs, jars, plates – all recall the dead who are associated with them and with her. In its intensity, Lois Roget's relationship with her objects shows another aspect of possession: just as she possesses them, so they possess her. They define who she is by embodying the social relationships that encompass the woman herself: "[T]o take possession of these objects is to risk being swamped by meaning. Their simple presence represents a daily, voluble insistence that the family is a lineage and Lois a descendent" (1988: 51). The merging of person, group and object that is apparent in the case of Lois Roget may be extreme in industrial societies, but its extremity is a matter of degree, not of kind. All possessions dissolve to a degree the unique and independent identity of the possessor, merging it into a group identity that defines and reflects the person, the object and those who previously possessed it.

At a more mundane level, Csikszentmihalyi and Rochberg-Halton (1981: 86) say that people's descriptions of the important objects in their lives are marked by the theme of "kinship; of the ties that bind people to each other – that provide continuity in one's life and across generations", a theme that was apparent in the intensity of the way people talked: "It is the cumulative effect of hearing people talk about their parents, spouses, and children, the depth of their emotion in doing so, that is impressive." For instance, they report how two women explained why different things that they had were important to them and how they embodied the giver and the relationship that bound them. One woman explained what it meant to have a quilt that her relatives had made and given:

> It means my whole family, that we all enjoy receiving these things. . . . And if somebody makes it and puts so much time in it, to me it's love that's been put into the object . . . that's more special to me than anything . . . if you know how many hours are put into it. [*Ellipses in original.*]

The other woman put it more succinctly: "Love, love. I can say that love covers it all because the people who have given them to me love me or they wouldn't have given me such things" (1981: 143).

The link between person and object is most visible in gift relations when giving goes wrong, when a present is rejected. For example, around Christmas every year there appear newspaper articles on what to do with unsuitable presents having titles like "Returning Unwanted Gifts Takes Much Tact" (New York Times News Service 1988). These articles are evidence that disposing of useless objects acquired as presents causes an embarrassment that no one would feel about disposing of useless objects acquired as commodities, such as paperback books that turn out to be boring or shoes that turn out to be the wrong style. People are uncomfortable about getting rid of an unwanted Christmas present because rejecting it rejects as well the giver and the giver's relationship to the recipient. This is apparent in extreme form in Theodore Caplow's observation (1984: 1314) of a marked association in

Middletown between open criticism of a spouse's Christmas present to oneself and subsequent rejection of the spouse in separation or divorce. This link between giver and gift – Mauss's point (1990: 12) that to give "is to make a present of some part of oneself" – is expressed by the unhappy parents who wrote to Miss Manners, an advice columnist, of their "concern when a gift [to an adult child] of hand-woven place mats was opened and held up to the wallpaper to ensure that it was a perfect color match .... It was, but our hearts were in our throats." These parents go on to ask the obvious question: does this scrutiny of the material nature of their gift mean "a rejection of us or our values?". Your children, Miss Manners replied, "ought at least to conceal from you even the possibility that your presents might not match their tastes". Finally, and appropriately, she says that if the parents want to assure a grateful reception of their presents, they might "give family mementos, whose value is beyond the question of mere taste" (Martin 1988).

In contrast to the inalienability of possessions is the alienability of commodities. I will use "ownership" and "property" to refer to this sort of relationship between person and object. Property, the form of ownership in a commodity system, speaks not of a "close relationship between person and thing", says Daniel Miller (1987: 120–1), but of "abstract relationships between anonymous people and postulated objects". Any person can own any thing, and ownership does not mark the object with the identity of the owner, nor does it mark the person with the identity of the object. Sheer property is without identity, which makes it alienable. This may explain why medieval sumptuary regulations are so incomprehensible. From the commodity view, an ordinary person wearing the clothes of the aristocracy, for example, is nothing more than a variety of emulation. From an older view of the relationship of people and things, however, the act comes to resemble transubstantiation, an altogether more serious matter.[1]

In a commodity transaction the object is alienated from the person who gave it. The bottle of wine that I buy at Safeway is not linked to them in any significant way once I pay my money and walk out the door; and if I do not like it after the first glass I can pour it down the drain. On the other hand, the bottle of wine that my mother gives me is her choice for me. It is a token of her concern and affection for me, a token that she is my mother, and thus bears her identity; and even if it were a wine I did not like, I would not simply throw it out. This is illustrated by the way a householder explained to Csikszentmihalyi and Rochberg-Halton (1981: 66, emphasis added) the reason why the painting was there above the sofa: "My parents gave it . . . to us. They saw the empty space above the sofa and one day they brought us this picture to fill it. *It's not my style, but they gave it to us so I keep it.*"

This distinction between inalienable gifts and alienable commodities parallels a distinction between the way people think about objects in gift relations and in commodity relations. The object as a gift is unique. What Mauss (1990: 24) says about the *kula* valuables of the Trobriand Islands expresses this in heightened form: they "are not unimportant things, mere pieces of money. Each one . . . has its name, a personality, a history, and even a tale attached to it." But even the most ordinary object given as a gift is unique because it is marked by the links between the giver, the recipient and the occasion of the giving. As Jean Baudrillard (1981: 64) puts it, "once it has been given – and *because* of this – it is *this* object and not another. The gift is unique, specified by the people exchanging it and the unique moment of the exchange." If I were to lose the cufflinks that my son gave me on my birthday and buy myself an identical pair as a replacement, they would be a cheat. They would not really be the same, for they would not be the pair he gave me and I would know, even if I kept it a secret from him. In contrast, in commodity relationships people think of objects as abstract bundles of utilities and values that are precisely not unique. If I were to lose a company envelope and had to get another from the supply room, it would make no difference because, from my point of view, the two envelopes are the same.

In other words, objects in commodity relations are fungible, a legal term that means capable of replacing or being replaced by another item meeting the requisite definition. Hence, when I place an order for a thousand barrels of Brent crude oil, an ounce of gold, a Mars Bar, I am not dissatisfied because I got this thousand barrels, this ounce, this Mars Bar, instead of that one. Instead, were I to consider the matter at all, I would be satisfied with any item that met the criteria of what I ordered, because each is freely substitutable within its class and hence is fungible. This, after all, is a goal of mass production and the basis of product advertising and mail-order catalogues.

The distinction between inalienable gifts and alienable commodities parallels another important distinction, that between the way people think about people in gift relations and in commodity relations. In gift relations people are thought of or identified in terms of their fundamental, inalienable attributes and relationships, and hence are unique. My brother is my brother because of our very biological substance (as our culture understands these things), not to mention the experiences we have shared, and he cannot be replaced by anyone else, even of the same age, occupation and general characteristics. He is unique. On the other hand, in commodity relations people are identified in terms of attributes that are not inalienably theirs. When I pay for my groceries, I give my money to the person behind the counter because that person occupies a position in an organization. That position is alienable. The person can be promoted or fired or can quit, and still be the same person. If a new face appears behind the counter, I will pay the new person and not the old. When I am trying to find someone to take my money, any competent clerk will do. This indicates that in commodity relations it is not only objects that are fungible; people are fungible too.

The point I have made in the preceding paragraphs is that in gift relationships the people and the objects involved are thought of as unique and inalienably linked to each other. As Mauss (1990: 33) says of gifts in archaic societies, they "are never completely detached from those carrying out the exchange. The mutual ties and alliance they establish are comparatively indissoluble", just as Lois Roget and her ancestors are never completely separated from the objects that they have in common and that bind them. On the other hand, in commodity relationships both the parties and the objects are fungible rather than unique and are alienable rather than inalienable: they are linked to each other in no enduring, personal way. I may like the old supermarket clerk more than the new one, but if I pay the new one, the groceries I buy become my property just as much as with the old one. The consequence is that commodities are alienated not only from the people who transact them, but even from the people who buy and own them.

My point that commodities and commodity relations are anonymous is a generalization, for the different things we buy are more or less perfect commodities, and so are more or less impersonal. In fact, Keith Hart (1986: 642) argues that in many circumstances even money is increasingly "bound up with tokens of personal identity", though appropriately these tokens are themselves impersonal: credit cards may bear our names, but they are awarded only after an impersonal assessment of our financial history and prospects. Some objects bought and sold do bear a personal identity, particularly of those who made them. Works of design, art and craft fall most easily into this category, and it is appropriate that they usually bear the maker's name or mark. The special relationship of creator and object is recognized in copyright law, as well as in continuing claims that creators should have a say in what they create even after it is sold: artists and writers should have a say in the use of their art, architects should have a say in the extension or modification of their buildings and so forth (see, e.g., Morrison 1988; Sutherland 1990). However, these qualifications do not contradict the point that commodities are impersonal. Instead, they show that not every-thing that we buy and sell is a pure commodity.

I have used the links between person and thing as a way of explaining how people transact those things. Because link and transaction are related, however, we can reverse the explanatory process and use the form of transaction to indicate how people see the links between person and thing. In particular, legal prohibition or moral censure of the buying or selling of something is a sign that the thing is so closely a part of the possessor that its alienation is not permitted. For example, one cannot sell one's vote, which is inalienably one's own as a consequence of one's citizenship: a person cannot go to a polling place four or five times and claim the right to do so based on the purchase of the franchise of three or four other people. Equally, one cannot sell one's decision on how to vote: the law will not enforce a contract in which Jones is obliged to vote as Smith directs in return for the payment of a sum of money. One can, however, give that decision as a gift. One cannot sell oneself, for that is slavery: one cannot, then, be alienated from oneself. But one can sell one's labor power, and that with relatively few restrictions.

In the United States, one cannot sell one's sexuality, for in almost all states that is the crime of prostitution, but one can give it as a gift. This list could be extended, but doing so would not add to the basic point, that restrictions on what can be sold indicate how society sees the link between people and certain sorts of things.

Thus far I have contrasted the inalienability of the gift relationship with the alienability and impersonality of objects and people in commodity relations. This leads to Mauss's (1990: 47) more general point that the evolution of society entails an increasing de-socialization of objects, their growing cultural separation from people and their social relationships: "We live in societies that draw a strict distinction ... between ... things and persons." With this evolution, people increasingly think of objects in terms of abstract and impersonal frames of value, particularly exchange value, of which monetary amount is the definitive, anonymous marker (Gregory 1980: 640). This is simply another side of what Karl Polanyi (1957) described as the spread of commodity markets for land, labor and capital in the nineteenth century.

In the extreme form of commodity transaction, the circulation of capital, this abstract impersonality means that only exchange value matters: a check, a bank draft, cash, debentures and electronic interbank transfers for the same amount all are the same, and the value of each is fully distinct from the instrument that bears it. In asserting this I do not mean that a customer seeking a loaf of bread will be satisfied with any commodity of an equal cash value. I am suggesting, however, that with the growing importance of commodity relations the customer is increasingly predisposed to reduce all loaves of bread to this single measure of value: money cost. This, after all, is the point of consumer-oriented reforms like unit-pricing in food stores: products of different qualities are reduced to the uniform measure of pennies per pound. Money is the great leveller, good for all debts, public and private. As Marx observed in *Capital*, "[e]very one knows, if he knows nothing else, that commodities have a value-form common to them all .... I mean their money-form" (in Tucker 1978: 313). In this sense, in this orientation toward exchange value, the transactors are indifferent to the concrete identity of the object used to meet an obligation.

I have described the second element of the definition of gift relations, that they involve inalienable objects. Objects as commodities are neutral and impersonal tokens of abstract value, given or withheld by autonomous individuals as calculation and self-interest dictate. However, objects as gifts bear, together with their use and exchange value, the identity of the giver and the relationship between giver and recipient, an identity that is not en-compassed by the more conventional sociological views of objects that I described in the Introduction. Implicit in the issue of alienability is another issue, the ways that people think of people. Those who transact and the objects transacted in pure gift relations are viewed in terms of their basic, inalienable identities and relationships, so that they are uniquely specified and linked to each other. In pure commodity relations, on the other hand, they are viewed in terms of their accidental identities and relationships, so that they are identified in terms of abstract and general structures, whether of utility or of exchange or sign value, and so are fungible rather than unique.

RELATED AND MUTUALLY-OBLIGATED TRANSACTORS

I turn now to the last element of gift relations: gifts are exchanged by related and mutually-obligated transactors. In a gift relationship, the parties are linked by their inalienable attributes, so that the relationship is part of their basic identity, as is their obligation to give, receive and repay gifts in appropriate ways. My mother and I are linked by what our society sees as inalienable attributes. Our blood relationship defines each of us and imposes on each of us the obligation to transact in certain ways in certain circumstances. Thus, gift transactors are social persons defined in significant ways by their inalienable positions in a structure of personal social relations that encompasses them. This is the import of Jonathan Parry's (1986: 456) observation that for Mauss "[i]t is not individuals but ... *moral persons* who carry on exchanges."

In many societies dominated by gift exchange the structure of kinship provides the basis for people's identities and their relations with each other, and thus their obligations to transact with each other. In industrial societies it is typically the structure of the household and family, and to a lesser extent friendship and neighborhood, that does these things (Barnett and Silverman 1979; Schneider, D. 1979, 1980). This moral personality within an encompassing structure is manifest by Lois Roget, the descendent in the encompassing lineages defined by the ancestral objects that she possesses. It is illustrated in a more mundane way by several of the English couples that Penny Mansfield and Jean Collard interviewed in their study of new marriages. These two sociologists wanted to interview husbands and wives separately, but met with objection: the couples "felt our request indirectly suggested a bias on our part toward perceiving them as two separate individuals rather than as a married pair, an issue about which we discovered a high degree of sensitivity" (Mansfield and Collard 1988: 38).

To stress the links and obligations between gift transactors is not to deny that people in commodity relations may also be linked and obligated to each other. But they are so in very different ways. Because commodity systems rest on "the social conditions of the reproduction of *things*" (Gregory 1980: 641), the parties to commodity transactions typically are defined and linked by their complementary positions in the system of production and distribution, which is to say the class system and the division of labor. Though people recognize that these positions are important, the fact that they value improving one's position in the occupational order indicates that they are not inalienable bases of identity. Those who transact commodities, then, are linked to each other only in an impersonal, abstract and general sense. Thus, I buy from Sally Jones because her position is store clerk, and I buy at all because my position as wage worker means that I do not make things to satisfy my need. My need to buy is a general one, and I need not transact with Sally Jones herself, for, as I have pointed out, she is fungible and fully substitutable by any other store clerk. She and I are linked only abstractly and fortuitously: she can change her job, I can shop elsewhere.

Likewise, the obligations between people in commodity relations do not bear on their inalienable beings, but on their accidental and alienable aspects. For instance, if I fail to make my mortgage payments the bank may be able to seize my property to recover its money, but it has no claim on me as a free and independent person: debt servitude does not exist. Similarly, completing the mortgage contract satisfactorily does not bestow upon me or the bank or any of the people who work there the right to make further claims upon each other. The bank and I may come away from our transaction with a good opinion of each other, which may increase the likelihood that I will re-mortgage my house with them. But the successful completion of the transaction itself does not mean that I have a link with the bank and its money or that the bank has a link with me and my house.

In gift transactions the bond of mutual obligation and relationship is reinforced by the inalienability of the gift, which gives the giver a continuing claim upon the object and the recipient. The extent of this will vary in different societies, and in extreme cases the giver will have a claim on whatever accrues to the recipient through the use of the object. Thus, in a famous passage Mauss reports the words of a Maori, Tamate Ranaipiri. To paraphrase what Ranaipiri said: if you give me a valuable item that I then give to someone else, and if that other person then reciprocates with a second item, I must return that second item to you, for it embodies the spirit of what you gave me. If I fail to do so, "serious harm might come to me, even death" (Mauss 1990: 11; see also Parry 1986: 462–6; Sahlins 1974b: ch. 4). On the other hand, the mutual independence of commodity transactors is reinforced by the fact that the object transacted is alienated. Once I receive a commodity, it is mine to do with as I please. I can destroy it wantonly, consume it or use it to create wealth, all at my own discretion. Those involved with the commodity's production or with the transaction in which I acquired it have no claim on it or me once the transaction is completed. I do not expect a letter from my bank, politely reminding me that it was with their money that I bought my house way back when, that they noticed that now its value has doubled and that they want their share of the increase. ("We aren't being unreasonable. Look, we only want a half of the increase! Not at all greedy, considering you wouldn't even have the house if it hadn't been for us.") On the other hand, in places where gift logic is more powerful, those who originally possessed something can and do make claims on the benefits others have gained from the use of that thing. Thus, in Papua New Guinea, indigenous land-holding groups who, so settlers thought, sold their land decades ago, presently lay serious claims to "compensation", a share of the wealth generated through the use of their land.

I have said that in commodity relationships the link between the parties is based on alienable attributes, while in gift relationships it is based on inalienable identities. People tend to see some sorts of identities as alienable and others as inalienable. For example, generally people see a job as insubstantial, and they expect people to change jobs freely if opportunities arise. People would not turn a hair if they heard someone discuss a job change like this: "You know, I fought it. I love this job, and I've been here for over ten years. But what could I do? The new job pays a whole lot better, it's in a really nice town, its a big-name company, and it will give me the chance for better jobs later on. What could I do? I had to make the change!" Conversely, people generally take being married as an identity that is inalienable. They would not know what to make of a man who discussed his divorce and new marriage like this: "You know, I fought it. I love my wife, and I've been with her for over ten years. But what could I do? The new wife is a whole lot better in bed and kitchen, she's in a really nice town, she's from a high-society family and it will give me the chance for better marriages later on. What could I do? I had to make the change!"

There are, however, important exceptions to such generalizations. People distinguish between a real marriage and a marriage of convenience, even though the mechanics of getting married are the same in both cases. Equally, some jobs are different. For example, people see the work of artists as the result of an inalienable "vision" or "gift". Likewise, some people in more mundane fields see their work as an expression of their inalienable identity (see, e.g., Ronco and Peattie 1988). A striking example is provided by an entrepreneur, Paul Hawken (1987: 9), who says that he started a health-food store because of his core biological being:

> Hindered by asthma since I was six weeks old, I had begun experiment-
> ing with my diet and discovered a disquieting correlation. When I
> stopped eating the normal American diet of sugar, fats, alcohol,
> chemicals, and additives, I felt better .... I was left with a most
> depressing conclusion: if I wanted to be healthy, I'd have to become a
> food nut. I bid a fond farewell to my junk foods.

Of course the notion of a calling (e.g. Weber, M. 1958: ch. 2) points to an older link between work and inalienable identity. However, like Hawken's explanation, with calling it is important to distinguish between the sort of work one does (calling or, less archaically, occupation) and the specific institution in which and people with whom one does it (job). For most people, especially wage workers, the latter is much less likely to reflect inalienable identity than the former (see Nakane 1986: 170–3).

Although a gift relationship entails inalienable identities, relations and obligations, these are not the automatic consequence of the core identity of the parties to the relationship. Instead, what is transacted, and how, can be important for defining transactors and their relationship to each other (e.g. Piot 1991: 411–12). As Marshall Sahlins (1974a: 186) puts it, "[i]f friends make gifts, gifts make friends". The task of establishing a friendship, for example, entails large amounts of the appropriate kind of give and take (see, e.g., Hunt and Satterlee 1986). Similarly, etiquette books and common understanding agree that the giving and acceptance of personal clothing between a man and a woman tends to define the relationship in a particular way, as one of intimacy. Alternatively, the rejection of such a present is a denial of that definition, as is the failure to give such a present when it is right to do so. This is recognized in the aphorism that "a man should not dress a girl unless he also undresses her" (in Shurmer 1971: 1244). More decorously, "Emily Post", an arbiter of etiquette, allows a boyfriend to give a girlfriend accessories like gloves or a belt, "but not 'personal' clothing" (Post, Elizabeth 1969: 604). To an earlier generation an earlier Post was more articulate about what the bride-to-be could accept from her affianced and what accepting the wrong present would mean. The woman can accept

> anything he chooses to select, except wearing apparel or a motor car or a house and furniture – anything that can be classified as "maintenance."
> ... [For] it would be starting life on a false basis, and putting herself in a category with women of another class, to be clothed by any man, whether he is soon to be her husband or not.
>
> (Post, Emily 1927: 311)

I said that for most Britons and Americans the core relationships that link them inalienably to others are those of household and family, especially marriage and parentage, and transaction is central to these relationships. This is most obvious in marriage, which requires more than just a formal ceremony. The couple also must transact, must give and take in an appropriate way, but although this may resemble transaction between individuals, it is more complex. The couple's relationship entails a communal existence, a structure that encompasses and defines the two people and makes them "moral persons" within the marriage. One spouse does not merely transact with the other, but at the same time contributes to that communal existence, that "us" that transcends and redefines "you" and "me". For example, in their study of newly married couples, Mansfield and Collard (1988: 113, 151) found this underlay much of what people said about their joint efforts to set up a home, as it appeared in the way working husbands came to see their work in terms of their obligation to contribute to their marriage. Even settled couples often experience the things they do as part of the creation and maintenance of a group and a communal existence. As one woman from a London suburb described her housework to Peter Willmott and Michael Young (1960: 132).

> I often feel at the end of the day that all my efforts have been of no avail. I remember all the polishing and cleaning, washing and ironing, that will have to be done all over again, and like many other housewives I wish that my life could be a bit more exciting sometimes. But when the evening fire glows, when the house becomes a home, then it seems to me that this is perhaps the path to true happiness.

Culturally, the husband and wife who live separate lives and go their separate ways and so have no "us" have a marriage as false as a marriage of convenience. In fact, the give and take and the creation of that "us" is, in some regards, more important than the legal form of marriage. In many industrial societies the rights to "palimony" by a *de facto* spouse (Oldham and Caudill 1984) and to inheritance by children born out of wedlock (Anderson, S. 1987) show that such relationships are coming to generate legal rights and obligations indistinguishable from those in formal marriage.

Transactions are even important in creating relations of parenthood. Many Westerners are predisposed to see parentage as a biological relationship that naturally entails affection and mutual identity. In extreme cases, people claim to feel this affection and identity on being united with the child that they had put up for adoption as an infant years ago (Modell, Judith 1986). However, David Schneider argues (1979, 1984) that in most societies, including the United States, parenthood is not just an expression of the consequences of sexual intercourse. Father and daughter are not so only and wholly because the germ plasm of one was instrumental in constituting the other. Rather, the relationship contains transactional elements as well. Parents look after their children, feed, clothe and house them, activities that bind the children to the people who care for them. One adoptive parent said: "There is only one reality. And that is the definition of parenting . . . . That is an action. It is not a title given to anyone because you have blood. It's a title given because you care, nurture and bring a child up" (Daily Progress 1993). As Diana Barker (1972: 585) put it in her analysis of the ways that parents look after their older children, in these activities "material goods and physical services are translated into lasting relationships" (see also Corrigan 1989). Thus, the relationship is inextricably linked to the transactions that take place within it, for those transactions express and recreate the relationship and thus the identities of the people and even the objects that are encompassed by it.

Indeed, in some ways transaction creates the very identities of those involved in it. For instance, my identity springs in part from my relationships with those around me. This is most clear with my relationships with my wife and children, my parents and brother. It is also true, to a lesser degree, with the relationships I have with colleagues in my department and elsewhere, and even with students I have taught. In an older and somewhat discredited terminology, I have distinct statuses and roles with relation to these sets of people, and over the course of time I internalize – think of myself in terms of – those statuses and roles. My identity, then, springs from those relationships. And those relationships in turn are not timeless things; rather, they are created, recreated and modified by the give and take that goes on within them. Although I have sketched the link between exchange and identity in very general terms, there is nothing mysterious about the processes involved.

VARIATIONS IN ACTION AND MEANING

The Maussian model provides a framework that allows us to consider transactions in terms of three variables: what is the degree of the obligation to transact; how is the object associated with the transactors; how are transactors linked and obligated to each other. While this model describes transactions, it also indicates the importance of a form of people's conceptions of objects that is distinct from the public structures of meaning and identity that have attracted sociological attention. While people see objects as bearers of sign or status value, they also see them as more or less impersonal, as possessions or commodities.

This identity of objects is shaped by the relationships and transactions in which they exist. However, objects have a past and hence have an identity before they are transacted. An object exists not only as it is transacted, but, in Igor Kopytoff's (1986: 68) words, also as "a culturally constructed entity endowed with culturally specific meanings and classified and reclassified into culturally constituted categories". This meaning can spring from the specific history of the specific object, its provenance: who owned it previously, what their relationship was to it, how I got it, what the nature of that transaction was. However, in the absence of specific knowledge it can come as well from a general understanding of a class of objects, an understanding that people use to interpret the specific object they confront and that springs in part from people's individual and collective experience with different classes of objects. Thus, while I may not know the history of a specific shirt or painting, I have a general sense that shirts are produced in factories by anonymous wage workers while paintings are personal expressions of individual artists. Thus, I am predisposed to see the shirt as an impersonal commodity and the painting as a possession.

Although it is convenient to speak of general understandings it can also be misleading, for people vary in the ways that they think about objects and social relationships. I deal with these throughout this book, but it is important to recognize them at the outset. Perhaps the most striking variation is between men and women, who appear to be oriented differently toward the realms of gift and commodity, though even the description of variation by gender obscures variation within genders. Kinship, the core instance of gift relations in industrial societies, is the province of women rather than men, for it is they who arrange the visits, write the letters and remember the relationships that those visits and letters mark and maintain (e.g. Firth 1956; Komarovsky 1987; Loudon 1961; Robins and Tomanec 1962; Willmott and Young 1960; Young and Willmott 1986). Similarly, Christmas, probably the most important celebration of family and kinship, is largely women's work. They are the ones who draw up the lists, buy the presents and cook the Christmas dinners (e.g. Caplow 1984; Caplow, Bahr and Chadwick 1983: 188–92; Cheal 1987). Given this, it is not surprising that women appear to think of the objects that surround them somewhat differently than do men. For example, Csikszentmihalyi and Rochberg Halton (1981: 60–1) found that while both adult men and women talked about objects in terms of a "concern for other people" and "responsibility for maintaining a network of social ties", men rather than women also tended to talk about objects in egocentric ways, in terms of "personal accomplishment, or an ideal they strive to achieve". (Helga Dittmar [1992] and Sonia Livingstone [1992] describe similar differences between men and women.) However, these differences did not appear among the children and adolescents they interviewed, who tended to talk uniformly about the sensual pleasure that objects gave them. Further, older adults, regardless of gender, tended to talk primarily in terms of social relationship.

These gender differences can involve more than who does what. For instance, Francesca Cancian has argued that adult men and women differ in the ways that they think about one of the strongest of personal attachments, love. She says that women tend to equate love with the emotional expression that comes with "talking about feeling", while men are more likely to express attachments through actions, and especially instrumental actions such as "providing help, sharing activities" (Cancian 1986: 692). Not only can this difference lead to misunderstandings between a man and a woman, it means that men are less prone to draw a sharp distinction between instrumental and expressive activities – a lack of distinction that, Cancian (1986: 695) says, also is more common farther down the economic scale.

In addition to these gender differences, and perhaps partly underlying them, are differences in people's experiences with objects in commercial realms, my subject in the next three chapters. Those chapters are not concerned just with the changing formal aspects of production and circulation, such as whether workers are wage employees or family members and whether purchasers pay with cash or barter for objects. These are important, but from my perspective they are so primarily as factors that affect the experiences that people have with the specific objects in their lives, experiences that are likely to shape their understanding of different sorts of objects in general. These experiences have changed markedly over the past three centuries, though changes have affected people of different social locations differently.

John Rule (1987: 104) points to the distinction between people's formal relationships with objects on the one hand, and on the other their interpretation of objects. He does so when he says that a skilled shipwright in the nineteenth century

> could often recognise his own work [in part of the ship] and describe it still as "his" work even when it had been alienated from him by sale. This hidden form of property, an element of continuing "creative possession" is missed by a concept of property limited to a nation [*sic*: "notion"?] of alienated material rights, yet it describes the property that skill invents.

Workers who experience the things they make in this way are likely to understand manufactured objects differently from those whose experience is more impersonal – a population where skilled work is the norm is likely to understand manufactured objects differently from a population where unskilled machine tending, much less office work, is the norm.

As I show in the following chapters, people's experience of the production and circulation of objects in Western societies has not always, or so uniformly, been one of commodity relations and commodity transactions. Instead, this experience is a relatively recent one for the bulk of the population, and for some the world of work is still overlaid with personal and family relations, as Betty Beach (1989) describes for homeworkers in the Maine shoe industry. These changes make it clear that the distinction between gifts and commodities such as exists in the modern West is an historical rather than a universal fact. In describing these changes, the following chapters help explain the changes that have occurred in the ways we think about people, objects and social relations.

2

CHANGING PRODUCTION RELATIONS

I said in the last chapter that the cultural distinction between gifts and commodities is affected by historical changes in the ways that people experience objects in production and circulation, my concerns in this chapter and the next two. The overall trend of these changes has been a growing alienation of objects from people.

In production this alienation has two distinct dimensions. One is the degree to which the individual producer controls and shapes, and hence is embodied in, the production process and the product. This is an element of the classic Marxian model of alienation, and Zygmunt Bauman (1982) argues that it is more important for understanding labor history, at least in England, than is the control of surplus product. At one extreme, the producer controls and determines totally what is to be produced, how it is to be produced and what is to be done with it; at the other extreme, the producer works at the direction of others in a production setting totally determined by others. The second dimension, which has attracted less attention, is the degree to which production takes place in the context of enduring, pervasive and personal structures and relationships. At one extreme, production occurs among those bound permanently and inalienably to each other in all aspects of their lives before, during and after they cooperate in production; at the other extreme, it occurs among strangers who come together only fleetingly to produce.

Understanding the changing nature of production is important for understanding the changing ways people think about objects. The common experience of production becomes transmuted into a common cultural understanding of the nature of production and of manufactured objects. When production is not alienated from producers, people are likely to think of objects as possessions, whether or not they know how any particular item is produced. Alternatively, if production is commonly alienated from producers, people are likely to see objects as commodities, anonymous and impersonal. This is the point Daniel Miller (1987: 115) makes when he says that "manufacture" has become "reified as having a separate and particular connotation", with the result that "manufactured objects" come to symbolize "a particular form of production and its attendant social relations".

39

The increasing alienation of production that I will trace entailed an increasing divergence between the organization and social relations that characterized production and those that characterized the household. The effect of this divergence was magnified by the fact that, during the same period, an increasing proportion of the population was entering paid productive work (Levine 1985: 172–3). One manifestation of this divergence is the growing distinction between the forms of social relations that characterized the economy and the household; another is the growing tendency for economic and household activities to take place in distinct institutions and places. With the growing differentiation of household and production, people came to define these areas of life in opposition to each other, the boundary between the two became more significant and crossing it required more work.

This chapter is a general description of changes in the social organization of production from the seventeenth to the twentieth century in Britain and the United States, but the issues and changes that concern me apply more generally to Western industrial capitalist societies (see, e.g., Bauman 1982; Medick and Sabean 1984; Polanyi 1957). The study of these changes is well trodden ground. Hence, I shall provide only a sketch of the more important ones, while attending more closely to how they affected the sorts of relationships in which people produced objects. In doing so I will demonstrate the growing impersonalization and alienation of production, while at the same time illustrating just what that impersonalization and alienation mean.

I will deal with four ideal types of production in turn. The first I will call cottage industry, production of objects for sale by households as independent economic units. The second is putting out, production by the household under contract with a merchant capitalist who provides raw materials and purchases the finished product. Third is early factory production, production in a central place but with much of the labor recruited and organized by production workers themselves, frequently using family relationships. The last is modern factory production, production in a central place with all labor recruited and organized by the capitalist treating labor as a commodity. Although I describe these as a sequence, they are not a set of uniform stages through which all branches of production necessarily progress uniformly. For instance, cottage industry disappeared only gradually in the West, and modern factory production did not arrive uniformly in all branches of industry. Equally, the overall progression does not reflect some inherent dynamic or search for objective efficiency (Sabel and Zeitlin 1985). But while these steps do not characterize production for the market as a whole at any one time, they do identify the general drift toward the increasing alienation of workers from production and the increasing differentiation of production from household institutions and social relations.

COTTAGE INDUSTRY

The first form of production for the market that I will describe is cottage industry, production within the household. I refer to this as "production for the market" rather than "commodity production" to avoid prejudging whether and in what ways the objects made are commodities in the Maussian sense. My discussion draws on practices in cloth production in England, but it must be remembered that for the bulk of almost all manufacturing "the basic unit of production remained the household" (Swanson 1989: 148). Cloth production was one of the first areas of manufacture to become intensified and industrialized, and the social historian Neil Smelser described it in detail in *Social Change in the Industrial Revolution*, on which I draw freely.[1]

At the beginning of the rise of industrial capitalism, the most common form of cloth production was cottage industry, also known as petty-commodity production (see, e.g., Scott 1986), in which objects are produced for the market using household labor and social relations (for this pattern in pre-industrial Europe see Medick 1976). In its basic form, production occurs within the household by household members using household tools, equipment and raw materials. Smelser (1959: 51–2) describes the technical aspects of cotton cloth production, so here I need refer only to the main stages. Cotton was carded (the cotton fibers combed to help clean them and to align them in a single direction), spun into yarn and woven into cloth by the family: "[T]he father wove and apprenticed his sons into weaving. The mother was responsible for preparatory processes; in general she spun, taught the daughters how to spin, and allocated the ... [subsidiary tasks] among the children" (Smelser 1959: 54–5) (some stages, such as fulling, had moved out of the household by this time; see Carus-Wilson 1966). The finished cloth was then sold to a merchant. This basic pattern was widespread and durable. It is the cottage craftsman system that Esther Goody (1982: 12) describes in Yorkshire woollen manufacture in the eighteenth century, and it was still being used in Europe long after the bulk of textile production had been mechanized, as is illustrated by Louise Tilly's (1984) description of linen weaving in northern France around 1900.

One reason producers are not alienated from the product is that their production is subordinated to their own need rather than the demands and rhythms of the market. This is reflected in the pace and timing of household production. Weaving families routinely had farm holdings as well, and produced cloth as a by-employment, as one of a number of occupations, some for money and some not, that together provided for their subsistence. By-employments were common in England through the eighteenth century and were important for the economic survival of the household (Thirsk 1978; Thompson 1967). Krishan Kumar (1988: 149) describes the common pattern when he says that among weaving families both husband and wife could be involved in "manufacturing" – he weaving, she spinning – as well as "agriculture" in the relevant seasons, while the wife could also do the domestic chores and probably also feed the livestock. The children would be employed as helpers in both weaving and spinning and would also do sundry domestic tasks.

When the demands of their farm were pressing or their need for money slight, they could slow or halt their cloth production. Alternatively, when money was tight or when other demands on their time were few, as in the winter months, they could work harder and longer. Again, this is a durable and common practice. Many of the linen weavers that Tilly (1984) describes produced cloth in the winter and worked in agriculture in the summer.

Alienation is low as well because production relations are household relations, so that the finished cloth was an embodiment of the household structure and the members that structure defined and linked. The obligation to labor is a family obligation, based on the inalienable relationships among people in the household, and the discipline used to coordinate and regulate production is family discipline. These are not fungible laborers who enter into a transient relationship in return for a wage. The woman who carded the cotton and spun it into yarn so that Mr Weaver could turn it into cloth did not do so for a stranger in return for a wage, but because she was Mrs Weaver, and she would not spin this way for anyone else. The child who helped his father weave did so as part of a family relationship that was life-long: he was helping the man who had produced much of the food the child ate, who oversaw his up-bringing and who was training him in his craft, who would have a say in his marriage, who would bequeath property to the boy in his old age, including perhaps the very loom with which the child was working (Tilly 1984), and whom, in time, the boy would help bury. Whether the son loved his father or resented him, he was bound to him in enduring ways.

This cooperation reflected that mixture of affective and utilitarian motives that characterizes systems in which economic and social relations are intertwined. Cooperation reflected the cultural value placed on mutual ties and obligations among family in the household, and so had a moral dimension. Equally, it came about because need drove family members to each other. Subsistence was sufficiently tenuous that households needed as much labor as possible if they were to survive with any degree of security. Martine Segalen's (1983: 78) point about French rural households applies to England as well: "The household had to produce in order to live, and often only lived in order to produce, production guaranteeing the perpetuation of the human grouping." In addition, common labor practices obliged parents and children to look to each other for support. Most training in most occupations occurred within the family household, even in crafts with formal apprenticeship (Rule 1987: 100–1), which helps account for the general tendency of children to follow in their parents' occupation, frequently for several generations (see, e.g., Everitt 1967: 489). So, children who wanted to acquire skills had to look to their parents, just as parents who wanted to secure their children's futures had to train them themselves. Similarly, when adults sought labor to assist the household, generally they looked to their own children.

Even the prosperous households that employed workers to assist in production were unlikely to treat them as impersonal laborers; instead, they lived with the family. And aside from family members, workers who lived with their employers "were probably the largest element in the labour force" in the sixteenth and early seventeenth centuries (Beier 1985: 23). This is how the historian Mervyn James (1974: 23; see also Beier 1985: 24–5) describes the relationship between employee and household among middling farming families in the area of Durham, England, in the sixteenth and seventeenth centuries:

> Servants were incorporated in the family, being housed, fed, and clothed, as well as paid wages, in return for their "fidelity" and "service"; and the developed Puritan (and Catholic) morality of the post-Reformation period required the householder to treat them as he would his children, and be responsible for their moral and spiritual, as well as material, welfare.

The observation that cottage production occurred in the household and that production relations were family relations may be taken to mean that family life, being thus strengthened and intensified, was more harmonious than it is in the present day. But there is no reason to think this. Indeed, as Segalen observes (1983: 2), "we do not know a great deal about the nature of relationships within the rural household", a point echoed by the tentative nature of many of the papers in Medick and Sabean's collection (1984) on emotional relations in pre-industrial societies. Even to say that household relations are embodied in a cloth is not to imply that the family was proud of what it made. They may or may not have been proud, but what is sure is that what they made embodied them and their social relations. To say that household members were linked by inalienable bonds and by need for each other is not to imply that family members loved each other. They may have, but one ought to remember that Cain and Abel lived in the same household. Indeed, a concern with genuine sentiment and emotion may be anachronistic, reflecting peculiarly modern interests that arise from the very divergence of household and economy that I trace in this chapter.

PUTTING OUT

In the simplest form of putting out, a merchant capitalist would supply a weaver, for instance, with yarn and specify the size and quality of the desired cloth as well as when the work was to be completed. The merchant might also provide a warp, yarn fixed to a frame and ready for weaving. In either case, the cloth was woven by the weaver in his own household with the assistance of his family. The merchant would collect it, inspect it, pay the weaver and perhaps supply yarn for another cloth. Putting out emerged from household production in part because cloth merchants sought greater control over production in order to ensure a more regular and uniform supply of cloths of the desired quality than independent producers supplied.

Smelser (1959: 58) says putting out began to appear in cotton production late in the seventeenth century and was common by the middle of the eighteenth century, though some textile production was put out in the Middle Ages (Walton 1991: 352). For other trades, Dorothy Davis (1966: 61) says that by the middle of the sixteenth century in the more crowded London guilds prosperous members who owned retail shops began to provide materials to poorer artisans without shops to be made up into goods, which the prosperous members would then buy back for sale in their shops (see also Earle 1989: 27). Even earlier, putting out appeared sporadically in crafts that involved intensive use of labor (Swanson 1989: 31). Equally, merchant capitalists were not alone in putting work out. Prosperous cottage textile producers themselves put out work to other households, particularly carding and spinning (Smelser 1959: 55–6; for other industries see Rule 1987: 102–4).

The technical operations of cloth production in the putting-out system were comparable to those of cottage industry, but the social relations were different in significant ways. Putting out entailed a prior commodity relationship with the merchant, and so entailed a differentiation of production and control that reduced the autonomy of the producer and hence led to a greater alienation from the product. For instance, the producer did not own the yarn being woven and so was obliged by law to surrender the cloth to the merchant. Some weavers did not even own their equipment, which was provided by the merchant (Smelser 1959: 59). Equally, putting-out workers were less likely to control production. The coordination exercised by the merchant tended to fragment production, which reduced the worker's influence on the product: the people who carded and spun were not likely to weave, and those who wove at times did not put the yarn to the frame but received it already made into warps. Similarly, cottage producers themselves decided what and when to produce and how to dispose of the product, though of course they had to take into account external factors over which they had no control. With the putting-out system, on the other hand, the merchant controlled the provision of yarn and collection of completed cloth, which gave merchants some control of the timing of production, one of the attractions that putting out had for them. Likewise, the merchant indicated the nature and quality of the cloth to be produced. Certainly independent household producers were likely to pay attention to what sort of prices were being paid for what sort of cloth, but they could exercise a discretion about what to produce that was denied to those who had entered into putting-out arrangements. Finally, the putting-out weaver had no influence over the social and market relations with the consumer of the cloth, for the merchant disposed of the cloth without regard for the interests of the producer or the relationship between the producer and the eventual consumer.[2]

Putting-out workers were more alienated from process and product than were independent household producers, but this alienation was only partial. Even though raw materials belonged to the merchant, most weavers continued to own the tools and equipment used to transform the yarn into cloth. Even though weavers had to produce within the time specified, they were being paid to perform a task, and so were able to exercise some discretion about the pace of the work. And, of course, the immediate social relations of production remained household relations. While the product may have been less an embodiment of the interests of the producers than it was in cottage industry, it remained an embodiment of the web of household relationships in which production took place.

The putting-out system, like cottage production, was not simply a passing stage in the evolution of industrial capitalism, but has remained up to the present. It is important to the making of objects that carry an aura of craft production, such as Harris Tweed cloth (Ennew 1982), but equally is important in many ordinary branches of industry (Benson 1989: 57–8; see generally Allen and Wolkowitz 1987; Boris and Daniels 1989; Pennington and Westover 1989). Modern forms are less likely to make use of household labor and household relations in the way that early cloth production did, but even so some modern putting out retains a distinct family air and occurs within the context of durable social identities and relations (Beach 1989; Benson 1989: 60–3). However, although putting out has continued to find a place in capitalist production, in most branches of industry its heyday is over, as it was superseded by forms of factory production, to which I turn now.

EARLY FACTORY PRODUCTION

The appearance of factories meant that production moved out of the household to a separate place more directly under the supervision of the capitalist (for a more detailed discussion of the emergence of factory production, see Robinson and Briggs 1991). Both the degree of control by the capitalist and the relative importance of commodity relations varied over the history of factory production, signalled by my differentiation of early and modern stages.

Much early factory production was patriarchal, the term William Staples uses in his description of Kenrick's, a hardware manufacturing firm near Birmingham, England, in the nineteenth century. Briefly, in patriarchal production capitalists employed contractors who agreed to produce a specified number of items within a specified time and were paid according to an established price structure. These contractors then hired their own assistants, and at Kenrick's, as elsewhere, these assistants were "mostly – though not exclusively – family members or relatives" (Staples 1987: 68). Typically, then, two sets of production relations co-existed, a commodity relationship between capitalist and contractor, and a personal or familial relationship between contractor and assistant.

This system appeared in the cotton-spinning factories that were established toward the end of the eighteenth century. Factory owners hired spinners, who in turn employed their own assistants, usually "their wives, children, near relatives", a practice that was regularized in trade-union rules of the time, which "explicitly prohibited members from recruiting assistants outside the narrowly defined classes of children, brothers, orphan nephews, etc." (Smelser 1959: 189). Consequently, work was a family affair. Smelser (1959: 185) found in one spinning mill at the beginning of the nineteenth century that twenty-six families provided 70 percent of the regular work-force of 136, over 3.5 employees per family. Family relations were important in Amoskeag Mills, in Manchester, New Hampshire, beyond World War I (Hareven 1982: 113) and through World War II in the textile industry in the American South (Blauner 1964: 76–8) and in England (Penn 1985: 65).

This pattern had long existed in coal mining. Owners employed miners at a piece rate, and miners drew on their own families for assistants. In her discussion of British mine labor in the early part of the nineteenth century, Jane Humphries explains the attraction of family assistants. The prime attraction was financial: the wage paid to an assistant did not go outside the family. In addition, family ties made it easier for the miner to supervise and control his assistants as they did their ancillary jobs: "[T]he need to *control* helpers explains the recourse to girls' labour, not necessarily because they were more docile, but because miners preferred to employ *daughters* over whom they had parental authority, rather than boys from another family" (Humphries 1988: 106). The strength of the familial bond appears again in the fact that miners felt safer with their own families, who were more likely to come to their aid in an emergency (1988: 107). But just as miners desired assistants who were family members, they were also compelled to look to their families, for often family labor "was the *only* source of labour. Other helpers were simply not available" (Humphries 1988: 106). Desire and need drove the family together.

Moving production to a central place facilitated a set of technical changes that were to have an important influence on the relationship between people and objects in production. Early patriarchal factories were little more than centralized workshops where workers carried out just about the same activities using the same equipment that they had under the putting-out system. However, centralization allowed the capitalist to introduce new productive technology, especially powered machinery, more readily than was possible for independent household producers, though equally it allowed workers to develop the habits and structures of collective organization and action that would benefit them when mechanization threatened their status as skilled workers later in the nineteenth century (see Penn 1985: 119–20).

Mechanization proceeded at different rates in different industries. However, when it occurred it undercut the control that workers had over production and so increased their alienation. First, it meant that workers were less likely to own their own tools and equipment. Second, it tended to convert individual producers from workers shaping what they made by the exercise of their skill into routine operatives. Smelser (1959: 128) says, for instance, that the introduction of the self-acting spinning mule in the 1820s "substituted the role of a 'minder' for that of a highly skilled spinner". Third, powered machinery reduced or eliminated workers' ability to pace production. Smelser (1959: 118) notes that with the introduction of steam-driven machinery textile workers

> became more subordinated to a work discipline, because the power-source lay in steam, not in their own muscles; they could no longer pace their industry in the cottage or even work sixteen hours a day during the last days of the week in a hand-mule shed to make up for a leisurely Monday and Tuesday.

Even without mechanization, the patriarchal factory system brought about important changes in the social relationships in which production took place. To begin with, those relations were more clearly hierarchical than they had been previously. While there were important inequalities in the households that were part of the putting-out system, with the patriarchal factory system a further layer of authority and control was added, represented by the capitalist factory owner. Furthermore, with production in a central place, the factory-owning capitalist could physically observe and oversee work more closely than the merchant in the putting-out system (this is discussed in Marglin 1974). Indeed, the emergence of industrial capitalism was associated with a general concern with observation, supervision and control (see Thompson 1967; Foucault 1979). This oversight allowed the capitalist to see and try to undercut practices that may have been necessary for the social survival of the work group but that slowed production, such as time contractors spent training their relative-assistants in their trades (cf. Grieco 1987: 11–14). In at least some industries capitalists implemented this knowledge and increased their control by setting the rate of pay at a level that would allow workers "their customary subsistence *if* they worked hard and *drove their assistants to similar heroic efforts*" (Humphries 1988: 106). Like the introduction of powered machinery, this made it harder for workers to set their own pace.

At the same time, the control by skilled workers over their production was being threatened by the spreading notion of free labor and associated attacks on the system of craft control of apprenticeship. In 1814 the legal support for this system was undercut when Parliament repealed sections of the Statute of

Artificers of 1564 and thereby allowed "free" apprenticeships, unregulated by craft associations and therefore freely manipulable by employers (see Bauman 1982: 56–9). John Rule, an historian, shows that in attacking the old system of craft-regulated apprenticeship in the skilled trades, the advocates of free labor were attacking the idea that skill and the use of it for gain was a possession of individual workers that was regulated by associations of workers. Critics denied that workers had rights in their skill and saw attempts to exercise these rights as an unjust restriction on individual liberty. Rule (1987: 110) points to Thomas Paine, who argued that this system denied people "the freedom to make bargains over the 'personal labour' which was 'all the property they have'".

Artisan groups claimed that individual skilled workers possessed the right to exercise their trade to earn a reasonable living, and that workers collectively had the right to regulate themselves and the exercise of the skills they possessed. Craft custom was taken as the guide to work practices, and the employer was not expected to interfere with production "so long as properly made goods were produced to the quantum regarded as normal by the trade" (Rule 1987: 109). Artisans resisted the interference by employers with their right to regulate their skills, just as they disciplined fellow artisans who worked for pay that was below the going rate, who worked in conditions that threatened the security and status of the trade, or who worked for more than the conventional hours (1987: 112). In disciplining individual workers artisans sought collectively to assure a fair livelihood for each individual craftsman and sought collectively to regulate and exercise the use of their own skills.

The right of individual workers to earn from their trade was acquired by serving an apprenticeship. Apprenticeships provided some craft masters with a cheap supply of assistants, as well as the premium that some were able to charge for taking on apprentices. However, masters had to pay the costs of looking after their apprentices, so that they may have cost more than their labor and premium. Certainly textile factories found them more expensive than hiring free labor (Smelser 1959: 187). However, when obligations to apprentices were reduced, employers could find apprenticeship financially attractive. Roger Penn (1985: 130–1) describes how English companies between the two world wars replaced journeyman engineers with lower-paid apprentices, and how they sacked apprentices once they qualified as journeymen and replaced them with a new batch of cheap apprentices.

But whatever the financial impact of apprenticeship on masters and employers, it served important functions for the craft community, though it is important to remember that the artisanal apprenticeship I describe here was organized and executed differently from apprenticeship in merchant guilds (see Earle 1989: ch. 3). It provided training in the skills of the craft; it marked those who were to be admitted to the body of recognized artisans, those with the right to live by their trade; and it regulated entry to the trade and so protected the property of skill of those who possessed it. However, while artisans' rights were exercised by individuals, they were maintained by the craft as a group, based on a common artisanal identity that cut across the specific links between workers, their assistants and their employers.

Thus, property in a craft was not a commodity relationship between artisans and their skill that was analogous to patents and copyrights, which can be bought and sold. Instead, it had aspects of a status identity, with the artisans collectively being the group embodiment of that identity. In part this is because, as the anthropologist Tim Ingold (1990: 11) argues, the production skills that apprentices acquired "are particular sedimentations of experience and, as such, are active ingredients of personal and social identity". Serving an apprenticeship, then, was not just the way to acquire a skill, it was the way that an individual acquired the appropriate social identity and the badges of that identity. These included special language, habits and clothing, the knowledge of artisanal custom and ritual, the obligations of artisans to each other, and a sense of the honor and dignity of the craft (Rule 1987: 108–10).[3]

The successful attack on this system by the advocates of free labor led to the substitution of an impersonal and more purely economic relationship between person and work for an older, more social one. Where workers as a group had collectively possessed and been possessed by their productive skills, free labor substituted the individual worker negotiating the sale of Paine's "personal labour", the ability to labor at the direction of the employer. As Bauman (1982: 8) notes, the repeal of the Statute changed "beyond recognition" the "very character of apprenticeship as an initiation into a totality of patterned existence of the closely-knit trade community: the craftsmen's resistance ... was a struggle for the restoration of such a community".

E. P. Thompson's discussion of the shift in the ways that people thought about time shows how the elements of patriarchal factory organization were reflected in and reinforced by broader cultural changes. He says that under the older, pre-factory regime time frequently was understood in terms of what he calls "task-orientation". It was defined by the task at hand and its inherent rhythms, so that the work-day "lengthens or contracts according to the task" (1967: 60). This appears in the custom of St Monday, which many producers celebrated by taking Monday as an additional day of rest, content to complete the tasks they needed to do by more and harder work at the end of the week. However, the spread of centralized manufacturing led to a novel understanding of work time as an external dimension, no longer a reflection of the task at hand but reliant only on the clock. Time came to be the factor that governed and coordinated the pace and processes of production, and so came to be the governor of the worker, who sold labor power for a time and submitted to the pace defined by the clock. Workers did not, however, submit happily, and even under a modern, repetitive production regime they try to impose their own structure on their undifferentiated work time in order to give it meaning and make it tolerable (see Roy 1960; see more generally Mars

1982: ch. 3). The subordination of workers to abstract clock time remains problematic.

I have described some of the ways that the emergence of patriarchal capitalist production led to a greater alienation of the producer from production and the product than had existed previously. Alienation was by no means as great as it was to become under modern factory production, and in the more skilled trades, such as metal working, workers could maintain a degree of control over production (Staples 1987: 71). Consequently, this system did not mark a total transformation of people's experience of objects in production. Instead, it marked a continuation and extension of the growing impersonality that I described first in the change from cottage industry to the putting-out system. The shift to modern factory production extended this alienation.

MODERN FACTORY PRODUCTION

The older patriarchal system gradually gave way to modern factory production, often through intermediate stages such as Staples (1987) describes for Kenrick's and as Hareven (1982) describes for Amoskeag Mills (see Edwards 1979: ch. 6). In the modern factory the capitalist did not merely supervise production, but controlled it directly, so that the worker became increasingly subordinated to production (see Stone, K. 1975). Modern factory production eliminated the older familial and craft-community relations between workers and their assistants, as it eliminated much of the need for skilled work. With the emergence of the modern factory system, workers were less likely to experience themselves as part of a durable web of relations that defined them in terms of their links with their co-workers and their tasks. Instead, they were more likely to experience themselves and their co-workers as isolated. Increasingly, workers were alienated from production and its products.

While I will describe the subordination of labor to capital as it existed in the factory, it had a cultural dimension as well. Workers were seen as different sorts of people from owners, and the two categories needed to be kept apart, just as in modern firms managers often think of laborers as a breed apart (Kanter 1977: ch. 3; Ouroussoff 1993). Thus, around 1900, Home & Colonial Stores in Britain forbade workers buying company shares without permission, "an offence the only adequate punishment of which is instant dismissal" (Mathias 1967: 143). A more substantial token of this cultural distinction is in education changes taking place at about the same time. In both Britain and the United States, advocates were urging, and schools were adopting, policies that segregated children of different social backgrounds and prospects (Carrier 1986). Although it had begun to appear earlier (Davidoff and Hall 1987), this separation of social classes became pronounced in the urban layout of the last decades of the nineteenth century, as more and more managers and professionals moved to homogeneous suburbs and as clerical and manufacturing districts became distinct from each other (for England, see Girouard 1990: 236, ch. 17).

Commentators often link the characteristics of modern factory production to a more thorough-going and efficient mechanization (e.g. Hounshell 1984: ch. 6). However, such a view ignores the social nature of technology, the social factors embodied in it and the social contexts of its use. The central elements of the modern factory regime do not spring from the complexity that machines entail, but from the way that machines objectify production (see Ingold 1990). This objectification can exist in the absence of mechanization. The changes in pottery production that Josiah Wedgwood introduced late in the eighteenth century illustrate this (see Forty 1986: 30–4; McKendrick, Brewer and Plumb 1982: ch. 3). Wedgwood marketed his pottery by displaying samples in showrooms, and in order to ensure that the pieces the customer received matched those displayed, he had to prevent the inevitable lack of uniformity that the reigning system of craft production entailed. He did so by breaking up the production process into a series of steps, each the job of a single worker who, following a model, shaped, modified or colored the pottery. With this scheme, Wedgwood separated the skill of production from the potter, objectified it and re-ordered it to suit his own ends. The results were the increased division of labor, reduced discretion and skill at each stage, and control of production that characterized the modern factory, all without significant mechanization. But whether the impetus was changes in equipment or in organization, the result was an extension of the fragmentation that had begun in the patriarchal system and an increase in the alienation of the producers from each other and from the objects they produced.

With encouragement from Harry Braverman's *Labor and Monopoly Capital*, greatest attention has been paid to the fragmentation of planning and execution in the modern factory, a key aspect of the objectification that I have mentioned. With the introduction of devices like the self-acting mule or processes like Wedgwood's pottery, the modern factory became a purpose-built tool in the way that Kenrick's hardware works was not, embodying the interests of its owners and designers. For Braverman (1974: 212) this meant

> the progressive elimination of the control functions of the worker, insofar as possible, and their transfer to a device which is controlled, again insofar as possible, by management from outside the direct process. It is this which dominates the new place of the worker in production processes.

Because production decisions were built into the very fabric and organization of the factory, workers needed less and less skill and judgement to carry out their tasks, which reduced their freedom of action and their ability to endow the objects that they made with their identity.

This rigid and alien environment is most pronounced in production using assembly lines to make objects from interchangeable parts, and Richard Edwards (1979: ch. 7) gives it an appropriate name, the technical control of production. He says this sort of control "is embedded in the physical and technological aspects of production and is built into the design of machines and the industrial architecture of the plant" (1979: 131). The classic example is the early Ford Motor Company plants on Bellevue Avenue in Detroit and, after 1910, at Highland Park (this discussion draws on Hounshell 1984: ch. 6). In these plants management sought to modify the work environment, to turn the factory into a tool that they controlled and that reflected their interests. In so doing management made it less likely that those workers involved in producing things would work in an environment that they themselves shaped and that embodied their own interests, identities and relationships.

In conventional factories all operations of a particular sort, such as milling, had been carried out in a single department to which parts were brought for the job and using machines with which the skilled operator performed a variety of tasks (Braverman 1974: 110–12). As a result, the factory was organized spatially around the different sorts of operations, and hence the different skills, tools and sets of workers used in them. The Ford factories, however, used machine-tools designed to perform only one job, extremely efficiently, laid out according to their place in the production process. Walter Flanders, who was responsible for laying out the Bellevue plant, "placed machine tools according to sequential operations on various parts .... If hardening or softening or any such nonmachine operation needed to be carried out during the sequence, Flanders placed a furnace or whatever in the correct sequential location" (Hounshell 1984: 221). The physical organization of the factory was subordinated to the flow of the production process, rather than to the skills and machines used in production. Thus, the design and spatial arrangement of the machine-tools used in production embodied as rigorously as possible, and furthered as much as possible, the production goals of Ford management. As a consequence, work discipline was built into the very factory itself.

Likewise, in conventional mass production individual workers or sets of workers performed a range of operations to assemble one unit at a time from parts provided for them at their work station, and Ford used this technique when the Highland Park plant was first opened. However, the development of the assembly line limited each worker to a single task, and so eliminated the work team and the cooperation that static assembly entailed. In one of the first Highland Park assembly lines, building flywheels for magnetos, the workers were

> to place one particular part in the assembly or perhaps start a few nuts
> or even just tighten them and then push the flywheel down the row to

the next worker. Having pushed it down eighteen or perhaps thirty-six inches, the workers repeated the same process, over and over.

(Hounshell 1984: 247)

Shortly after this line was set up, in April 1913, the flywheels were placed on a moving belt, forcing workers to work at a uniform and more efficient pace. The result of these changes was that the labor time required to produce a magneto dropped from twenty to five minutes (Hounshell 1984: 248). This was not simply an application of Frederick Taylor's scientific management, which focuses on training the worker to get the task done more efficiently (from the capitalist's perspective). Instead, it was an attempt to change the worker's task. Producers were subordinated to the production process: "Ford engineers mechanized work processes and found workers to feed and tend their machines." The result was that "the machine ultimately set the pace of work . . . . This was the essence of the assembly line and all the machinery that fed it" (1984: 252–3).

This subordination of labor did not come about solely because Ford rearranged equipment and installed the moving line. It occurred as well because Ford was able to do away with workers' skills, and hence with their residual ability to influence the pace, process and product of production. In this, free labor finally triumphed. This was possible in large part because tools had only recently become good enough to turn out nearly identical parts. Prior to this, assembling a machine from metal parts required skilled fitters, who gave parts the final shaping they needed to fit properly. To circumvent this, Ford engineers pressed for greater and greater precision in production equipment. When Max Wollering began his supervision of the Ford Bellevue plant in 1906, he directed his mechanics to design equipment such that the parts produced with them would fit together without any need for the skills of the metal worker. Wollering called these devices "farmer tools", says Hounshell (1984: 221), "because with them he asserted that he could make a farmboy turn out work as good as that of a first-class mechanic". The skill of manufacture became embodied in the machines and the parts they produced, and was no longer necessary or even desirable in workers: "[T]here was no fitting – and therefore no fitters – in any Ford assembly department" (1984: 234).

The assembly line, especially the single-purpose Ford line at Highland Park, is not that common. However, in its very extremity the Highland Park plant makes especially clear some of the distinctive features of modern factory production, though these were continuations of changes that accompanied the move to the patriarchal factory: the breaking-down of production into more and simpler steps and the increasing subordination of the worker to production.

These changes meant that those who labored ceased to be agents of production, people oriented toward the task of making things. Instead, they became instruments of production, sources of labor power that the company purchased as commodities and applied to specific production operations for specific lengths of time (see Ingold 1988: 170–3). A corollary of this is the elimination of the need, which existed under the patriarchal system, for workers to cooperate with each other in order to produce. The engineers who laid out Highland Park sought to replace this cooperation among workers as agents with their coordination as instruments, governed by management and mediated by the physical processes of making cars, the placement of machinery and the moving belt of the assembly line, intended to "speed up the slow ones, restrain the quick" (Hounshell 1984: 248). The social interactions among workers that are necessary for cooperation disappeared; coordination required only that workers interact with the machines they tended or the parts they assembled. This does not mean that they were mute during their whole 9-hour shift, only that the plant was designed as much as possible to allow them to remain mute without affecting production, which could be carried out just as well with silent strangers. This facilitated the disappearance of social bonds between workers (cf. Zetka 1992 on the persistence of those bonds where workers must cooperate in automobile production). Assembly-line workers are so constrained that their ability to shape their work is reduced to "the various withdrawals from work such as absenteeism and sickness", and "sabotage – 'the conscious act of mutilation or destruction' that reduces tension and frustration" (Mars 1982: 87).

Not all factories are as impersonal as Highland Park, not all workers are as alienated as Highland Park workers (see Harris 1987; Piotrkowski 1979). Indeed, even Ford ended up abandoning single-purpose production for a more flexible system (Hounshell 1984: ch. 7). But this does not mark a retreat from the double alienation of the workplace, because workers are enmeshed in a set of bureaucratic rules and procedures that structure work in a way that is less concrete but no less effective than the physical structuring of the Ford works. The result is what Edwards (1979: ch. 8) calls "bureaucratic control", which the sociologist Michael Burawoy describes in his *Manufacturing Consent* and calls the "corporate internal state". Burawoy (1982: 72) says such a system reduces "antagonism between worker and shop management", but increases "lateral conflict among different groups of workers". Edwards (1979: 145) makes the same point when he says such policies "push workers to pursue their self-interests in a narrow way as individuals".

Since World War II, another source of alienation has become more important, as the division of labor has begun to take on a form qualitatively different from much of what existed before. When Wedgwood fragmented the making of pottery, he separated planning from execution and turned his workers into instruments rather than agents of production. However, those workers could still understand the various stages of pottery production and how they meshed with each other to produce a final product. Broadly speaking, the same was probably true of Highland Park workers. However, with more recent technical and organizational changes in a growing number of industries, planning itself has become fragmented and the production process has become so complex that workers decreasingly are able to understand, except at a general level, how the various stages in production mesh to produce the final product. Production is becoming opaque to producers.

In the 1980s commentators became more vocal in their criticism of the alienation of workers from the firm and their work that characterized technical and bureaucratic control. Those commentators sought instead ways to make the firm a social unit to which employees were bound in durable ways, a unit that would be more than the sum of the commodity relations that constitute it. Business books like *In Search of Excellence* (Peters and Waterman 1982) were urging executives to involve workers more closely in the firm. For example, in *Vanguard Management*, James O'Toole (1985: esp. ch. 4) urged executives to see workers as "stakeholders", people with an interest in and claim on the company that employs them. He applauded companies that encouraged or subsidized ownership of stock by their employees, that involved workers in corporate decisions, that gave them freedom and responsibility to determine their own work practices, that encouraged them to see the way that their work related to the overall goals and operations of the company, and so forth. Many of these policies would reduce alienation by giving workers a greater control over production and may very well make going to work more pleasurable and interesting. However, these suggestions do not herald the end of alienation in Western industrial capitalism, as a number of scholars have noted (e.g. Blanchflower and Oswald 1988; Braverman 1974: 445n.; Grenier 1988; Kelley and Harrison 1991). In fact, O'Toole himself said that only a handful of companies have instituted these sorts of policies, though people have been advocating them since the beginning of the twentieth century in the United States (Edwards 1979: 91–7) and Europe (e.g. Campbell, J. 1989). One important reason to be skeptical of the appeal and impact of these reforms lies in the historical blindness of the advocates. In their successive attempts to subordinate workers and alienate them from production, owners and managers were following a compelling commercial logic. Until reformers begin to address the historical question of why modern forms of control over workers and production emerged, they are unlikely to be able to propose realistic alternatives.

But in any event, these policies would not restore workers' control or reduce their alienation to the level that existed before modern factory production, for workers would remain confronted with an extensive division of labor and they would continue to produce with others in relationships derived overwhelmingly from the workplace itself rather than pre-existing structures. Indeed, for O'Toole key functions of these policies include the continued, albeit perhaps less oppressive, subordination of labor to management. As he said (1985: 127–8) of one company that he applauded, "[a]s employees started to participate in managerial decisions, they came to identify with the needs and goals of top management – they came to understand why and how to carry out better the company's mission."

IMPERIUM

I have sketched a set of stages that highlight the growing alienation of objects from people in production. While this sketch points to an important set of changes, it is important to remember that people's experiences were never uniform. In the heyday of cottage cloth production there were casual, unskilled laborers who had no real say in the work they did. Equally, workers in modern factory production are not all so alienated as those on the Highland Park lines. To flesh out and qualify my schematic discussion of modern production, it is useful to look at one company in some detail, "Imperium", David Halle's pseudonymous chemical plant in northern New Jersey in the late 1970s.

Halle's study is useful because it focuses on the ways that workers seek to evade management's effort to control production and its attendant impersonality, and so exercise their own control over production. Rosemary Harris's (1987) anthropological study of an English chemical works, ChemCo, also addresses this issue, and echoes many of the points I make here. Indeed, Halle (1984: 145–9) uses his description to challenge Braverman's assertions about the loss of worker control in twentieth-century Western capitalist production. However, it is worth remembering Robert Blauner's (1964: esp. 6–7) point that there are important differences between continuous-process production, as in chemical works such as Imperium, and assembly production, as in plants like Highland Park, and that these standardized production techniques differ fundamentally from unique-product manufacturing (1964: ch. 3).

The Imperium plant was designed to incorporate the most modern production equipment. Although management issued detailed instructions on how work was to be done, workers exercised a significant amount of control because, like skilled workers in early factory production, their collective knowledge of how the plant worked was greater than the knowledge of those who designed and managed it (Halle 1984: 119–25). For example, workers knew better than management the effects of the many minor and often unrecorded modifications that had been made. Most important, workers learned operating shortcuts that were easier and quicker than the formal production instructions but that produced a product that satisfied the laboratory technicians who assessed the output.

> In many cases workers come across such devices by accident. A chief [of a production team] forgets to do something the formula card [that

adding an ingredient – and the laboratory does not comment, so the "accident" becomes a technical discovery, a useful component of the men's practical knowledge.

(Halle 1984: 121)

To recall my earlier point about the growing opacity of production, this knowledge is only practical, for workers had no systematic understanding of how or why these accidents produced the results that they did. Even so, it allowed Imperium workers a significant amount of control over production, which gave them an advantage over management in their attempts to influence the ways that production took place. This was most spectacular in strikes, when managers tried to run the plant and frequently failed, but it occurred as well when managers saw that their attempts to overrule production decisions by workers often produced disastrous results. Workers used this knowledge to organize production to suit their ends in a tacit agreement with management, which left them alone so long as output was regular and met specifications.

Equally, the relationships among Imperium workers were not merely reflections of their common commodity relationship with their employer. Instead, many were linked through kinship, for membership in family and friendship networks was important for being hired in the first place. This pattern, moreover, appears fairly often among blue-collar workers, and frequently management consents to or even encourages it (Grieco 1987). Thus, Halle found (1984: 5) that of 121 blue-collar workers, 37 percent were closely related: "[T]here are twenty-three brothers and seven brothers-in-law. Ten men are cousins, twelve fathers or sons, and six uncles or nephews." Not only were personal relationships often important for getting a job, workers interacted socially with their fellows intensely. They spent much of the work day talking to one another, about "work, sports, fishing, hunting, food, politics, sex, and local gossip"; they played cards and they cooked and ate together (1984: 141; for clothing workers cf. Roy 1960).

Clearly, many industrial workers do exert control over production and are linked with their colleagues. Even so, there have been profound changes in production that have led to a greater and more widespread alienation between worker and product. First, the relationships developed in the workplace frequently did not extend outside the Imperium plant. This was particularly so for married workers, who "spend more and more time with their families. They tend not to stop at the tavern after work or to spend much of their leisure time with male friends from work" (Halle 1984: 44). Likewise, pre-existing relations among workers had a different meaning from those among workers in older systems of production. Though many at Imperium were related and perhaps even beholden to relatives who helped them get jobs at the plant, production relations did not reflect personal relations. The fathers who got jobs for their sons did so as a part of their personal relationships with their children, not because they had to draw on close kin in order to produce or needed to pass on skills; the sons whose fathers worked at Imperium did not work for their fathers, they worked for Imperium; they were not paid by their fathers, they were paid by Imperium. Here, then, sociality was added on to the more purely economic relations that existed at Imperium; it did not permeate economic relations in the way that occurred in older production regimes.

The position of many workers may resemble Imperium more than Highland Park, and work in different segments of the economy is organized in different ways (Baron and Bielby 1984). However, these variations are just that, variations on a central theme of increasing alienation of workers from each other, from the production process and from the things that they make. If Imperium workers have surreptitious influence over production, it hardly compares to the recognized and extensive control exercised by the skilled artisans that Rule describes, much less household weavers. If Imperium workers are beholden to relatives for their jobs, the link that unites them neither orders production nor reflects the need of workers to draw on their families in order to produce.

CHANGING RELATIONS OF PRODUCTION

I have described different relations of production that emerged with the development of Western industrial capitalism. These do not form a unified sequence or set of stages, but they do mark a general trend that affects people's experience of objects in production and so affects their understanding of the social identity of objects. The most obvious change is that production and things produced gradually became more alienated from the workers who made them.

As might be expected, workers frequently resisted this trend, though here I can only allude to the complexities of that resistance (see, e.g., Brecher *et al.* 1978; Penn 1985; Price 1983; Stepan-Norris and Zeitlin 1991). Textile workers frequently used violence against their employers and the machinery they were expected to use, most spectacularly in the Luddite movement early in the nineteenth century. Skilled artisans agitated against the repeal of the apprenticeship statutes and disrupted the work of those who violated craft custom. Workers responded to modern factory production with growing unionization and strikes, and less spectacularly by simply quitting. At Highland Park in 1913, labor turnover associated with the installation of the moving assembly lines was so high that it was necessary to hire more than 950 people in order to achieve a net increase in the work-force of 100. The other 850 people refused to stay at their jobs. At the end of 1913, less than 5 percent of the company's 15,000 workers had been at Ford for three years or more. The only way the company could keep workers was by raising wages, by more than 100 percent between October 1913 and January 1914 (Hounshell 1984: 257–9; note, however, that labor turnover generally was quite high in manufacturing firms early in the twentieth century [see Jacoby 1985: 115–17]).

This resistance to the changes I have described was not simply resistance to technical modifications of production processes or equipment. Instead, it was resistance as well to a reconceptualization of the relationship between the worker, the work and the product. What Craig Calhoun (1982: 65) says of Luddite agitation applies more generally. The Luddites

> were concerned with more than machinery. They campaigned for the right of craft control over trade, the right to a decent livelihood, for local autonomy, and for the application of improved technology to the common good. Machinery was at issue because it was used in ways which specifically interfered with these values.

Underlying these specific complaints was a resistance to a radically different understanding of people and their work.

Two anthropologists, Steve Barnett and Martin Silverman, describe this new understanding as one that sees people as having two distinct aspects. One is a core, of "things which people believe to be real things, which are in an important sense thought to be internal to the individual or continuous with the individual as a concrete being" (Barnett and Silverman 1979: 51). This core is the inalienable self, distinct from the second aspect of the self, a superficial collection of attributes that can be separated from the core. These relate not to one's being but to one's performance at specific tasks. This is the aspect of the self that is pertinent in modern production relations, which exist among "individuals (more or less) freely entering into agreements to do certain things in accordance with certain standards and rules" (1979: 51). Describing ChemCo, their pseudonym for the agricultural chemicals factory in England that Harris also studied, Theo Nichols and Huw Beynon (1977: 193) report that "the men we talked to ... knew that they, as individuals, weren't really needed by ChemCo – that others could come in 'off the street' and do their job. They were told this day after day" (but cf. Harris 1987: 73–84). This is just another way of saying that, in production, people have become fungible suppliers of labor power, and that they are to be assessed on the quality of what they have to sell.

The corollary of this alienated self in work is the alienation of work and its products. As the employer hires only an alienable part of the self in production, so things that people make are divorced from them. They are divorced legally for they are the property of the capitalist. They are divorced technically because the capitalist control of work processes means that workers have little effect on the things they make. They are divorced socially because workers do not produce in groups linked by enduring and pervasive personal relationships. They are divorced culturally because the self that engages in production is not the real, core self, but an alienable attachment.

Although this separation is pronounced, it may reflect less the reality that people experience than the dominant rhetorics that are used to talk about it. Even though what Barnett and Silverman describe is a powerful element of Western culture, at the same time many people seek to colonize the alienated realm of work with more durable, less alienated relationships. Ernest Beaglehole (1932: 132) argues that there is a general tendency for people to form "an enduring and intimate relation" with the objects in their work lives, as when

> the workers and machine tenders . . . speak of the instrument of labour and the products thereof as their "own." In many cases the worker will rationalise . . . this identification of himself with the objects with which or upon which he works. But since he usually speaks of his "love" for his machine or his tools, he shows that other than utilitarian considerations are influencing his relations with the machine he calls his own.

Similarly, Mark Granovetter (1985: 490) says that economic relations between people in different firms are not in fact alienated and impersonal, but tend to develop a clear social and moral component, as they come to trust each other and come to restrain their own opportunism. Equally, Gerald Mars (1982) describes how many groups of co-workers form social relationships that reduce their alienation from each other, just as he shows how workers frequently manipulate their work to gain greater control over it. These colonizations show that workers respond actively to the alienation that characterizes industrial capitalist production, but it is important to recognize that in many cases these colonizations are only partial. They may stress or strengthen links between employees and their colleagues, their equipment or their work, but often they do so by stressing the separation of these things from the firm itself (e.g. Harris 1987). The alienation, then, may be from the firm rather than from the workplace.

I said in Chapter 1 that understanding the ways that people think about objects requires considering their experience of the objects around them. In this chapter I have described briefly the complex history of changes in the social organization of production that have occurred as part of the rise of Western industrial capitalism. However, production is not the only way that people experience objects in social settings, and indeed as a smaller and smaller proportion of the population is engaged in the actual manufacture of things the social experience of production is likely to have a smaller and smaller impact on people's cultural image of manufactures. In the next chapters I turn to another important way that people experience objects – buying and selling them in retail trade.

3

CHANGING CIRCULATION RELATIONS
The Emergence of the Market

I turn now to a key way people deal with objects in circulation – retail trade. As production moves out of the household, retail trade becomes the main way that many people acquire the objects that they use. Equally, as a declining proportion of the work-force is engaged in manufacturing, retail trade becomes a more important source of people's understanding of objects.

Although retail trade is important in the West, few sociologists and anthropologists have paid attention to it, and they are not much further along than Marx's very general comments on the relationships among production, distribution, exchange and consumption in the *Grundrisse*. Those who study stores and shopping tend to focus on the symbolic issues of consumption, not the social relations of circulation (e.g. Benson 1979; Miller, M. 1981; Williams, R. 1982). Even when writers do describe these social relations, the subject is usually tangential to their main interests (e.g. Benson 1986, concerned with gender; Williams, B. 1988, with community; Zukin 1990, with forms of capital). This inattention is particularly unfortunate in the case of anthropologists. Anthropology has devoted much attention to circulation and has generated an extensive and interesting body of knowledge and ideas. In slighting retail trade, anthropologists of the West have forgone the chance to use Western cases to refine and reflect on that knowledge and those ideas, just as they have forgone the chance to make a fruitful contribution to the study of the West.

It is important to remember that forms and relations of circulation can have their own influence on the ways that people are related to and think about the objects that surround them. A person who gets an object in a durable, personal relationship is likely to see it as bearing a personal identity and being embedded in a social relationship, even if the object is produced by anonymous factory workers. To point to a distinct role for circulation in shaping people's understanding of objects is not to deny the importance of production as an influence. It is, rather, to argue that those who ignore circulation can understand only part of what is involved. Here I am only repeating a point made in different ways by Josephides (1985), Kelly (1992) and Strathern (1988), among others: the study of production itself is an inadequate basis for understanding how people deal with objects in particular and economic activities more generally.

Attention to circulation also can help extend and qualify our understanding of the sign value of objects. As I noted in the Introduction, many writers see objects and people in terms of their locations in a structure of types of objects and people. This orientation does not help us to see how people relate to and deal with the objects in their lives, and especially how they transact them with each other. These transactions are important, because they can endow objects with a personal specificity that weakens their impersonal symbolic meanings, their sign values. There is, then, an opposition between the object as sign and as gift. This opposition is not absolute: the object as gift still carries its sign value, but in attenuated form. This opposition suggests that when people acquire the greater proportion of things through more personal transactions and relations, they are less likely to see objects as sign values. Thus, modern consumer culture – the world of objects as signs – would be relatively unlikely to emerge before the spread of the neutral commodity and impersonal trade. This does not mean that objects in Western Europe bore no impersonal sign values before the end of the eighteenth century. Obviously they did (see McKendrick, Brewer and Plumb 1982: ch. 2; Schneider, J. 1978). It does suggest, however, that consumer culture did not depend solely on developments in production and mass media; changes in circulation played their own part.

This chapter and the next describe aspects of the history of retail trade over the last few centuries, showing how alienation in circulation has increased. Buyer and seller were increasingly likely to be autonomous strangers. Sellers were increasingly likely to be passive and impersonal intermediaries between producers and consumers. Buyers were increasingly likely to transact with wage laborers alienated from their employers, the objects they sold and the selling that they did. In short, the circulation of objects in retail trade was increasingly likely to entail commodity transactions in impersonal relationships between people and objects. I write of likelihoods here, because these changes have not been absolute. In the West there has always been impersonal trade, just as there is likely always to be personal trade. However, the relative frequency of these sorts of trade changed markedly.

Because the history of circulation is less studied than the history of production, my presentation must be discursive and tentative. None the less, one can discern two important stages in that history. One, which I describe in this chapter, occurred in the decades around 1800, primarily in London, though it was common at different times in different countries (for parallel changes in France see Miller, M. 1981; Williams, R. 1982). It was at that time that a significant number of stores began to cater to anonymous, casual customers, and the impersonal concept of "the market" began to displace older understandings of trade and older, more durable relationships between shopkeeper and customer. The second stage, which occurred in the decades around 1900 and which I describe in Chapter 4, is the embedding of market rationality in the structures and relations of retail trade and associated commercial activities. This embedding increased and gave institutional form to the impersonality of people and objects in commercial transactions.

CIRCULATION AND MORAL ECONOMY

To understand what the emergence of modern retail trade entailed, it is useful to understand the older order. This older order was neither simple nor static, as the economic historian Joan Thirsk (1978) demonstrates, and it has not attracted extensive attention from historians of trade. Even so, it is possible to sketch the main understandings of trade and the main trade practices that were to be displaced.

Before the eighteenth century, most English people were peasant farmers living in villages or hamlets. Their orientations and their village institutions were dominated by the linked values of localism and self-sufficiency. As Dorothy Davis (1966: 4) notes, their "dream of perfection was not a chest full of coins to spend, but to farm wide acres" in order to produce what was needed, a dream of a "house economy" (cf. Gudeman and Rivera 1991; Eugen Weber 1976: 35 makes similar points about self-sufficiency in rural France in the nineteenth century). People could and did travel beyond the village in order to trade; they were not forestalled by poverty or lack of transport (see Britton 1977: ch. 15; Hodges 1988: 133–9). However, compared with the later eighteenth century and after, there was relatively little trade, and the bulk of it took place between people who were known to each other, defined and linked by a common local social structure. The image of this trade is the local market, bringing together local producers and consumers. Furthermore, most market towns were oriented toward local rather than specialist trade (Biddick 1985; Hilton 1985: 18–19), a pattern that persisted into the second half of the nineteenth century (Brown 1986: 65).[1] This local orientation was reflected in vagrancy and settlement rules and acts that made it difficult for people to establish residence in a new locality. Parish officials were suspicious of strangers and were quick to turn them out (Beier 1985: 32).

Households and localities could not produce everything they wanted and needed, and their ability to do so declined in the later medieval and early modern period. Some counties had long relied on grain grown elsewhere, as had the growing urban population, and there was a marked expansion in regional trade at the end of the sixteenth century (Willan 1976: chs 2, 3). The result in much of England was a dual economy, one with two distinct spheres (Biddick 1989; cf. Kula 1976). One sphere revolved around subsistence production and was based on the village and its small-holding peasantry; the other revolved around commerce. While some householders were more oriented toward one economic sphere or another, it is probable that most households were engaged in both to a degree. Demand for petty consumer goods was rising, and a growing number of householders, rural and urban, devoted some of their time to producing such objects (Thirsk 1978). Likewise, a growing number of agents were invading the countryside in search of agricultural produce to feed urban dwellers (Fisher 1966: 136–9), where they were met by a growing number of large farmers producing especially for trade. Empirically and conceptually, however, such production and commerce were the exception. The commercial agricultural sector was dominated by a fairly small group of relatively rich farmers and merchants (Everitt 1967: 553), and it was centered on brewing and textiles and related trades (Hilton 1985: 8). For most English people the local market town was the furthermost point in their economic lives.

Localism and self-sufficiency were embodied and reinforced by regulations that sought to secure local produce for local people, partly in order to reduce the chances of unrest in times of dearth. At the simplest level, the structure of market tolls, which often cost foreigners twice as much as local sellers, helped channel local products to local consumers (Everitt 1967: 487). Further, outsiders traveling to markets, unless they were established merchants, were likely to be seized as vagrants, as happened frequently to petty traders (Beier 1985: 74). Equally, producers usually had to offer their wares to local householders before they could sell to traders or elsewhere. In fishing villages, for example, people frequently were required first to offer their catch in the market to local buyers. Even in the London markets in the seventeenth century, as in urban markets elsewhere, the first hour or two of trade was restricted to local householders: traders, hawkers and shopkeepers were excluded (Davis, D. 1966: 78; Fisher 1966: 150; Swanson 1989: 10; Westerfield 1915: 209).

National legislation in the sixteenth century tried to ensure that goods passed direct from farm and artisan's shop to consumer and generally restricted purchasing other than for domestic consumption or immediate use in manufacturing (see Westerfield 1915: 137–41). These regulations were part of a general condemnation of the practices of engrossing, the buying of an entire stock of goods (e.g. a farmer's grain crop) in order to gain a market advantage, and of forestalling and regrating, the buying of goods before they arrived at the market (forestalling) and re-selling them later (regrating) at a higher price – key elements of modern retail trade. Thus, manufacturers were regulated to prevent them re-selling the materials they had bought unless they had substantially modified them. For example, ironmongers could not sell the metal they bought unless they had transformed it (Westerfield 1915: 241), just as bakers had to convert into bread the flour or meal that they bought, instead of re-selling it.

To assure that trade was carried out in conformity to these rules, "secret" or "private" deals, trade outside the market and hence outside official scrutiny, were prohibited: London grain importers, for instance, were prohibited from trading from their homes (Davis, D. 1966: 68–9). It was this concern that trade be visible that underlay the stress on the "open market", chartered and regulated buying and selling. Market officials were supposed to test weights and measures, to control large-scale traders, to enforce standards of quality and price, and to ensure fair trade generally (Hilton 1985: 15–16). Perhaps just as important, the sheer visibility of trade in the open market "afforded at least a measure of protection to both consumer and tradesman. The fact that transactions became the common talk of the town discouraged, if it did not prevent, wholesale cozenage" (Everitt 1967: 571). As Jean-Christophe Agnew (1986: 31) puts it, "[w]ith its cross, weighing beam, booths, stalls, pillories, and tumbrils, the market made of its publicity the basis for its claim of utility, security, and equity."

The open market was intended to ensure that trade be fair rather than free, and many traders who operated outside the market were criticized for an acquisitiveness that led them to shirk their social obligations. A complaint against a private cattle dealer in London was that he traded "not respecting any conscionable course of dealing, but altogether his own private gain" (in Everitt 1967: 569). A conscionable course of dealing required that the deal be equitable. If completing it would work serious hardship on one party, then the contract was invalid, even if drawn in proper legal form (Everitt 1967: 570). Thus, commercial activities had to meet moral, rather than more purely economic, criteria. As J. E. Crowley (1974: 6) put it in his analysis of economic thought in early colonial America, "[i]t was the traditional view that exchange . . . was a social matter involving reciprocity and redistribution: competition, in the sense of one man's gaining at the expense of another, was a violation of this traditional ethic."

It is important not to exaggerate the uniformity of people's adherence to this understanding. In London playhouses early in the seventeenth century audiences, consisting of a high proportion of apprentice merchants, were regaled with the Gallant. He was a rapacious young man who, with guile and lack of scruple, took advantage of his more moral friends and relations to achieve both his own self-interested ends and the acceptance of his elders and betters (Griswold 1983; see also Agnew 1986). Earlier, and more soberly, some writers began to advocate the expansion of petty manufacture and commercial agriculture as a way of generating and spreading wealth. Thirsk (1978: 13–14) dates this from the middle of the sixteenth century, though such projects did not begin to flourish until later in the century, only to wilt in scandal in the seventeenth century. Defoe summarized one of the principles of these writers around 1700 when he said that "trade ought to pass through as many hands as it can" (quoted in Thirsk 1978: 147), the better to spread the wealth throughout the kingdom. These marked alternative understandings and evaluations of trade that are closer to our own; but these were signs of divergence, not yet of displacement.

In this early period, then, material transaction and social relation were not separated conceptually in the way that they later became. Instead, before the eighteenth century trade was regulated to try to make it conform to an economic model very different from our own. This was the model that E. P. Thompson (1971) calls a moral economy, which he distinguishes from the political economy of theorists like Adam Smith. So far as possible, transactions were to be direct transfers from local producer to local consumer. Any trading practices that seemed likely to encourage non-conformity, such as secret trading and even manufacturing, were suspect, watched and regulated closely. The same applied to traders who did not conform to this model. Middlemen of any sort were suspect, and while people "recognized, perhaps grudgingly, that [some of them] offered a genuine service, . . . a suspicious eye was kept on their behaviour" (Swanson 1989: 10). Pedlars and hawkers of all sorts, who were intermediaries, itinerant and frequently poor, were tolerated even less, and often declared vagrant and jailed (Beier 1985: 89). From our perspective, though probably not from theirs, regulators were seeking to protect the moral order from the intrusive, corrosive effects of impersonal market rationality of the modern sort.

However, regulation and restriction, which persisted to the end of the nineteenth century, could not prohibit private dealing (Agnew 1986: 49; Brown 1986: 30). These deals predominantly were part of long-distance trade in commercial goods within the kingdom and overseas, and in the later sixteenth and early seventeenth centuries this trade grew markedly in response to the demands generated by the London markets, the growing export trade, and the victualling and provisioning requirements of the royal household and armed forces. This trade involved sophisticated commercial techniques and large quantities that were alien to ordinary market dealings (on credit, see Postan 1966; see generally de Roover 1974). Here were the agents of London fruiterers who "came down into Kent . . . [and] purchased in springtime the prospective crop of . . . [growers], sometimes for several years in advance". These were the transactions

> of a Hertfordshire knight sending 2,000 quarters of malt to London in four years; of a Smithfield cooper buying 8,000 boards from a Sussex yeoman; of a Cheshire drover sending 600 cattle a year to be fattened in Essex; and of 1,700 or 1,800 veals being sold in Cheapside every Saturday.
>
> (Everitt 1967: 511; see also Biddick 1989: 130–3)

But while these deals were large and complex, typically they were between relatives, friends and neighbors. Just as need and sentiment drove family members to look to each other in the early forms of production that I described in Chapter 2, so need and sentiment drove kin to look to each other in these commercial deals. Because this trade took place outside the open market, beyond the public eye and the security that it provided, kin and community were more important than in local market trade, for these links among traders were a key basis of the moral structure that regulated this trade (Everitt 1967: 558).

Alan Everitt illustrates the bonds of kin and community in the agricultural trade, noting that a

> group of Thanet farmers who sent malt to the capital in James I's reign were not only themselves related, but operated through London factors who were their own nephews and cousins . . . . [Likewise, the] purchase of Kentish fruit by London fruiterers, and their ownership of orchards in the countryside around Teynham, often arose from their inter-marriage with the daughters of Kentish farmers and from the fact that they were themselves sons or cousins of Kentish yeomen.
>
> (Everitt 1967: 513)

The same was true of military victualling, royal provisioning and the export trade. Patents and contracts were awarded to royal courtiers, dependants and relatives, who themselves were likely to re-grant them to their own dependants and relatives. The man who had the final task of arranging the purchase and transport of goods "set on foot a similar process in his own town, forming a working partnership from among his own relatives and neighbours" (Everitt 1967: 530). Everitt sums this up (1967: 557) when he says that such trade "necessarily operated through a network of neighbours, friends, relatives. Sons, fathers, brothers, cousins, wives, uncles, mothers, brothers-in-law: all were drawn into the circle" (see also Mauro 1990). Such webs of personal relationship remained significant in core areas of English commerce and manufacture well into the nineteenth century, strikingly so in the case of Quaker firms (Davidoff and Hall 1987: 215–22).

The common practices, regulations and beliefs that I have described indicate that the circulation of objects was relatively unalienated for most people most of the time. The things offered for sale were likely to be the possession of the seller, who was the person who grew them, made them or transformed them in significant ways. Further, seller and buyer were not likely to be anonymous individuals, but neighbors or fellow locals, seen frequently by and known to each other, and jointly subsumed by the web of identities and relationships that defined and bound the local community.

Just as the goal of local self-sufficiency reflected and reinforced deeper values, so did the form and regulation of trade. The concern that producers and consumers trade direct, without the intervention of forestallers and regraters, was articulated in the economic philosophy of mercantilism, which sought the development of commerce, but not free markets (Polanyi 1957: 70–1). Instead, it subordinated commerce to the common weal, particularly the material wealth of the nation. In this philosophy, most intermediaries served no purpose. As one mercantilist pamphleteer in the early nineteenth century put it, "but their meer *handing of Goods one to another*, no more increases any Wealth in the Province, then Persons *at a Fire* increase the *Water in a Pail,* by passing it thro' Twenty or Forty hands" (in Crowley 1974: 88). Even Adam Smith, no mercantilist, objected to intermediaries in trade, and in analogous, though hardly identical, terms (Lubasz 1992: 49). Smith held that retail and, to a lesser degree, wholesale trade were inferior to agriculture and manufacture because they employed relatively little of the society's labor per unit capital and increased the wealth of society only by the level of the trader's profits.

The social evaluation of trade entailed a moral evaluation of traders: those who aided the common weal were good, those who were purposeless intermediaries were bad. This moralization is expressed by an Elizabethan writer (in Willan 1976: 50) who said that the merchant adventurer involved in foreign trade

> is and maye be taken for a lordes fellow in dignitie, as well for hys hardye adventurynge upon the seas, to carrye our plentye, as for his royall and noble whole sales that he makes to dyvers men upon hys retourne, when he bryngeth in our want . . . . [But retailers were] not worthy the name of merchaunts, but of hucksters, or chapman of choyse, who, retayling small wares, are not able to better their own estate but wyth falsehode, lying and perjurye.

This moralization helps explain attempts to define retailers, in order to distinguish them from their betters, as the Merchant Adventurers Company defined retail trade around 1600 in order to deny membership to those who engaged in it. Their definition contained two elements. First, retailers were those who keep an open shop or display of their wares. Second, retailers were those who traded in small quantities, "small" varying with the item involved. For London members, this meant "[t]he minimum quantity of many imported cloths was the piece; of currants, prunes and dates, wax and flax, battery and ironmongery it was the hundredweight, and of small haberdashery it was the gross". For provincial members the stipulation was they "should not sell by less than the yard or the pound" (Willan 1976: 51, which also describes the Spanish Company regulations of 1605).

While mercantilist thought may have represented important elements of commerce in this late pre-capitalist era, it needs to be supplemented by a sense of the underlying values that commerce embodied and shaped. These are illustrated in an anecdote published in the seventeenth century and related by Thirsk (1978: 15):

> An English vessel once put into Caernarvon with a cargo of apples. The townsmen were so outraged at being offered apples where they had looked for good corn that the town council forbade the inhabitants to buy them, and the cargo lay in the harbour untouched until the apples rotted.

The townsmen had intended to trade "their best Welsh wares: friezes, broadcloth, and wool", and had looked to do so for English grain. Why were they outraged?

I suggest that the Caernarvon townsmen saw honest wares – grain, cloth and wool – as things that people produced by honest work, the extended application of skill and will to the materials on which they worked (this differs somewhat from Thirsk's interpretation). In this work, the farmer and the grazier, like the weaver, guided and applied their own skilled efforts to transform or shape the transformation of something: seed corn into grain, lambs into sheep, fleeces into cloth. In terms of the issues raised previously in this book, they produced objects that embodied them. This is what gave these wares value. But what about apples? These were not things that people made: "Fruit grew naturally on trees, and was there for the taking" (Thirsk 1978: 14). Cloth and apples were not comparable morally, and should not be traded for each other: they belonged to different spheres of exchange. To compound the insult, picking fruit required little skill and was not even performed by those who owned the trees, but by wage laborers – "Employing the idle to pick the fruit" (1978: 14) – which did not confer value on the fruit that justified trading it against honest wares. This incident suggests that people thought that the value of an object in trade consisted of its cost to the seller (which for artisan-traders frequently meant the cost of its raw materials) plus the amount of intentional effort it contained.

This understanding includes how objects in trade ought to be linked to the people who trade them: honest wares embody the honest effort of honest people. As it did for the artisans I described in Chapter 2, this meant working to embody one's own skills and intentions rather than working merely at the direction of others. The work that is acceptable is work that imposes the self on the object in transforming it. Passing the pail of water through twenty hands, like employing the idle to pick the fruit, results in things of little value.

EARLY SHOP TRADE

Although local self-sufficiency was desirable, it was not possible, particularly in urban areas, and as towns expanded they had to draw more and more from larger and larger hinterlands. London's imports of wheat from the rest of the country tripled from 1500 to the middle of the seventeenth century, its oat imports increased nine-fold and malt sixteen-fold, primarily in the second half of the period (Everitt 1967: 507; see also Willan 1967: 78; Fisher 1966). It is not surprising, then, that shop trade, the precursor of modern retail trade, emerged first in urban areas, though it did so only slowly. In the Middle Ages, a town the size of Leicester would have had only two or three pure retail shopkeepers (Davis, D. 1966: 18; Eugen Weber 1976: 223 notes the near-absence of purely retail shopkeepers in rural France in the nineteenth century). During the course of the seventeenth century retail shops became an ordinary, if not very common, feature of life in English towns (Chartres 1977: 49; Davis, D. 1966: 60; Willan 1976: ch. 3).

The typical early shop was not a pure retail establishment. It was the place where an artisan sold his or, less commonly, her wares. The typical early trade relationship was markedly personal. The setting, the objects sold and the transaction all involved and even required close personal involvement by the buyer and seller.

To begin with, shop trade did not occur in special places devoted only to economic transactions and bearing the mark of that devotion. Instead, trade occurred at the home of the seller, for typically shops were part of people's houses and were not distinguished architecturally from private residences.[2] Shop traders usually lived "over the shop", a pattern that is memorialized in the design of a vast number of buildings that still contain shops in modern England, though it is less common in the United States. Artisan shopkeepers usually had a work room on the ground floor of their houses, and sold their wares from a front room on the ground floor or from a covered space on the pavement. Even in London, "the commonest kind of retail shop occupied the ground floor of a house" (Davis, D. 1966: 101). This pattern prevailed as well in Paris, but was breaking down in Holland by the seventeenth century (Rybczynski 1988: 39, 59).

As a part of this unity of home and shop, shopkeepers made relatively little distinction between family and business. Shopkeepers did not see their shops as a corporation in Gudeman and Rivera's (1991) sense, an autonomous business that the shopkeeper happened to own. Instead, the household was a single economic unit, with the shop living off the family and the family living off the shop as need and opportunity arose: "[H]ousehold expenses were often charged to the business ... [and] business expenses were often charged to the household. The business and the household can be separated only for analytical purposes: in reality they were interwoven parts of a single function" (Alexander, D. 1970: 189; see also Carruthers and Espeland 1991: 45; Clark 1979; Earle 1989: 112–13).

Similarly, the household was a single social institution. The integration of hired workers into the family that I described in Chapter 2 occurred as well in shops. Such a household would contain kin, both closer and more distant, and outsiders "'adopted' into the shop-household complex .... [T]he tradesman assumed responsibility for educating the apprentice in the trade and for promoting his moral and physical well being" (Alexander, D. 1970: 189–90). Just as the people of the family and shop were integrated, so were the activities. Spouse, children and servants worked in the shop during crush times; shop workers, usually apprentices, lived and ate with family members and worked in the household during crush times. In other words, when people bought in a shop they confronted household members in household space doing household work, though this conjunction of shop and family means that "household" meant something different from what it does now.

Moreover, the identity of the shopkeeper was likely to be stamped on the objects for sale, so that they were the shopkeeper's possessions. This is because shopkeepers invested their wares with their personal judgement and skill (I return to this point in Chapter 4). They did so in the difficult task of locating and securing supplies of the necessary quality and in the processing and even the manufacturing of what they sold. This was obviously the case with shops run by craft workers. However, cloth merchants worked on the cloths they bought before selling them, as wine merchants blended and sweetened their wines before selling them (e.g. Earle 1989: 41; Willan 1976: 108–9, 143). Likewise, in the food trades butchers predominantly bought stock live, killed and dressed it, sold the meat to consumers and the waste to industrial buyers (Alexander, D. 1970: 121; Blackman 1962). Even grocers, who traditionally had dealt "almost entirely in foreign produce of dried fruits, spices, and a variety of teas, coffees and sugars" (Blackman 1967: 110), had to "prepare the goods for sale, [so that] considerable skill was necessary in processing, sorting, and blending" (Mui and Mui 1989: 219; see generally Alexander, D. 1970: 110–12).

Not only were shopkeepers likely to have stamped their wares with their identities in significant ways, their relationships with their customers were likely to be relatively personal. Partly this was because shops served a small clientele. The earliest reasonable British data are from a government survey of 1759, which under-counted small shops. The survey showed that in England and Wales as a whole there were 43.3 people per shop; for southern England there were 35.5 people per shop; for London there were 30 people per shop (Mui and Mui 1989: 40). For comparison, in 1840 the United States had about 290 people per shop over all (Hower 1938: 93).

These personal relations between buyer and seller should not, however, be romanticized. At the upper end of trade, many shopkeepers found themselves dependent upon aristocratic or gentry customers, which frequently placed them in "a highly vulnerable, occasionally humiliating and certainly weak position" (McKendrick, Brewer and Plumb 1982: 198). At the lower end customers could find themselves dependent on traders for credit, which was necessary generally and was relatively long-term: six months or more was common (Earle 1989: 115–17). Customer and tradesman were not, then, independent economic actors but were linked in a durable, personal, social and economic relationship, even if it was one that each struggled to control.

Indeed, in the absence of such a relationship customers could find it difficult to buy reasonable goods at a reasonable price, for often traders would not deal with just anyone. One such trader was Robert Gray, of London, early in the seventeenth century. When he went to Exeter on business he left his wife to look after trade, and in one of his many letters, he wrote to her, "I pray see that when any of our costomares com to London ... be verye carfull to sarve them that ar good men; and for the other lett them goe" (in

Willan 1976: 123). Furthermore, as nothing was standardized or guaranteed, everything had to be thrashed out between shopper and trader.

> The shopper of those days, whatever he needed, had to buy a lot of personal service along with the goods, for he depended very heavily on the shopkeeper's knowledge and skill and honesty. To shop successfully it was important to choose a reliable shopkeeper and come to terms with him. Not necessarily friendly terms; acrimonious terms would do just as well; but at least personal terms.
>
> (Davis, D. 1966: 181)

The personality and durability of the relationship between customer and shopkeeper appears as well in the practice, common at least in rural areas, of customers working off part of their debt. William Wood ran a village shop in the 1780s in Didsbury, and many of his customers performed services for him, the value of which was credited to their accounts. Ann Bancroft and George Fletcher paid off parts of their debts by "'spreading mole hills' at 1s. 2d. a day", while William Birch's wife and daughter did haying (Mui and Mui 1989: 40). In such a situation, shopkeepers and customers bought and sold with each other, each transaction building on previous transactions and anticipating future ones in a way very different from the fleeting cash sale of the modern supermarket, pharmacy or discount store. This pattern persisted into the nineteenth century in the Connecticut River Valley in Massachusetts (Clark 1979) and indeed through the nineteenth century and into the early twentieth century in country stores in the United States (Harvard University 1919: 47–8). Gerald Carson (1954: 97–8) summarizes common rural trade practice in the United States in the nineteenth century when he says that

> [i]n the ledger the customer who received goods on tick was marked debtor . . . . Frequently there would be an entry in both [debt and credit] columns, the buyer of merchandise receiving credit for live chickens or shoeing the storekeeper's horse. The accounts were continuous, and settlement infrequent, though the almanacs advised settlement annually, around December or January.

Consonant with this pattern of durable relationships, traders appeared not to have thought of "consumer demand" as an abstract aggregate. Instead, it was a set of people with ties to individual shopkeepers. Such an attitude helps explain why shopkeepers wanted to have an established body of customers and disliked poaching the customers of others. For example, William Stout, a Lancaster shopkeeper late in the seventeenth century, thought it improper to invite into his shop "any of my master's or neighbour's customers" (in Mui and Mui 1989: 11), customers of the merchant to whom he had been apprenticed or of nearby merchants. Likewise, a draper who traded in Bristol at the beginning of the nineteenth century said that merchants valued a regular patronage over an impersonal trade with higher volume, and that this concern with stability was felt by customers as well, who were reluctant to take their custom to a stranger. The draper said that

> a man commencing business in the country, unless he had lived in one town a number of years as an assistant, and had made a connexion or succeeded to some old-established trade, or become a partner in a house, did not stand a very good chance in a country town, unless he went to very great lengths to make himself known.
>
> (in Alexander, D. 1970: 162)

This was as true of relations among merchants as it was of relations between customers and merchants. Running a respectable retail business required a range of dealings with different sorts of merchants, manufacturers, wholesalers and the like who could be trusted and who could trust the shopkeeper. Such a web of durable relationships emerged only slowly, often in years spent as an apprentice to an established merchant, and it was not lightly disrupted (see, e.g., Mui and Mui 1989: 219).

This conception of customers as a stable body of individuals went hand in hand with the idea from moral economy that "since every man occupied an appointed place or degree in the body politic, every man had a claim on that body to provide him with the means of livelihood" (Everitt 1967: 570), which means sufficient to maintain an appropriate level of consumption. People had not, in other words, institutionalized scarcity by assuming that desires are infinite (see Macpherson 1979; Sahlins 1974b: 3–4). The historian David Alexander (1970: 161) translated this into economic and commercial terms when he said that there existed the "assumption that demand curves are inelastic, and that competitive pricing will not increase sales sufficiently to maintain profit margins; or, looked at from another point of view, that the size of the retail market is fixed, and that increased sales in one shop means losses for others". These assumptions existed among Parisian retailers early in the nineteenth century (Miller, M. 1981: 21–3) and remained important in England through the 1890s (Winstanley 1983: 81). This set of attitudes helps explain why shopkeepers practiced fair trade rather than free, sought to maintain established prices and restrict price competition. For example, in the eighteenth century petitioners to parliament argued that itinerant pedlars should have to adhere to the "'established' or 'fair' price, the changing of which would wreak havoc on dealer and customer alike .... Open price competition was a distasteful and destructive practice in the eyes of traditional shopkeepers" (Mui and Mui 1989: 83). Even in London early in the nineteenth century some merchants were arguing that prices charged by different shops for the same item should vary only when one sold for cash and the other credit (Alexander, D. 1970: 163).

To the community that held to it, this system of beliefs about levels of consumption and trade relations would tend to be self-perpetuating, because self-evident. If demand were relatively fixed, it would make no sense for a shopkeeper to try to stimulate sales. Doing so only shifts demand, it does not generate it. A draper who reduced the price of cloth for a month might sell more, but the extra demand would have only two possible sources. One would be the customers of other drapers, which would result in the impoverishment of one's fellow traders and the censure of the moral community for denying them the means of livelihood. The other source would be the future: one's own customers buying more cheaply what they would not use until later, when their need for it actually arose. The result would be the impoverishment of oneself in the future, when those customers would fail to buy what one had sold them already. Equally, if shopkeepers made no effort to attract new customers, instead offering comparable wares at comparable prices according to the custom of the trade, then demand would likely appear stable and customers would likely continue to patronize the same shops. Obviously perfect stability did not occur in practice. Traders complained about each other's unfair practices and parliament enacted and re-enacted sumptuary laws to stabilize consumption (Baldwin, F. 1926). However, trading and consumption patterns were relatively stable and it was thought proper that they were so.

I have described a system in which most retail trade was embedded in durable personal relationships. Objects were possessions of the seller; seller was linked to the place and act of selling; buyer and seller were linked to each other. The structures and practices of this trade expressed and reinforced the value placed on localism and on trade as a social relationship. Even those engaged in large-scale and long-distance trade did so within a web of personal relationships. Recurring complaints about unfair practices indicate that other forms of trade were taking place. Equally, however, these complaints show that there were common assumptions about how trade should be carried on, and the available evidence suggests that these assumptions matched trading practices reasonably well most of the time (Thompson 1971).

THE EMERGENCE OF IMPERSONAL TRADE

The legal structures supporting localism had largely disappeared by the start of the eighteenth century (Beier 1985: 173), and during the second half of that century the gradual weakening of this older system began to accelerate. Trading practices started to change more quickly in urban areas, and a growing number of people began to espouse a newer, more impersonal view of commerce (see, e.g., DeBolla 1989: ch. 4.; Dumont 1977; Pocock 1975: ch. 13; 1979; Thompson 1971). Both conceptually and practically, economy was becoming increasingly differentiated from society. In retail trade this meant that buyers, sellers, objects and relations were becoming increasingly impersonal. This was true particularly in London. It is difficult to realize how different London was from anywhere else in England. Peter Borsay's (1989: 3) observation, referring to the beginning of the eighteenth century, gives a hint of this difference: "At the turn of the century there were scarcely seventy settlements of over 2,500 inhabitants, and a mere three cities of over 20,000. One of these was the 'monstrous city' of London with half a million souls."

While there had been a steady growth since the seventeenth century in the sheer number of objects that English people owned (Weatherill 1988), it was in the decades around 1800 that the social relations of circulation in which people acquired those objects began to change significantly. It was in those decades that something very like the modern store selling anonymously to a mass market began to appear, albeit only on a small scale in certain branches of trade. Household and shop began to separate, as shops came to be distinguished from houses architecturally and spatially. Mass (in the sense of anonymous) marketing appeared, as shopkeepers increasingly sought individual transactions with unknown buyers rather than extended patronage by established customers. Customers were increasingly acquiring objects in impersonal interactions in impersonal institutions.

These changes in forms of circulation were shaped in part by changes in forms of production, and especially the growth of factory production that occurred in the second half of the eighteenth century and thereafter. For instance, the historian Neil McKendrick (1974) says that the spread of factories led to the growth of female and child labor, which in turn increased the number of households with two, three or even more wage earners. Such households were able to spend more; and because they had less labor available for subsistence production, for making and mending, they *had* to spend more, to buy what they could no longer do for themselves (Heyman 1994 describes how this process can become self-sustaining). The resulting growth in demand led to a sharp increase in retail trade.

The spread of factory production did not just affect households in the way McKendrick describes. It also affected the nature of objects for sale, making them more uniform. Frank Fanselow (1990), an anthropologist, says that when goods are not standardized, branded and packaged, the purchaser is likely to be unsure of the nature of what is for sale. As was noted previously, in such a situation the purchaser who develops a personal relationship with the trader is better able to avoid deception and over-charging than the passing buyer. With the spread of standardized mass manufactures, however, purchasers were better able to rely on their own experience, rather than the trader's claims, when assessing goods. Close relationships with traders were becoming less necessary, and impersonal forms of trade were becoming more possible.

Paul Alexander (1992: 86–8) objects that Fanselow exaggerates both the ability and the tendency of buyers to assess the nature of goods for sale. Equally, Alexander argues that the increasing specialization of production and division of labor associated with mass production means that buyers are less able to assess quality than they had been. Moreover, Alexander notes that in systems of mass production, retail sellers increasingly are able to set prices independently of buyers, without bargaining. He argues that this is because sellers have privileged access to wholesale price information. Whether or not Alexander has identified the important causal factor, it is true (as I describe below) that retailers were increasingly offering to sell wares only at non-negotiable prices that they themselves had set.

Alexander simplifies somewhat the way that factory production affects the knowledge of price and quality available to seller and buyer. However, he is correct in pointing out that it makes objects more opaque to buyers, especially the buyers likely to be shopping in the emerging new-style stores in London around 1800. With this opacity it became easier for seller and buyer alike to impose new, symbolic meanings on commodities (cf. Williams, R. 1982). It became easier for objects to acquire sign value. Thus, to return to a point I made earlier in this chapter, changes in both production and circulation facilitated the emergence of sign value for objects, though this emergence took place only slowly over the nineteenth century. Changes in both realms meant objects that people bought were less likely to be embedded in older systems of meaning, whether of quality in production or of social relationship in circulation.

I said that one factor facilitating change in retail trade was the growth in demand that McKendrick identified. This growth, coupled with sheer increase in urban population, meant that cities had to draw more on distant producers, which increased the role of intermediaries and reduced the likelihood that the householder would purchase objects from their makers. Intermediaries became ubiquitous during this period, though not universal even in the London food trade (Alexander, D. 1970: 232; Fisher 1966; cf. Sheffield, described by Blackman 1962). Families spent some of their rising income at markets. However, as cities expanded outward, shops, together with itinerant traders, became much more convenient than urban markets, which usually were near the center of the city (Shaw, G. 1985: 293–4). Thus, though many urban food markets continued to flourish through the twentieth century, their number decreased significantly between 1750 and 1900 (Blackman 1962: 96; Brown 1986: 14). As well as this urban demand, Jane Humphries (1990) indicates that enclosures induced a greater reliance on purchased items in many rural areas.

The growing importance of intermediaries was killing the old belief that trade ought to pass through as few hands as possible. As early as the seventeenth century some began to argue that "occupations which passed work through many hands benefitted the nation more than those which involved one process only and passed directly from producer to consumer" (Thirsk 1978: 146). The view emerging seemed to be that while handing buckets from one to another may not have increased the water in the buckets, it made for more work for bucket-handlers. But the debate was becoming pointless, overtaken by events.

Retail shop trade was increasing, though there is disagreement about the amount of that increase (contrast Alexander, D. 1970: 92–3 and Winstanley 1983: 12–14). Much of the increase in trade was for goods, like clothing, that had not previously been sold retail very much; much of the demand was from people who had not previously been very significant as shop customers (e.g. Mitchell 1981: 45). This increase brought new people into the trade and facilitated the development of trade techniques and orientations that formed the basis of a new retail order. One token of the emergence of this order is that this period saw the appearance of several stores that were to remain significant in retailing in London through the twentieth century: Flint & Clark (later Clark & Debenham) in 1790, Heal's in 1810, and Swan & Edgar in 1812 (McKendrick, Brewer and Plumb 1982: 86). Equally, this was the period that saw the development of the shopping arcade as a novel form of trading (MacKeith 1986).

It was in this period that a significant body of shopkeepers began to operate in terms of what we, though probably not they, would think of as "the market", consumer demand abstracted from the particular people with whom the shopkeeper dealt (but see Agnew 1986: 41). Traders at the upper level sought to free themselves from their dependence on powerful customers by banding together for mutual support in the middle of the eighteenth century (McKendrick, Brewer and Plumb 1982: 222–4; aristocratic domination of traders also weakened in France in the later eighteenth century [Williams, R. 1982: 48]). By the middle of the nineteenth century, merchants were sufficiently secure, even in provincial towns, that they could vote in opposition to the local social elites (Winstanley 1983: 23). On the other hand, poorer customers tried to end their dependence by banding together to put collective pressure on shopkeepers, such as occurred during the agitation of the 1830s (e.g. Foster 1974: 53–4, 150, 169).

Shopkeepers' changing attitudes and orientations were matched by a growing differentiation of the shop from the household, which made the shop less of an embodiment of personal, familial relations than it had been. This differentiation took a number of forms. The simplest was the emergence of a distinct appearance for shops late in the eighteenth century. Previously, buildings devoted to shopkeeping were almost identical to residences, the main difference being that the former were likely to have somewhat larger windows. By the second half of the eighteenth century, however, the two sorts of buildings began to diverge (Kalman 1972), and it was at this time that the classic single or double bow-fronted Georgian shops appeared, buildings that remain clearly recognizable as shops in a way that most earlier shop buildings do not (Alexander, D. 1970: 202).

Differentiation of shop from household took a more direct form as well. This was the appearance of the lock-up shop and the non-resident shopkeeper. Whereas shopkeepers had lived above the shop, during this period some of the more prosperous began to live in the suburbs and commute. The first significant lock-up shops in London were stalls rented in the new Royal

Exchange, built in 1568, but such shops were rare throughout the seventeenth and eighteenth centuries. The new, commuting shopkeeper was most visible in London's West End, which was emerging as the main fashionable shopping area (Davis, D. 1966: 196).

By the middle of the nineteenth century, the shop in the West End and similar areas "was much less a house from which its inhabitants traded than a commercial building", albeit one in which the shopkeeper still occasionally lived (Alexander, D. 1970: 202). This growing spatial differentiation was part of a general segregation of residential and commercial areas in English towns in the eighteenth century (Borsay 1989: 107, 294). It continued into the nineteenth century, when central commercial areas became devoted to retail shops and other service functions as manufacturers moved elsewhere (Brown 1986: 55; e.g. the description of Chester in Mitchell 1981: 46), and it continued into the twentieth century with the appearance of the shopping center and the shopping mall. However, it is important to remember that the non-resident shopkeeper and the building that was only a shop were uncommon outside of wealthy areas around 1800. For poorer people, the local retail shop frequently was what the Excise called "inward rooms", without a separate door to the street or passage-way, often enough the family's parlor (Mui and Mui 1989: 131). Janet Blackman (1967) describes such a shop in Sheffield in the middle of the nineteenth century; Eugen Weber (1976: 223) describes comparable shops in rural France.

As shopkeepers came to think in terms of the anonymous and impersonal "market", so they began to adopt practices intended to attract what they called the "dropping trade", casual trade from strangers who were passing and dropped in to buy (Alexander, D. 1970: 196–7). This catering to the passer-by had existed previously to some degree. From late in the seventeenth century the elite spa town of Tunbridge Wells had shops along its leisure walking areas, as did the queen of spas, Bath, by the middle of the eighteenth century (Borsay 1989: 166, 168). However, these elite shops and their passing customers were oriented rather differently from their later, more aggressive London counterparts and their customers. In the spas, shopping was emerging as a social leisure activity of the upper ranks of society.

Elite shopping was the seeing and being seen of the social parade such as Alison Adburgham (1981: 101–3) describes of fashionable shopping areas in the West End in the middle of the nineteenth century. Anticipating Rosalind Williams's (1982) point that Parisian department stores were enveloping their wares in pleasurable glamor and romance, one commentator near the end of the nineteenth century said that the grand London department stores were a place "for one to take one's friends and meet one's friends; a fashionable resort, a lounge, an art gallery, a bazaar and a delightful promenade" (in Winstanley 1983: 35). However, this elite shopping was different from the anonymous window-shopping of the mass market, in which shoppers were less likely to be able or willing to pay the price of what they saw, and were less likely to be a socially homogeneous and mutually known set of people enjoying not just the display of goods but also each other's company and chance encounters with friends and acquaintances. The spread of enclosed shopping malls designed to attract distinct segments of the buying public suggests a reversion to the older pattern of more homogeneous buying spaces (Kowinski 1985; on the idea of these spaces, see Zukin 1990).

The growing desire to attract the dropping trade underlay the new forms of shop display that began to appear around this time. Shop windows got larger and retailers devoted more attention to producing an attractive display of their wares. In 1786 the German visitor Sophie von la Roche (in Davis, D. 1966: 195) wrote home about the sights of Oxford Street in London's West End:

> The spirit booths are particularly tempting . . . . Here crystal flasks of every shape and form are exhibited: each one has a light behind which makes all the different coloured spirits sparkle. Just as alluring are the confectioners and fruiterers, where, behind the handsome glass windows pyramids of pineapples, figs, grapes, oranges and all manner of fruits are on show . . . . Most of all we admired a stall with Argand lamps . . . forming a really dazzling spectacle. Every variety of lamp, crystal, lacquer and metal ones, silver and brass in every possible shade.

Such displays were not limited to the West End, but appeared as well in other, more established parts of London where better-off customers made their purchases. A provincial tradesman (in Alexander, D. 1970: 162–3) visiting in the City in 1810 reported that he was

> no longer able to discern the neat but unadorned shop which formerly bespoke the habits of its dweller, which was now entirely changed; the windows were such as Gulliver would describe as a glass case in Brognibog, each pane being no less than plate glass a yard square, and instead of his name in plain Roman capitals, with his trade of chemist and druggist; after a quarter of an hour's decyphering, I could make out —— and Co. Chemicals and Galenicals in that kind of distorted characters which are pourtrayed on the Egyptian monuments of antiquity.

These stylish signs, these colorful and bright displays behind large glass panes, often illuminated to be visible in the long London evening, were very different from the old style of shop, which had little glass and less need for it. Mayhew (in Fraser 1981: 175–6) describes this contrast in display and the attitudes that it expressed as they survived late into the nineteenth century:

> The quiet house of the honourable tailor, with the name inscribed on the window blinds, or on the brass-plate on the door, tells you that the proprietor has no wish to compete with or undersell his neighbour. But

at the show and slop-shops every art and trick that scheming can devise or avarice suggest, is displayed to attract the notice of the passer-by, and filch the customer from another. The quiet, unobtrusive place of business of the old-fashioned tailor is transformed into the flashy palace of the grasping tradesman.

In this passage Mayhew brings out what is implicit in the spreading concern with the dropping trade. The new orientation presumed not only an alienation of merchant and purchasers, but also an alienation of merchants from each other. Fair trade and the desire of William Stout not to poach the customers of other merchants had no place in the world of Mayhew's grasping tradesman.

Fancy displays may have been intended to bedazzle the shopper with glamor and romance, as Rosalind Williams (1982) says was the case for early French department stores. But while the glamor and romance may be significant, it is important not to lose sight of the people for whom these visual delights were intended: strangers. Established customers had no need for such displays, and merchants like Mayhew's honorable tailor who saw themselves dealing with a body of established customers disdained them. Further, the fact that these displays were oriented outward, toward the anonymous passing public, distinguishes them from luxurious shop interiors. Elaborate and luxurious shop fittings may have helped secure custom. However, the historians Lorna and Hoh–cheung Mui may not be correct in asserting (1989: 221–2) that the existence of such shop interiors early in the eighteenth century illustrates the newer market orientation. It is certainly plausible that fancy interiors of shops, like fancy interiors of houses, had their effect much more privately, in terms of a different set of values, processes and relationships.

Orientation toward an impersonal public emerges as well in three novel pricing practices. These are fixed pricing, open ticketing and single pricing. Fixed pricing meant that the price of the object had been determined by the merchant in advance. This eliminated the possibility of haggling, and so made the buying transaction more mechanical and less personal, as it reduced the discretion of sales staff, and so made their work more impersonal. (Fixed pricing began to appear in Parisian stores in the 1830s and 1840s [Miller, M. 1981: 25].) However, fixed pricing did not necessarily mean objects had a single price. Instead, there may have been a number of prices in the shopkeeper's mind, "one for the man who paid cash, one for the man who paid on payday, one for the man who had to be dunned before he paid, and one for the man who had to be sued for the bill" (Carson 1954: 93). Single pricing (a policy of no "abatement" or price reduction) presupposed fixed pricing together with a single price, which would not be abated (reduced) for different sorts of customers, though the claim of single pricing could mean "not one price to all but only that a salesman would never differ from the first price named to a customer" (Resseguie 1965: 309–10). Finally, open ticketing meant that the price was plainly visible to the customer considering a purchase. But again, open ticketing did not necessarily mean a single price: it might have been a first or highest price, subject to reduction for favored customers (Carson 1954: 93), just as on the fringes of a black economy the official price may be for the customer who pays by check or credit card, with another, lower price for the customer who pays in cash.

All three of these pricing practices began to appear during this period, though as I have indicated, they were not always as straightforward as their names imply. By the late 1780s, London shops began regularly to announce that they had goods "ready made, for ready money, and at a fixed price" (McKendrick, Brewer and Plumb 1982: 83; see also Mui and Mui 1989: 232, 234). In the United States this appears to have been uncommon before the 1850s (Hower 1938: 95; Resseguie 1965: 310; but see Walsh, L. 1983: 113). Taken together, these practices betoken an impersonalization of the buying transaction. It was becoming possible to buy without negotiating the nature of the object, its price, the method of payment or the reliability, or even the identity, of customer or shopkeeper: complete strangers could buy as easily as established customers. This is illustrated nicely by the 1876 catalogue for the American mail-order firm of Montgomery Ward, which stated that the company would not "refuse the patronage of any person . . . . We sell our goods to any person of whatsoever occupation, color or race" (in Hendrickson 1978: 222). These changes meant the disappearance of the need for what Richard Sennett (1976: 142) calls the "stylized interplay [that] weaves the buyer and seller together socially". And it did not just mark the end of the *need*, it was the foundation of the end of the *practice*, for it made possible the appearance of the competitive pricing that was "essential to the success of the 'monster shops' and the 'cutting shops'" (Alexander, D. 1970: 172) that relied on aggressive mass retailing.[3]

Such shops began to appear in the last quarter of the eighteenth century. A wave of them started up in London in the 1780s, calling themselves "warehouses" to imply that they charged cheap, wholesale prices: tea warehouses, linen warehouses, muslin warehouses, blanket warehouses and so on (Mui and Mui 1989: 64). The stereotype was the London draper selling to the bottom part of the growing middling sort. Such a shop aimed at high sales volume and low mark-up, and it did so by appealing to strangers who had never bought there before. Appeals were made by press advertisements, handbills pushed through letter-boxes, window displays – all novel techniques used for touting cheap prices for ready money to an anonymous public (Davis, D. 1966: 258; Mitchell 1981: 52). Again, Mayhew (in Fraser 1981: 176) describes this late in the nineteenth century:

Every article in the window is ticketed – the price is cut down *to the quick* – books of crude, bold verse are thrust in your hands, or thrown into your carriage window – the panels of every omnibus are plastered with show placards, telling you how Messrs —— defy competition.

What may be the apotheosis of monster shops, Schoolbred & Co., of London, had 500 employees, and such a shop could have an annual turnover in excess of a million pounds (Alexander, D. 1970: 168, 189). By comparison, the largest store in the United States in the 1840s appears to have been Oak Hall, a men's clothing store in Boston, with an annual volume of only $500,000 (Hower 1938: 92), a bit over £100,000.

These pricing practices appeared in settings less spectacular than the monster shops. For instance, late in the eighteenth century a few manufacturers began to advertise proprietary products, ranging from teas and china ware to razor strops and exotic sex aids (McKendrick, Brewer and Plumb 1982: ch. 4; Mui and Mui 1989: 278). These were part of the move toward fixed and open pricing, for the advertisements announced the prices of what they touted. At a more mundane level, ordinary grocers, drapers and mercers, without pretence of being monster shops, were adopting single, fixed prices for their wares (Mui and Mui 1989: 234–5). This was not restricted to the lower end of the market. While shops that aimed at an exclusive clientele still adhered to the older system of pricing, those that served the respectable middle classes in London had generally adopted fixed, open pricing by the time of the Napoleonic wars (Davis, D. 1966: 291).

These different trade practices, together with changes in the design and use of shop premises, point to the key changes in retail trade that occurred around this time. I said that the first of these was the growing differentiation of the shop from the household and family of the shopkeeper, which made the shop more of an impersonal economic institution. The second of these was the growing reorientation of traders, away from a distinct body of customers linked to them in relatively enduring ways and toward the "market" in the modern sense, an anonymous and impersonal mass of isolated individuals who only fleetingly interact with the shopkeeper. These changes are, of course, intertwined. The large windows and artificial lights of the new-built Georgian shop both distinguished it from a residence and lured passers-by. Conversely, the shopkeeper who ran a lock-up shop away from his residence, less able to rely on personal links with those who lived near the shop to secure trade, was obliged to attract strangers (Alexander, D. 1970: 11).

Linked to these changes in turn was a changing conception of why people bought things. The older understanding of objects as part of a relatively stable customary level of consumption was breaking down. The older moral economy of stable orders was being replaced by the newer political economy of aspiring individuals. As people's expectations about consumption were becoming more fluid, so did their sense of what they wanted and needed to buy, the symbolic delights they expected from their purchases (Campbell, C. 1987). In these changed circumstances, the older style of trade, relatively invisible, was no longer enough. Shopkeepers had to lure customers in. In doing so they began to compete with each other for trade. Thus, not only was the moral bond between shopkeeper and customer breaking down, so was the moral community of shopkeepers, further depersonalizing retail trade.

CONCLUSION

People in England had bought and sold things impersonally for money long before the middle of the eighteenth century; indeed, if Alan Macfarlane (1978) is correct, they had been doing so since the thirteenth century. However, the evidence I have presented indicates that when ordinary people bought foodstuffs, cloth and the like, generally they did so in relatively personal and durable relations, at least until the eighteenth century. It was in the closing decades of that century and the first part of the nineteenth that there began to appear clear signs of a change to more alienated forms of circulation. These changes were only beginnings, and they were centered on London, by far the biggest city in a country still dominated by villages and small towns. Likewise, they appeared most clearly in trade aimed at the middle classes. Exclusive traders with rich customers, like small shops serving the poor, were less touched by these changes.

But though these signs are only local, they mark the visible beginnings of a fundamental change, the emergence of the notion of the anonymous, mass market in retail trade. This trend to increasing alienation continued well beyond the middle of the nineteenth century. Certainly it was resisted by people in different parts of society, and certainly a significant number of people continued to acquire a significant proportion of what they had in shops and markets where older understandings and practices prevailed. Nonetheless, by the middle of the nineteenth century the new, alienated form of trade was entrenched, seemingly ineradicably, and familiar to almost everyone.

As trade understandings, practices and patterns began to change, so people's common experiences with and transactions of objects began to change. In the period around 1800, this change touched most the urban middling groups, whose shopkeepers were the ones most likely to adopt the emerging orientations and practices. It seems likely that it was among these groups that things were most rapidly losing their particularistic social identities as possessions and becoming impersonal commodities, just as it was among these groups that people had little direct experience with the making of things. For these people, objects became free to take on the abstract allure of the sign value, an allure that department stores were beginning to exploit by the middle of the nineteenth century.

4

CHANGING CIRCULATION RELATIONS
Institutionalizing Alienation

Chapter 3 described a set of changes that appeared only in restricted areas of retail trade in a restricted number of localities. They did not remain restricted. From the middle of the nineteenth century they spread to more and more branches of retail trade in more and more different areas. As they spread they became manifest in a set of institutional practices that increased the impersonality of retail trade, and hence of the objects that people acquired through it. I describe that spread and those practices in this chapter.

Although just about all areas of retail trade grew and changed in the decades around 1900, change was most pronounced in trade that drew on and reflected the growing working-class demand, itself the consequence of growing, relatively secure industrial employment and rising real wages (Jefferys 1954: 7). This demand constituted the mass market in the statistical sense that complemented the mass market in the conceptual sense that I described in Chapter 3. For England, this meant that the center of change was not the shops in stylish streets of the West End or the prosperous areas of the City. Instead, it was the branch store, part of a large retail firm specializing in inexpensive common wares, whether foodstuffs, household goods or tobacco, in the industrial areas of the Midlands, the North and lowland Scotland. For instance, Peter Mathias (1967: 39–40) reports that the main companies that eventually merged to form the large British retail food group, Allied Suppliers, were founded during the 1870s, a decade of rising working-class income and relatively low unemployment. And they were founded in Glasgow and Newcastle upon Tyne and their environs, Manchester and Birmingham. Just as significant, none "was established in the middle-class suburbs of its town of origin, but in the high-density living and shopping areas of its central districts, immediately within the precincts of working-class residential districts".

The prosperity that lifted the industrial working class in England and the United States during this period lifted the middle classes as well, and affected the ways they bought and the stores that sold to them. This was most notable in the appearance of department stores in the second half of the nineteenth century, stores that embody some of the changes that I describe in this chapter. Department stores have attracted much more scholarly attention than the stores that draw on the working class (e.g. Benson 1979, 1986; Chaney 1983; Miller, M. 1981; Williams, R. 1982). However, the organization of these two sorts of stores differed markedly, and the relationships between people and objects were much less impersonal in department stores than in the stores that catered to the working class. Commentators who link the department store with a growing impersonality of consumption might look more closely at the less spectacular but more important trade catering to the working class.

James Jefferys (1954: 32–3) says in his history of modern British retail trade that the main reason for the difference in organization lies in the difference between middle-class and working-class demand (parallel points from a different perspective are in Cherington 1913: 188–91). The wares that department stores sold may have been made in factories in bulk and been cheaper than their predecessors, made by hand for specific purchasers. However, the prosperous middle class was using its growing wealth to seek a more varied array of higher-quality and stylish items, and was seeking to buy them in pleasant surroundings. Those who catered to this demand successfully did not stress price, they stressed style and variety. The organization of department stores reflected this concern. Although these stores were large, they consisted of a number of relatively small and independent departments, each with its own staff, its own internal hierarchy and its own buyer, who bought from suppliers and usually took overall responsibility for the department. Thus, the department store resembled a collection of shops under one roof – the older shopping arcades or the modern shopping mall. One student of department stores in New York City in the 1920s said that the buyer "resembles ... the proprietor of a small shop" (Donovan 1929: 194). In Edward Filene's aphoristic definition, "a department store is a holding company for its departments" (in Resseguie 1965: 302).

On the other hand, the working class was using its growing wealth to buy inexpensive staples, often of a sort not bought before. The stores that catered to this demand attracted customers by emphasizing low prices. Their concern for efficiency led them to sell a small range of mass-produced commodities. For example, in the United States A&P stores stocked only tea, coffee, sugar, spices, canned milk and butter in the 1880s (Walsh, W. 1986: 22–3). A more extreme case is Maypole Dairy, which became part of Allied Suppliers. In 1913 this firm had almost 800 shops, selling only eggs, condensed milk, tea, margarine and butter, and in 1914 they abandoned eggs (Mathias 1967: 172). In the way they traded large quantities and in the way they centralized and routinized their selling operations, these firms pursued the same impersonal economic efficiency that motivated the Ford Motor Company.

One result of these changes is that the buying and the things bought became impersonal. This is most apparent in the selling of food. Outside London, New York and a few other large cities, the householder in the middle of the nineteenth century typically bought dairy products, poultry, eggs, fruit, vegetables and meats from those who grew them, made them or butchered them. In other words, the object was the possession of the person who sold it, and it was bought in a relatively personal relationship. By the middle of the twentieth century, householders typically were buying their food in a supermarket, which is only the passive distributor of objects produced and advertised by other institutions located elsewhere. The store itself, like the clerk, is only tenuously linked to what the customer buys.

Although supermarkets are the stereotype of the new retail trade, their origin is not clear. By 1912 the Alpha Beta stores in Los Angeles were self-service, and other stores advertised themselves as "cafeteria groceries" and "groceterias" (Barger 1955: 31; Furnas 1974: 172). However, conventionally the Piggly Wiggly chain, based in Memphis, Tennessee, is considered the first supermarket firm. It was operating self-service food stores by 1916 (Strasser 1989: 248). By about 1920 the supermarket had come into its own, with just under 200 in Los Angeles alone (Zimmerman 1937: 4). In Britain supermarkets emerged much more slowly. Apparently, the Allied Suppliers group had no self-service food stores before 1949, and only 250 by 1957. However, most of these were small: by 1959 the company had only 12 shops that fit the minimum criterion for supermarkets of 2,000 square feet of selling space (Mathias 1967: 394). In the United Kingsom as a whole there were less than 600 supermarkets by 1961, accounting for less than 4 percent of retail food trade (they accounted for 56 percent in the United States in 1958) (McClelland 1962: 135).

As the new impersonality spread and matured, different changes occurred at different times in the different branches of trade, reflecting the peculiar economic, technical and organization histories of different areas of production and distribution (for Britain, see especially Jefferys 1954). However, there were five core changes that appeared in just about all branches. The first of these is the growing scope of retail firms, as stores got bigger and chain stores (in the United States) and multiples (in the United Kingdom) became more common. This growth made it less likely that the storekeeper and customer would be linked in a personal relationship. The second is the change in the nature of credit, which severed an important link between storekeeper and customer. The third is changes in labor relations, which increasingly alienated the clerk and the storekeeper from the store and from his or her work. The fourth is the shift to passive distribution, as stores were less and less actively involved in selecting and transforming their wares, a change that helped alienate the shopkeeper and clerk from the objects being sold. The fifth is a related phenomenon with a similar effect, the appearance of manufacturers' brands and advertising. These five changes cannot be treated as a single event, but require separate consideration. Even so, they are part of a recurring process, the replacing of personal with commodity relationships in retail trade and buying.

The changes I describe in this chapter, like the changes in production I described in Chapter 2, are important. However, like changes in production, they may not generate as much impersonality as they appear to at first glance. As I describe in Chapter 5, people find ways of generating personal relationships in shopping. The image of the impersonal branch store, like the image of the impersonal factory, contains both truth and self-deception.

SCOPE OF STORES

Although some large shops had appeared earlier, it is only in this period that many ordinary shops and shopkeepers expanded their orientation beyond a small body of regular customers and concerned themselves instead with the dropping trade. As a result, shop staff were less able and less likely to focus on individual customers and transactions. As Robert Prus (1987: 359–60) argues, based on his sociological studies in Canada, shopkeepers are aware of the value of a regular clientele. However, their cultural understanding of their work stresses economistic impersonality – making sales rather than having customers. This increasing scope took two main forms: stores got bigger and chain or multiple stores became more common.

The classic retail shop was small. Often it was only 10–15 feet wide and 20–40 feet deep, into which had to fit the shopkeeper and perhaps a clerk, shelves and cabinets, the counters over which buyer and seller faced each other, and of course the customers themselves, not to mention the storage room at the back.[1] This suggests that the shop served a relatively small body of customers. Staff and customers frequently knew each other and their interactions were as much social as economic. One writer recalled shopping in middle-class London before World War I:

> It is difficult nowadays to realise how very personal then was the relationship, even in London, between shop-keeper and customer . . . . All my female relatives had their own favourites, where some of them had been honoured customers for more than half a century and their arrival was greeted by frenzied bowing . . . and where certain of the older assistants stood to them almost in the relationship of confessors.
>
> (Lancaster 1953, in Adburgham 1981: 281–2)

Personal relationships existed at the other end of the social scale as well. One woman who ran a small shop in a working-class area in the North of England during the Depression put it this way:

> They like a place where they can come in drunk and know you'll give them the stuff they want even if they've forgotten what they've come in for . . . . They want a place they can come in with their curlers or in their slippers and dressin' gowns. They know ye aren't goin' to diddle them by bamboozlin' their little bairns if they send them in with a message.
>
> (Robinson, J. 1977: 140, in Johnson 1985: 146–7)

Shop size increased in the last quarter of the nineteenth century. This is illustrated by early F. W. Woolworth's stores. In the first year of operation, 1879, the company opened three stores. Their average size was 360 square feet and the largest was 14 x 35. Nine years later, in 1888, the company opened five stores. These averaged 1,350 square feet, almost four times the size of the earlier stores; the smallest was larger than any of the 1879 shops and the largest was 17 x 110. For comparison, its manager reports that my local supermarket, not markedly big or small, has 27,000 square feet of selling space.

Equally impressive were the food stores run by Thomas Lipton, the founder of an important constituent company of what became Allied Suppliers. He opened his first shop in Glasgow in 1871, and by the end of the decade his shops were large:

> [T]he Paisley store in 1879 . . . [had] a large horseshoe counter served by twelve assistants . . . . The Dundee branch in 1878 had twelve to fifteen salesmen and three cash boys . . . . His main Glasgow market, in the same year, had a horseshoe counter 100 feet long, and it was claimed that 200 people could be packed into the shop at a time.
>
> (Mathias 1967: 46)

These larger shops were busier shops. For instance, the gross annual sales per Woolworth's store were $6,012 in 1879, $20,565 in 1889 and $81,761 in 1899 (Woolworth 1954: 8, 17). More space, more customers and more transactions made it more difficult to interact personally with customers or to develop personal relations with them: "[S]heer size does effectively destroy much of the opportunity for interaction . . . . It is harder to remember faces if there are many of them" (McClelland 1962: 139; Sofer 1965: 189–90 describes some of the psychological aspects of selling space).

A firm can increase its scope without increasing its floor space. It can sell by mail, a form of trade that became popular in the second half of the nineteenth century. In the United States, Montgomery Ward began trading by mail in 1872, while Sears, Roebuck began in 1890 (Scull 1967: 166, 169). In Britain, the large stores in London and Glasgow expanded their country trade in this period, shipping orders throughout their regions (Mathias 1967: 47; Winstanley 1983: 35–6; Yamey 1954: 36). Traders in market towns increased their scope by filling the orders of a growing number of English villagers who paid local carrier services to do their shopping, a practice that expanded until the introduction of extensive motor-coach services in rural areas after World War I (Brown 1986: 10; Winstanley 1983: 203).

The other main way firms increased their scope was by becoming chains or multiples, a form of organization that emerged in the last quarter of the nineteenth century. Chain outlets tended to be large, as the examples of the growing size of Woolworth's and Lipton's stores illustrate. Not only were these stores relatively large, they were distinctly concerned with economic efficiency, with facilitating the economic transaction of selling. This is illustrated by an American study around World War I, which found that the volume of sales per clerk was frequently twice as great in chain grocery stores as it was in independent stores (Harvard University 1919: 21).

In the United States the earliest mass chain stores appear to be the general merchandise firms J. C. Penney's and F. W. Woolworth's (Furnas 1974: 169–71), which began trading around the 1880s. (A&P was founded earlier, but did not appeal to the mass market until 1912: Bullock 1933; Darby 1928: 13; Furnas 1974: 71.) American chains spread steadily. In 1923 the 65,000 branches of the 4,000 American chain firms accounted for about 8 percent of total retail trade (Nystrom 1925: 158). As might be expected, they took a much larger share of trade in urban areas, and in some lines rather than others. Thus, a survey of eleven cities in 1927 found that chains took only 8 percent of dry goods and notions sales, but at least 30 percent of automobile, department store, grocery and delicatessen, and restaurant sales. These were the highest-volume branches of trade, accounting for 40 percent of total retail sales in the cities surveyed (Nystrom 1930: 226).

In Britain, as in the United States, there had been companies that owned more than one shop since early in the nineteenth century. However, typically these were no more than "a main shop in a market town . . . with satellite shops in surrounding villages" (Alexander, D. 1970: 103; see also Davis, D. 1966: 255). The Rochdale Pioneers, established in 1856, is taken as the first multiple firm in Britain, for it had both branch stores and centralized wholesale buying (Davis, D. 1966: 280). The Pioneers was a cooperative, dealing mainly in food, serving industrial areas of Lancashire and Yorkshire. It marked the beginning of something that remained important in British retail trade through the middle of the twentieth century, a vast number of cooperative stores linked to central, cooperative wholesale organizations. By 1862 there were about 400 cooperative societies in Britain with about 100,000 members, rising to over 1,000 with about 550,000 members in 1882 (Jefferys 1954: 17).

According to Jefferys (1954: 28), however, by 1875 there were only twenty-nine multiple firms, operating less than a thousand shops, though his figure is frankly an underestimate: it excludes cooperatives and includes only firms with ten or more branches. These firms were dominated by three specialist companies: W. H. Smith's and John Menzies's, operating newspaper stands at railway stations; and the Singer company, with shops selling its sewing machines. There followed a marked expansion. In 1900 there were over 250 multiple firms with over 11,500 branches, accounting for about 3.8 percent of all retail trade. By World War I there were 433 firms with almost 23,000 outlets, accounting for about 7.8 percent of all trade (Jefferys 1954: 22, 23, 29). The largest, James Nelson & Sons, sold frozen imported meat at over a thousand branches, more than the national total just forty years earlier (Winstanley 1983: 38). At the middle of the twentieth century there were about 640 firms with about 45,000 branches, accounting for about one-fifth of all retail trade (Jefferys 1954. 61, 73).

The spread of firms with multiple outlets increased the alienation of shopkeepers by reducing their involvement with their shops and the community. Most obviously, this was because the shop did not belong to the manager. Some companies had sought to link managers to their stores by giving them part-ownership, but the leading American advocate of this approach, J. C. Penney's, abandoned it in 1927 (Darby 1928: 33). Equally, many companies moved managers frequently from location to location in order to broaden their experience (1928: 56, 113) and develop a body of loyal and career-oriented branch managers (e.g. Walsh, W. 1986: 30–1 for A&P). Frequent moves oriented managers to the chain and their career in it rather than to the locality, clerks and customers. Further, managers' freedom of action was restricted by many corporate policies, which were concerned with the economic goals of volume and profit. Branch managers were not the only shopkeepers who were alienated by these policies. Independent shopkeepers were affected as well. Even those who valued durable, personal relations with individual customers and saw such relations as an important part of their work were obliged to adopt more profit-oriented and alienating practices if they were to stay in business (Sofer 1965: 189).

This alienation was apparent to people at the time. As early as the middle of the nineteenth century, some English writers were arguing that in large shops relations with customers were anonymous and impersonal (Alexander, D. 1970: 109). Similarly, some American critics of large chains and mail-order companies stressed their alienation, and charged them with "predatory pricing", "destroying local independent businesses", "taking money out of the local communities" (Walsh, W. 1986: 21), which was probably true in many cases (for a modern example, see *The Economist* 1990). Some commentators objected explicitly to the impersonality of these firms in terms that echo the older, moral economy that I described in Chapter 3. In the first decade of the twentieth century, the American writer William Allen White complained: "There is such a thing as 'tainted' dry goods, 'tainted' groceries and 'tainted' furniture . . . . All of such that are not bought at home, of men who befriended you, of men to whom you owe a living, are 'tainted' because they come unfairly" (in Strasser 1989: 216). Indeed, chain firms themselves saw that their uniformity and size, so important for economies of scale, could repel customers. Some firms gave their branch stores different names and designs to make them appear more individual and local (Darby 1928: 29). Equally, branch managers objected to the alienation and constraint imposed by corporate policy, which obliged them to act toward customers and competitors in aggressive ways that they found distasteful (Sofer 1965: 186). And finally, many shoppers felt that they should avoid buying at the chain stores run by large, alien corporations, preferring instead to buy from local shopkeepers (Boone, Kurtz, Johnson and Bonna 1974; Stone, G. 1954).

CHANGING CREDIT

Just as the growing scope of the shop and shopkeeper tended to make buying more impersonal, so too did the change in the nature of credit. During this period, especially in urban areas, credit became restricted to the point that it ceased to be an expected part of many sorts of retail trade. Gradually, and not really until well after the middle of the twentieth century, store credit was replaced by the ubiquitous credit card. However, the card, unlike the sort of credit that is of concern here, bespeaks no personal relationship between shopkeeper and customer. Indeed, its impersonality is its strength (Hart 1986: 642): the shopkeeper who accepts it need know nothing about the customer who presents it.

I said in Chapter 3 that there was a growing tendency for shops to sell at fixed, single prices that were posted publicly, which implies a growing tendency for sales to be for "ready money" only, for cash. This was certainly the case by the middle of the nineteenth century with the high-volume drapers' shops in London, as it was with the corresponding dry-goods trade in New York (Hendrickson 1978: 28; Scull 1967: 79–82; but cf. Resseguie 1965: 312). Credit was expensive for stores, and the early chain and multiple firms, seeking to keep costs down, were natural adopters of a cash-only policy, as were the cooperative stores in England (Alexander, D. 1970: 184). For Lipton's food stores in the 1870s, "[q]uick turnover, rapid returns, minimum book-keeping, and a maximum insurance against the risk of bad debts all implied cash sales" (Mathias 1967: 47).

Credit disappeared with the spread of high-volume, low-markup selling. Consequently, it was the broad, and growing, urban middle group, from better-off workers to the upper-middle classes, who routinely paid cash. For these people, a credit account became, not an expected aspect of buying, but a mark of special esteem and privilege (Benson 1986: 90). As the twentieth century progressed, store credit became rarer and rarer, until it was replaced in large part by the credit card.[2] However, merchants who sold to other sorts of people were not so quick to abandon credit. Many English drapers' firms employed itinerant traders in London as well as in rural areas, pedlars who had a regular circuit. These traders routinely sold on credit (Johnson 1985: 154; Rubin 1986). At the other end of the scale, through the beginning of the twentieth century women buying from exclusive clothing stores "might not know what they had spent until the bill arrived six months later" (Adburgham 1981: 207). Similarly, small merchants were more reluctant to abandon credit. In England, small shopkeepers felt that they had to offer credit if they were to attract customers (Winstanley 1983: 55), just as the English urban working poor needed the small shops that offered the credit that was not available at the multiple shops and department stores (Johnson 1985: 145). In the United States, 90 percent of independent grocers surveyed in 1918 offered credit, and of these, 90 percent did half or more of their business on credit. Most grocery chains did not offer credit, and independent grocers with branch stores were somewhat less likely to grant credit than were those without. Among rural general stores, credit was no more common than in their urban equivalents, but the length of credit was not the one month that was routine to grocers; half gave credit for two months or more (Harvard University 1919: 25, 46–7).

Credit did not simply fade in the decades around 1900, only to reappear as the credit card. It was transformed, and it is this transformation that marks the changing nature of credit as an important aspect of the growing alienation of objects in circulation. The granting of credit by merchants through the early nineteenth century was not simply the result of a dispassionate assessment of the customer's financial status, in the way that a modern credit card is given to those whose credit record and financial standing satisfy impersonal criteria, and is issued and administered, moreover, by someone other than the shopkeeper. Certainly a financial assessment was involved: shopkeepers frequently demanded cash for the first few purchases, or until they got to know the customer (Alexander, D. 1970: 182–3). However, the decision that a customer deserved credit was as well the decision to enter into a personal relationship of trust. It was not just a matter of the shopkeeper being willing to extend credit to a customer, it was a matter of shopkeeper and customer becoming linked to each other. Those who, like Susan Strasser (1989: 241), describe retail credit in the early twentieth century in terms of modern business rationality miss the importance of this social dimension and anachronistically impose an impersonal economistic logic that only later became dominant.

Because the shopkeeper's judgement rested on personal knowledge of the customer, credit was scarce for those not known in the neighborhood. Indeed, Gareth Stedman Jones (1971: 88) argues that the inability of working-class people to transfer their reputation for creditworthiness from one area to another was an important factor restricting the geographical mobility of labor in England around the start of the twentieth century, and presumably also in the United States. The need for credit restricted mobility because the credit relationship was reciprocal in a way that it no longer is. The parties to that relationship expected that each would support the other in good times as well as bad.

This is most obvious from the perspective of the customers, who expected that the shopkeeper who gave credit would not just carry them on "tick" until payday. In addition, they expected, or at least hoped, that the shopkeeper would carry them through bad times. This meant through bouts of illness or injury, through spells when there was no work to be found, through strikes and bad harvests, through times of extraordinary expenses like medical bills or funeral costs. In short, they expected the shopkeeper to trust them to repay when times got better. The shopkeeper was entitled to proper treatment as well. At its simplest, this meant loyalty to the shop, buying there when times were good and purchases could be paid for in cash, even though the multiple shops might have the same goods for less. The importance of this mutual support helps explain why small shopkeepers had to extend credit if they were to get custom, and why Jewish immigrants in London's East End late in the nineteenth century would patronize local shops, even though a two-minute walk would bring them to stores that would sell for less, but only for cash (Johnson 1985: 145).

In such a relationship between customer and shopkeeper, buying carried an air of gift, rather than just commodity, transaction. Buying a tin of milk was not the exchange of equivalents, self-contained; rather, and echoing an older pattern of trade, it was the recreation of a durable personal relationship, harking back to previous transactions and anticipating future ones. This appears to have been marked commonly by the fact that customers never quite paid off their debt; the small balance remaining marked the continuation of the relationship of trust between shopkeeper and customer. Lorna and Hoh–cheung Mui (1989: 215) found this in village shop records from the eighteenth century, though they did not consider its social significance: "In settling their accounts almost all customers left a credit balance, and paid in round figures." Gerald Mars (1982: 173) describes the same practice around World War II:

> [W]hen a trust relationship does break up the debt *has* to be paid off – precisely and immediately. The open-ended transaction is closed, and the method of final settlement reverts to normal market exchange. The transaction is, in effect, depersonalised ... as it was among working-class families in the north of England where I grew up. The credit account at the local store would be broken through dispute. Then the bill was paid and the family's custom removed to another shop.

Abandoning credit, then, involved more than just a tidying of financial loose ends by the shopkeeper concerned with the neutral and objective goal of increased efficiency. Instead, it involved a decreasing willingness on the part of retailers to engage in durable relations with established bodies of customers. In some cases, doubtless, this occurred because shopkeepers preferred to offer lower prices instead, feared a steady defection of their customers to chain or multiple branches, or simply wanted to be up-to-date. Regardless of the motive, however, the restriction of store credit and its ultimate replacement by the impersonality of the credit card reduced the likelihood that people would buy in enduring, personal relations and in-creased the likelihood that the act of purchase and the thing purchased would be impersonal. Shopkeepers may have been pleased to be free of personal bonds to their customers, just as customers may have been pleased to be free of bonds to shopkeepers "who often knew details of the health and wealth of the whole family" (Jefferys 1954: 92) or who had the power to break them in bad times (Winstanley 1983: 23). But better pleased or not, the relationship between shopkeeper and customer, like the object they transacted, was more impersonal than it had been before.

LABOR RELATIONS

The appearance of the commuting West End shopkeeper around 1800 marked the beginning of a change in labor practices and relations that became pronounced in the decades around 1900. This change took a number of forms, but the common effect was to alienate those working in the shop from their work and the goods they sold. This in turn meant a growing impersonality of the act of buying and of the objects bought.

Changing labor relations affected the shopkeeper as much as the assistants. As I have already noted, increasingly the local shopkeeper was a paid employee of a chain or multiple organization, and likely to be alienated from shopkeeping. The older, independent shopkeeper had been apprenticed in the trade, learning its craft mysteries and identifying with it like any other skilled worker. However, many chains saw this bond between person and trade as a hindrance, producing hide-bound and backward retailers unable to move with the times and keep up with the new techniques. The chains often were right. Cyril Sofer (1965), an English social psychologist, found that established English shopkeepers who had sold out to multiple firms frequently were obliged by their new employers to follow practices that they found distasteful and opposed to the values that they had learned in the trade. In the early part of the twentieth century A&P sought to avoid these problems by hiring "young men with no retail experience" as store managers, for they had "no built-in bad retail habits" to be overcome (Walsh, W. 1986: 30). Like factory workers, these managers were allowed little discretion in their work. A&P dictated the layout, equipping and stocking of new stores, and prohibited managers from buying stock locally without prior authorization (1986: 29, 30). No doubt many managers were attached to their occupations and looked forward to a successful career within the firm. But that attachment was to the career and the corporation rather than the shop, and was unlikely to be as durable as that of the man who had been brought up in the trade. Running a store "was becoming an occupation with starting and finishing times permitting a separate existence for the retailer away from the shop, instead of a life's work that was never completed" (Jefferys 1954: 36).

Changes were more pronounced among clerks, increasingly those with whom customers interacted when they made a purchase. Clerks, who used to be apprentices being raised in a trade and bound to a master, became wage laborers without skills, unlikely to learn any, employed by but not a part of the organization that hired them (see, e.g., MacLean 1899). As A. T. Stewart is supposed to have said of the army of employees who worked in his dry-goods store in New York City in the middle of the nineteenth century, "[n]ot one of them had his discretion. They are simply machines working in a system that determines all their actions" (in Resseguie 1965: 314; cf. Mars 1982: ch. 3). Some companies did seek to produce a personal relationship with their employees, as Michael Miller (1981: ch. 3) describes for the

Parisian department store, Bon Marché. However, these policies could not overcome the alienation of workers within what was ultimately and necessarily a very impersonal firm.

The change in labor relations was slow and aspects of the old system were tenacious. For instance, in the middle of the nineteenth century even Schoolbred & Co., the largest drapers in England, continued to have its clerks, over 500 of them, "live in" – receive bed and board in company lodgings – even though they were no longer apprentices in any real sense (Alexander, D. 1970: 108). Living in continued into the twentieth century. Gordon Selfridge, an American who worked at Marshall Field, in Chicago, before moving to London and founding the massive Selfridges department store in the West End, complained about the practice precisely because it established a durable bond between clerk and firm (Lanchester 1913: 579). Personal labor relations persisted past World War II in marginal businesses and geographic areas. In 1950 about one-tenth of the 9.5 million people working in retail trade in the United States were unpaid family members, but mostly in smaller businesses, especially general stores in small towns (Barger 1955: 17–18). Older patterns persisted and remained significant, but for the visible core of retailing, impersonal wage labor became the norm.

As apprentice clerks became wage workers, the firm came to monitor their cost and efficiency in a way that was alien to the older system. Thus, in the beginning of the twentieth century the National Cash Register Company was touting its machines as a way of monitoring the efficiency and honesty of individual clerks (Strasser 1989: 236–7; Winstanley 1983: 66). National Cash Register was part of a growing chorus that was urging retailers to adopt "sound business practice". While advocates saw these practices as self-evident technical improvements in business operation, they entailed a reconceptualization of the store as an independent, self-reproducing capitalist enterprise in the modern mode, alienated from the owner. The reluctance of the owners of small businesses to change their practices, which many reformers derided, suggests that many small retailers saw their shops as nothing of the sort (e.g. Harvard University 1919: esp. 16–19).

As was happening in manufacturing, the transformation of the clerk into a wage laborer was associated with, and facilitated by, making the clerk's job simpler and more routine (Bluestone, Hanna, Kuhn and Moore 1981). Consequently, clerks could not reasonably look forward to moving upward into the ranks of shopkeepers and managers in the way that the older apprentices could, further alienating them from their work. To see what simplification meant, consider skilled English grocer's clerks around World War I. They knew how to process and transform the teas, coffees, sugars, cheeses, fresh and dried fruits, and all the other stock that the shop sold, and knew how the customer should prepare and serve what was sold: "They could tell them what sauces to use with various things and, of course, where you had a shop ... with a license, they could advise on wines to go with a meal"

(Winstanley 1983: 132). In the exercise of these skills, clerks were more closely linked to their trade, to the objects sold, and to the act of selling than were the unskilled clerks who replaced them. Such clerks could never be marshalled in the way that A. T. Stewart had boasted. They were inseparable from the operation of the shop and the act of purchasing. In contrast, by the 1950s commentators could argue that the unskilled wage-laboring clerk was more of a hindrance than a help, and the less seen they are, the happier the customer and the more profitable the store (Weiss 1956; cf. Fortune 1956). Being a clerk had become casual work, even for those who found themselves doing it full time.

The transformation of the clerk's job was marked in the same way as the transformation of the manager's. Chain and multiple firms preferred employees ignorant of retail trade, "inexperienced people, on the grounds that they are more easily taught" (Darby 1928: 53). Max Zimmerman (1937: 107), a sympathetic observer of early American supermarkets, summarized their operators' viewpoint this way:

> All our help is composed of young men and boys .... We can train a man on stock in an hour – on cashiering, in a few days. We can start with an entire new crew and operate very efficiently even to having one of them make out the orders. The less they know about the grocery business, the better. We have and want a large turnover in regular help because the work is monotonous and hard and as the boys develop, we place them in new markets. Better positions of course are not many. This is a condition that we recognize as not being conducive to building a loyal organization because of limitations in advancement.

Such employees offered the same advantages to retail traders that they offered to manufacturers. They could be paid little, were unlikely to remain in the job for long enough to raise their wages substantially, and could be fired during slack periods. They were unlikely to have the sense of their work as a craft with standards and rights that could lead them to resist management control.

The unskilled clerk was not unique to food stores. Between the two world wars, variety stores like F. W. Woolworth's selected, organized and displayed their stock in a way that "brought a revolutionary simplification of the selling function. The sales talk and the selling work are either eliminated or strongly reduced" (Pasdermadjian 1954: 50). Equally, department stores so standardized and routinized their organization that it became "possible to use for the lower positions [i.e., clerks] ... less qualified personnel" (1954: 13–14; see also Benson 1979: 213–16), which likewise restricted the chances of promotion into management (Donovan 1929: 197–8).

With the transformation of the labor came a change in the laborers. There was a growth of child labor during this period in Britain, and presumably in the United States, primarily "to fetch and carry, to provide the short-distance

delivery service in urban areas .... After leaving school their job specifications changed little until they were sacked on reaching adulthood or
demanded men's wages" (Winstanley 1983: 69). Equally, this period saw the
spread of women in retail employment.[3] In the United States in 1870, women
were 15 percent of the entire labor force but only 2 percent of those employed
in distribution; by 1950 they were 28 percent of the labor force but 34 percent
of those in distribution. These figures, moreover, understate the degree of
feminization, because within distribution women were about twice as common in retail trade as in wholesale (Barger 1955: 15). In Britain feminization
was especially pronounced in World War I, which created a severe shortage
of male labor (Winstanley 1983: 68; French department store clerks were
overwhelmingly male late in the nineteenth century [Miller, M. 1981: 78]).
Feminization was not uniform. Women were more likely to occupy retail
positions that called for less skill and commitment (Benson 1986: 24). The
result often was a two-tier clerkship, with different requirements and
expectations for each tier. For instance, in the early part of the twentieth
century in the United States, J. C. Penney female clerks were to be hired
directly by the store manager. However, "male help – or associates, as they
are called – from whom the company expects to recruit its managers and
higher executives, are hired by headquarters, or ... must be approved by
headquarters" (Darby 1928: 90; see also 107).

These changes in labor relations increased the alienation of shop workers
from the shop, the objects being sold and the act of selling, though as with
factory workers, store clerks could find ways of asserting their personality in
their work (Mars 1982: ch. 3). Consequently, for the customer the purchasing
and the thing purchased became more impersonal. This does not mean that
shop workers became less happy with their work or less cheery in their
interactions with customers, or that clerks in less alienating trades had
pleasant jobs (French 1960). The checkout clerks at a supermarket can be
friendly and smiling and still be wage laborers with no durable links to the
boss, the company, the customer or the goods.

PASSIVE DISTRIBUTION

At the same time that shop labor became more alienated, the shift to passive
distribution was also increasing alienation in the relationships between people
and objects in retail trade. The shift meant the withdrawal of shops from the
work of selecting, processing and packaging wares, a change that was
associated with the spread of manufacturers' brands and advertising, discussed later in this chapter.

As I described in Chapter 3, in the older style of trade the shopkeeper
frequently was involved actively in selecting, acquiring, processing and even
manufacturing the things he sold, typically within a web of fairly personal
relations. The result is that the objects the shopkeeper sold were his

possessions, stamped, figuratively and often really, with his identity and his social relationships. In the decades around 1900 the older-style shopkeeper was replaced with the modern retailer who purchased wholesale in impersonal relationships and did little processing. Further, although most modern shopkeepers could choose from among a broader range of suppliers than before, that freedom is somewhat illusory. This is because the shopkeeper is obliged to cater to impersonal demand, rather than actively shaping demand in personal relationships with customers. Shops came to restrict themselves to merely passing the bucket from hand to hand, so the objects the customer bought were alienated from the shop, the shopkeeper and the clerk.

Those who ran anything larger than a small, back-street shop had been active intermediaries between producer and consumer, and much of their job consisted of meeting the desires and needs of their customers by selecting and securing goods from different manufacturers. Doing so required personal relations with wholesale merchants. Retailers had to know the wares merchants offered, how reliable and predictable suppliers they were, how quickly they would fill an order. Equally, merchants had to know the retailer, either directly or by repute, before they would grant the credit the retailer needed to operate (Alexander, D. 1970: 117). Acquiring this knowledge and reputation was an important part of a shopkeeper's apprenticeship (Mui and Mui 1989: 219), and maintaining and extending these relationships was an important part of shopkeepers' social clubs (McKendrick, Brewer and Plumb 1982: 222–3).

The shopkeeper who acquired his wares through personal effort in a web of personal relationships stamped them with his identity in that web and appropriated them. This was true not only of the trader of the later eighteenth century seeking out sources of sugar, but true also of rural shopkeepers through the middle of the nineteenth century and even beyond. American country-store operators often made but a single annual buying trip to New York, Philadelphia, or wherever they got their supplies. The trip itself, its hardships and adventures, served to make the objects bought the shopkeeper's possessions.

> [T]he returning merchant would be endlessly cross-examined on his experiences; and he would be expected to deliver a lively account of the ways of travel, of how Philadelphia looked, of the crowds, the gaiety, the scandals . . . . The men back home would want to know that it had been a cold, late spring; that collections were slow, buyers cautious; that the jobbers were heavily supplied and able to move only small lots. Personal contact and experiences endowed the goods of the merchant who bought in the East with intangible values.
>
> (Carson 1954: 150)

The emergence of large wholesale and jobbing organizations in the nineteenth century reduced the need for personal relationships (Strasser 1989: 19), but they did not disappear. The wholesaler's agent still had to assess how creditworthy the retailer was, and the retailer had to learn the strengths and weaknesses of the different firms and their different agents. Beyond all this the retailer still had to make the essential decision of what to order for his customers, still confronted "the choosing of a firm that made products he knew they [i.e. his customers] would like" (Strasser 1989: 191).

The shopkeeper further appropriated stock by transforming it into a state suited for sale and consumption. Shopkeepers had to work to prepare the vast majority of what they sold. In the British food trades, the serious retailer or skilled clerk had to carry out a range of activities: "Blending tea (still a major profit spinner), grinding and roasting coffee, cleaning, sorting and stoning dried fruits, bottling beers, maturing cheeses, ripening bananas, smoking bacon and patting butter" (Winstanley 1983: 125; see also Brown 1986: 52). Equally, butchers only slowly were being differentiated into the wholesale or "cutting" butchers who slaughtered livestock, and retailers (Blackman 1962; Winstanley 1983: 140). But even here, as late as World War I "the skilled butcher selecting and buying livestock on the hoof, slaughtering, and retailing remained the dominant figure in the home-killed [as distinct from imported] trade" (Jefferys 1954: 183).

As the nineteenth century came to a close, however, shops increasingly dealt in goods that were processed and packaged ready for sale by the manufacturer or wholesaler. The spread of packaged goods was linked to consumers' movements and the politics of public health. Branded and packed goods were presumed to be purer and cleaner than bulk goods (see Furnas 1974: 509–11; Strasser 1989: ch. 8) and brand names were seen as a form of consumer protection (Schudson 1984: 158), though books like Upton Sinclair's *The Jungle* suggested that shoddy and dangerous foodstuffs could come from a branded package as well as from an anonymous barrel. But whatever its causes – public health or manufacturers' profits – the appearance of processed and packaged goods underlay much of the simplification of shop work. Many of those in the food trades resented this trend, fearing quite rightly that if it continued, "their trade would become 'fatally facile': 'Any untrained adventurer or group of tinkers think they can attempt its mysteries in a week'" (from the 1890s, in Yamey 1954: 35). And this trend threatened their self-respect. Sofer (1965: 190) reports one grocer's complaint: "Bacon cutting is a measure of how good a man you are. Anyone can put a can on a shelf."

In the United States the earliest substantial packaging was the "paper", "a 'paper' of coffee, a 'paper' of dry yeast – and shipped ... twenty-four or thirty-six to the case, in wooden boxes" (Carson 1954: 268). These goods began to appear after the Civil War, but the first large-scale packaging by the manufacturer was Smith Brothers cough drops in 1872 (Scull 1967: 43), and it was not until the Centennial Exhibition in Philadelphia in 1876 that displays of packaged goods attracted widespread attention (Carson 1954: 270). By this time, coffee, oatmeal, starch and spices were packaged, though they were still usually sold loose.

The packaging of sugar followed after 1880, but print butter did not appear until around 1900 .... Even after 1900 much coffee was still sold loose, but Domino sugar in 1902 was already advertised as "never sold in bulk." The packaging of cheese and bacon seems to have begun after 1900.

(Barger 1955: 32)

A survey of independent grocers around World War I found a marked decrease in the number of shops that sold in bulk: flour, sugar, breakfast cereals, crackers, coffee, tea and butter were getting hard to find in bulk form (Harvard University 1919: 31–2).

Packaging in Britain emerged at about the same time. It was late in the nineteenth century that "[j]ars of pickles and sauces and jams, tinned goods of all kinds, packets of powder that could be turned like magic into custards and puddings and gravies and substitutes for porridge were all being made in factories" (Davis, D. 1966: 284). Packaged tea was common by 1890, but the wrapped loaf of bread did not become common until the 1920s, and then primarily for the country trade, as wrapped loaves last longer (Mathias 1967: 101, 319). However, packaging was less common in the industrial North, where householders commonly prepared their own food, including bread, until around 1920 (Mathias 1967: 74, 83–4, 90). Equally, there were class variations. The richer families who bought butter resisted packaging through the 1930s, while the poorer families who made do with margarine accepted packaging by around World War I (Mathias 1967: 217, 304). In spite of these variations, by World War II only dairy and bakery shops still produced what they sold (Jefferys 1954: 47). Even the farmer's wife who brought her butter, poultry, eggs and fruit to market was being replaced by the professional trader (Brown 1986: 45).

The shift to passive distribution contains a number of elements, each reducing the likelihood that objects will be transacted in durable social relationships or that they will be produced or transformed in significant ways by those from whom the customer acquires them. In other words, these changes reduce the likelihood that objects will be possessions rather than commodities. Shopkeeper and clerk increasingly found their work reduced to the routine of breaking bulk, of handing the bucket from the distributor to the customer.

MANUFACTURERS' BRANDS AND ADVERTISING

A factor that encouraged passive distribution was the emergence of manufacturers' brands and advertising. In the food trades this followed the development of mass production in the second half of the nineteenth century. However, the emergence of manufacturers' brands is not simply a consequence of the sheer need by manufacturers "to dispose of their huge outputs" (Strasser 1989: 19; see also Shaw, A. 1912: 708). Mass manufacturers have other ways of selling what they make than starting their own brands, and in any event manufacturers' brands appeared before mass production (see McKendrick, Brewer and Plumb 1982: chs 3, 4). But whatever the causes, this branding affected the organization of retail trade and the personality of objects.

Until manufacturers' brands became ubiquitous, most people were unlikely to associate their purchases with the makers or merchants whose names were branded on the case or barrel in which the shopkeeper received them. Instead, they were likely to think of objects in terms of their geographical origins (French lace, New Orleans molasses, Stilton cheese, Scotch whisky) and of course the retailer who sold it to them (Carson 1954: 262). As a corollary, shopkeepers were the origin of most advertising. Usually this was restricted to announcements that shipments of stock had arrived and were available for customers who wanted to buy. Thus, shops' advertisements in newspapers were "[o]ften simply a sort of inventory of the store's stock, with no specific information, no mention of price . . . . Copy often appeared for weeks or even months without change" (Carson 1954: 266; an example is in Hood 1991: 66). This was appropriate given the prevailing notions of the nature of demand and the relationship between retailer and customer. However, by the middle of the nineteenth century street advertisements and posters began to appear, both for local firms and for emerging manufacturers' brands (e.g. Sampson 1875: ch. 2), and display advertising in newspapers began to appear in the last quarter of the century (Strasser 1989: 90–3; for England see Adburgham 1981: 232; for the United States see Hendrickson 1978: ch. 10).

In the United States there had been some branded goods since before the Civil War: Bartlett's lye, Burnett's vanilla, Robert Burns cigars, Eagle condensed milk, and of course Singer sewing machines. However, brands did not become widespread until the last quarter of the nineteenth century, encouraged by postal regulations of 1875 that cut the cost of shipping printed matter and so encouraged periodicals and the advertising that they carried (Carson 1954: 166, 262; Scull 1967: 186–7). By the 1870s, Ivory soap and Quaker oats had appeared, and the spread of brand names had expanded sharply (Carson 1954: 266; Scull 1967: 180; Strasser 1989: ch. 2). By 1920, brands had entered the common consciousness:

> In 1917, . . . every one of three hundred men interviewed could think of at least one brand of fountain pen, watch, and soap . . . . By the early 1920s, studies showed that people asked for brands at stores, and that brands dominated sales in many industries. Ninety percent of Chicago grocers interviewed in 1920 said that more than three-quarters of their customers requested baked beans by brand name.
>
> (Strasser 1989: 52)

And it was in this period that courses on sales and sales management began to appear in colleges and elsewhere in the United States (Maynard 1951).

The pattern was similar in Britain. Branding was rare through the middle of the nineteenth century, one of the first branded lines being candies (Adburgham 1981: 130; Alexander, D. 1970: 126). However, late in the nineteenth century branded foodstuffs were common:

> By 1900 there were over 360 types of biscuit on the market baked by nationally known firms . . . . There were jams from Keiller, Hartley, and Crosse & Blackwell, pickles of Lazenby's, W. H. Lever's "Sunlight Soap" and Hudson's, Bovril. . ., Van den Bergh's margarine, Cadbury's cocoa essence . . . the list, if not endless, is exceptionally long.
>
> (Winstanley 1983: 124)

By World War I even small village shops were likely to carry more than one brand of cocoa, tea, salt, jam, sauce, gravy mix and custard powder (Winstanley 1983: 206). However, Mathias (1967: 379) notes that it was only after World War II that manufacturers' brands finally came into their own in the multiple shop firms in the food trade, winning a place next to the house brands that had held sway previously. This was the result of rising standards of living and greater brand advertising. These

> reduced the pull of the multiple shops based on price advantage alone – which was fading through the thirties – and forced them to seek expansion of turnover by moving towards national proprietary articles. National advertising costs (adjusted for price changes) were running four and a half times higher in relation to production in 1957 than in 1938, a crude index of the rise in the power of the branded article.

In creating and advertising their brands, manufacturers were creating novel identities. Manufacturers may have created them for fairly simple commercial reasons, but these acts of creation had important consequences. The consequences that have attracted the most attention revolve around the changing social meaning of objects, the ways that brands become badges of identity, as I described in the Introduction. However, there were also important consequences for the operation of retail trade. Manufacturers sought to pre-sell customers – encourage them to go to the shop and ask for a specific brand. Indeed, manufacturers encouraged customers to *demand* the brand, warning them against perfidious clerks who might try to sell them a substitute (Strasser 1989: 83–7). This reduced the clerk to a mere filler of orders and the shopkeeper to a mere stocker of brands. The clerk may have found it easier and more enjoyable to sell to the pre-sold customer (e.g. Donovan 1929: ch. 5), but it required less skill. What a clerk knew of the qualities of different products was of no interest to the customer who came into the shop wanting a can of Campbell's chicken soup. The shopkeeper's knowledge of local tastes and the web of contacts that allowed him to locate suitable products was equally pointless. The ability of both to judge the quality of products and prepare them for sale was never exercised when the only work was unpacking cases of ready-to-sell and ready-to-use products (Bluestone, Hanna, Kuhn and Moore 1981: 18; Winstanley 1983: 33). "A century ago a shopkeeper could say with conviction, 'This is a sound article,' while his descendant today only dares to say 'We get asked for a lot of these'" (Davis, D. 1966: 277). The irrelevance of shopkeepers was implicit in the advertising material that manufacturers supplied them with. Often this suggested that the manufacturer was conferring an honor on the retailer by allowing him to carry the branded good, and it quietly ignored the possibility that the retailer had used his judgement to select a product that he thought his customers would like (Strasser 1989: 191).

In fact, manufacturers used branding and advertising to oblige retailers and even wholesale merchants to abandon their old roles. "To the manufacturer who advertises", wrote one American publicist in 1905, "it makes no difference what jobber or what commission man buys his goods. All of them will have to buy them in the end" (Calkins 1905, in Strasser 1989: 81; for Britain see Jefferys 1954: 12). Equally, retailers were put under pressure to stock brands that they may have thought unsuited to their customers' needs and tastes, inferior in quality to other brands, or more expensive than and indistinguishable from other forms of the same commodity – as they often were.[4] The *Grocers' Review* in 1904 complained about "bare faced attempts to get between the grocer and his trade", and company salesmen are said to have routinely told reluctant retailers that they may as well buy the branded item now, as advertising would make local demand irresistible in the end (Schudson 1984: 167; Strasser 1989: 193–4). This resentment continued into the 1950s. Sofer (1965: 185) said that the British food shopkeepers that he talked to "felt that the manufacturers and their associated marketing companies determined demand by direct communication with the public . . . and left them to cope with the consequences of their actions". One American commentator put it more decorously, when he said that with its own advertising the manufacturer assumes some of the functions of distribution (Shaw, A. 1912: 740–4).

Brands allowed manufacturers to constrain retailers in other ways as well. By advertising their wares with prices listed, manufacturers could control both the wholesale price at which they sold to shops and the retail price at which shopkeepers could sell. This allowed them to put pressure on retail profit margins. At the very least, shopkeepers were aware of this power, which pointed out the adversarial relationship between shopkeeper and manufacturer in a striking way (e.g. Cherington 1913: 128–34). More subtly, as Sofer (1965) illustrates, the shopkeeper could be put under pressure to reorganize his shop in ways that he did not like, solely to reduce costs and stay in business. Even when retailers made use of manufacturers' brands and prices for their own purposes, they did so in a way that increased their alienation from each other. This occurred when retailers used brands and prices in their competitive advertising. When supermarkets spread in the United States between the world wars, they advertised brands almost exclusively, these being standard items that would show to best advantage the lower prices that these stores offered buyers (Zimmerman 1937: 49–55).

ALIENATION IN TRADE AND PRODUCTION

The changes in retail trading practice that I have described in these two chapters resemble many of the changes in production practice that I described in Chapter 2. In each case, work became simplified as a growing proportion of the decisions involved came to be made by those not actually doing the work, so that work required less skill and involvement on the part of workers. In each case as well, relations among workers became less personal, so that work increasingly took place among sets of people who were linked only through their work.

The increasing impersonality of production and trade affected people's experience with objects, and hence the common cultural understanding of purchased manufactures. In each case that experience became more impersonal, but the changes in these two realms were unequal and came about in different ways. Growing impersonality in production affected production workers. However, growing impersonality in retail trade affected both trade workers and the large number of people who transacted with them. There is another reason to think that alienation in retail trade had the greater impact. Alienated factory workers were producing objects that likely they would never see again. The impersonality of the process may have colored the worker's general understanding of manufactured objects, but it did not have the immediacy of the impersonality that the shopper confronted. The impersonal objects people bought in stores did not disappear into never-never land in the way that automobiles, shirts or cardboard boxes did for factory workers. They got carried home and brought their impersonality with them. Those who search for the historical sources of impersonality in modern life might look, then, at the monster shop, the dropping trade and the supermarket, rather than just the factory.

I have stressed the growing impersonality of retail trade and the economic advantages of the newer practices. However, these do not mean that circulation became stripped of social content or control, responding only to the individual, primeval economic lust that is supposed to motivate a free market. There are two reasons for this. One is that trade remained embedded in social structures and permeated by social values. These, though, were the impersonal structures of state regulations governing purity, health and safety, discrimination and the like, and the impersonal values of the commodity-sign. The other is that the logic of economic rationality stressed by advocates of the changes I have described was not accepted by all retailers, clerks or customers. Small shops continue to exist and even in large stores customers and staff can find ways to make their tasks and relationships more personal. However, it remains the case that for most retail trade this personality is optional, no longer so obligatory a part of the way people acquire objects in commercial exchange.

5

THE WORK OF APPROPRIATION

In the three preceding chapters I described a set of historical changes in the ways that people produce and circulate objects. Not only did these changes affect people's common conception of objects, they mark a growing differentiation in social life. Put briefly, the dominant forms of production and circulation, the economic aspects of social life, came to involve a type of social relation that was more impersonal than it had been. Furthermore, this type of social relationship appeared distinct from the type that characterized other areas of life, a type that was itself changing as it lost many of its earlier links with production and circulation. Put in other terms, life became differentiated into two spheres, each with its own distinctive form of social relationship. I shall call these spheres "economy" and "society". In making this point I am only echoing the Maussian observation that the emergence of the modern West meant that "the economy becomes progressively disembedded from society, . . . economic relations become increasingly differentiated from other types of social relationships" (Parry 1986: 466).

Cultural conceptions came to reflect this disembedding. People came to construct and see the realm of the commodity, economy, as distinct from and opposed to the realm of the gift, society. However, the dominant cultural constructions of these realms exaggerate the changes that occurred and the resulting differences between realms. Dominant understandings of relations and transactions proper to the social and economic realm appear to be defined in dialectical opposition to each other. The results, though doubtless containing a truth, are stylized and exaggerated. David Schneider, an anthropologist, points to this dialectical exaggeration in his summary of one rendering of the opposition in the United States, the distinction between "home" and "work":

> The family as a symbol is a pattern for how kinship relations should be conducted; the opposition between "home" and "work" defines these meanings quite clearly and states them in terms of the features which are distinctive to each and opposed to the other.
>
> (Schneider, D. 1980: 45)

The distinction people draw between these realms is reflected in many

106

different ways. Constance Perin (1977), for example, shows how the separation of residential areas from commercial and industrial ones manifests this distinction in land use and urban layout. Chaya Piotrkowski (1979: 87–98) shows how many individuals organize their daily lives to maintain and even exaggerate the distinction between the different realms of their activities, changing identities as they return home from work, shrugging off their job and refusing to let it impinge on their domestic lives.

People generally see their identity in the family as part of their being and not related to their general competence or their performance of their roles. I have already related how Steve Barnett and Martin Silverman (1979: 51), drawing on Schneider, explain that in this realm people see themselves and each other in terms of "things which people believe to be real things, which are in an important sense thought to be internal to the individual or continuous with the individual as a concrete being." As Schneider (1980: 47) puts it,

> even if a spouse rates low on every measure of competence or productivity which can be applied, from the output of clean shirts per week to the number of fond endearments issued each month, this in itself is not proper or sufficient grounds for terminating a marriage.

Schneider is not saying that Americans ignore endearments and clean shirts at home. They are important, but they are subordinated to the relationships they are taken to express. Too few clean shirts per week, by itself, is sufficient grounds to change your laundry, but not your spouse. But too few clean shirts per week can mean that love is gone and the marriage dead.

Work is very different. For Barnett and Silverman (1979: 51), this is the realm of "individuals (more or less) freely entering into agreements to do certain things in accordance with certain standards and rules." Thus, work involves an insubstantial aspect of the self that relates to the goal of the company and to the task at hand, but not to one's true self. What is engaged at work is only the loose skin of work identity and relations that we put on when we go to work. "[A]t work, it is what one does and how he does it that counts. Who he is is not supposed to really matter" (Schneider, D. 1980: 47). To an earlier generation, Talcott Parsons (1959: 261) made a similar point when he said that work

> roles are organized about standards of competence or effectiveness in performing a definite function. That means that criteria of effective performance ... must be predominantly universalistic and must be attached to impersonally and objectively defined abilities and competence through training.

Thus, people do not base their marriages on clean shirts, but they surely base their pay on it, because at work clean shirts per week is all there is.

Not only do these two realms entail different types of relationship and involvement of the self, the values and transactions that characterize them are very different. Work is about money; home and family are about love.

> Home is not kept for money and, of those things related to home and family, it is said that there are some things that money can't buy! The formula in regard to work is exactly reversed at home: What is done is done for love, not for money! And it is love, of course, that money can't buy.

> (Schneider, D. 1980: 46)

And again, Talcott Parsons's earlier formulation (1959: 262) says pretty much the same with less punch:

> Broadly speaking, there is no sector of our society where the dominant patterns stand in sharper contrast to those of the occupational world than in the family. The family is a solidary group within which status, rights, and obligations are defined primarily by membership as such and by the ascribed differentiations of age, sex, and biological relatedness. This basis of relationship and status in the group precludes more than a minor emphasis on universalistic standards of functional performance. Similarly, the patterning of rights and obligations in the family is not restricted to the context specific to a positively defined functional role; rather, it is functionally diffuse . . . . Finally, instead of being defined in impersonal, emotionally neutral terms, the family is specifically treated as a network of emotionally charged relationships, the mutual affection of its members in our society being held to be the most important basis of their solidarity and loyalty.

It is important to recall that Schneider is not reporting people's actual experiences in or considered judgements of home and work.[1] Instead, he is concerned with cultural constructions, "the system of symbols (or signs) and meanings which inform social action and the norms of social action. I do *not* mean patterns *of* action, nor patterns *for* action" (Schneider, D. 1979: 155). In fact, these two realms are not as isolated as the idealized opposition between them suggests, an opposition that many social scientists have adopted unthinkingly from popular culture (see Millman 1991; Piotrkowski 1979: 6–9).

The world of work is, in spite of this construction, larded with social relationships. For example, a popular variety of books on how to find a job (e.g. Jackson 1978; Lathrop 1977) advise their readers not to rely on an impersonal job market, but to establish personal relations with possible employers. This reflects a belief that the job market is impersonal in important ways, but it suggests as well that people are attempting to impose the self onto the world of work (see also Granovetter 1973). To recall a point I made in Chapter 2, for those lower down the occupational hierarchy personal relations can be important for getting access to work. Further, many employers make overt use of kin and friendship links to recruit such workers (Grieco 1987). Equally, many things that appear to betoken impersonal rationality at work serve functions that are as much social and symbolic. Contracts between firms may define legal rights and obligations, but often these are ignored if they interfere with the sales representative's reputation and relationships (Macaulay 1963). Thorough bookkeeping often is a way of signalling that a firm is orderly and competent, rather than just a way of keeping accounts (Carruthers and Espeland 1991). In fact, many firms are under pressure to adopt popular practices largely in order to maintain their reputation in their industry (DiMaggio and Powell 1983).

The exaggerated opposition between these realms also ignores the ways that social relations have a substantial material and utilitarian dimension. Within the family, parents are bound to their children and are supposed to love them, but they also feed, clothe and house them. Beyond the household, people are supposed to get along with their neighbors and kin, but they also help them in material ways, as illustrated by different sociological studies in North America. The resources that friends, relatives and neighbors transact in these relationships typically are much smaller than those they transact in more formal economic relations of employment or shopping. However, they can be substantial even so. People who dig out a friend's garden, who look after a neighbor's child every other day, who help a relative repair a house, are engaged in transactions that affect the subsistence of the recipient and provide things that would cost a lot if purchased in commercial transactions (Wellman and Wortley 1990). Likewise, people facing financial crisis often receive substantial amounts of money, services, and material objects from neighbors, friends, and kin. Whether it is a holiday turkey, rent money, or a bag of groceries, and whether it is given without being asked, loaned freely and without much concern for repayment, or only loaned grudgingly, this assistance can have a significant impact on these people's basic subsistence (Uehara 1990). Social relationships carry a significant economic load (see Hofferth 1984).

The cultural opposition between economic and social relationships, then, is an exaggeration that most people contradict every day of their lives. But exaggerated or not, it has an important consequence. The very opposition that makes home life so distinctive and valued in relation to work means that the products of the world of work are tainted by their origin. The result is that in their raw state, as people first approach them, they are inappropriate for use in household relations. As I said in Chapter 2, Daniel Miller makes an analogous point. He says (1988: 115) that for many people "manufacture", like its corollary of "manufactured object", has come to connote the alienated commodity, and that people are likely to see certain sorts of objects as manufactures without knowing how the actual object has been made. Doubtless this is facilitated by the decline in industrial employment in

advanced capitalist economies, which has meant that an ever-smaller proportion of the population has any direct experience of making things, and
hence any direct knowledge of the impersonality or otherwise of the
manufactures that they buy and consume.

Miller is not arguing that all people in industrial societies think they are
alienated, separated, from impersonal objects and institutions any more than
he is saying that they react to that separation in the same way. "Alienation"
has negative connotations, but what it denotes can also be glossed with a word
with positive connotations, "freedom". At the least, then, people are likely
to be ambivalent about the separation that goes with alienation, as they are
about the joining that goes with durable social relations. In their different
times and places, each is necessary in people's lives; moreover, the degree of
necessity, which times and which places vary, as I note at different places in
this book. Within societies people of different class, gender and culture will
differ in the degree to which they see things as alienated from them and they
will differ in their response to that alienation. Equally, however, those
variations can be submerged in a dominant rhetoric. There are differences
between societies as well. To a marked degree, Americans stress their
autonomy and individuality, as commentators have noted repeatedly over the
centuries. In contrast, and at the risk of over-simplification, many Europeans
seem much less concerned with these issues. Perhaps this is because they see
impersonal institutions not as threats to their individual freedom, but as ways
in which they can pursue collective goals. As my European conjecture
indicates, the question of gift and commodity relations that this book
addresses bears on more than people's perception of and relationship with
objects and others in exchange; or, perhaps, those perceptions and relationships are more fundamental than they appear at first glance. (I return to
this issue in my concluding chapter.)

FORMS OF APPROPRIATION

My presentation of the cultural separation of the realms of home and work
indicates that the object that a person confronts is not neutral and inert, but
is "a culturally constructed entity endowed with culturally specific meanings
and classified and reclassified into culturally constituted categories" (Kopytoff
1986: 68). In the economic world outside the household, the things that people
confront carry the cultural meaning of commodities, and people are obliged
to convert them into a different cultural category – possessions – in order to
make them suitable for use within the household.

Until it is sold, the object is construed and considered in commodity terms.
What price will it fetch? What demand is there for it? What are its costs? It
is a stock item subject to bulk discounts in orders over 100 gross; marketed
to 25–34-year-old semi-professionals; part of the Christmas product line;
assembled in Toledo from components made in Singapore, Springfield and

Aberystwyth under license from a Düsseldorf company; just like the other 839 produced in the factory that day, so if this one is defective for some reason we can get a replacement in 48 hours. After it is sold, however, gift terms come to the fore. Is it what suits me? Will my family like it? It is the kind of hot dog young Sally always likes after school; a necktie that I picked out because it goes so well with your grey suit; something that we got when we were in Monterey, to remind us of the harbor; a pair of cufflinks my son got for me when he was in London – aren't they nice? Converting the object from commodity to possession is the work of appropriation, "the means whereby an enduring and intimate relation between an object and an individual is initiated and perpetuated" (Beaglehole 1932: 132).

Appropriation occurs in a variety of ways, the variation reflecting a range of factors. One factor is the nature of the object. Does it have a history, and is that history interesting? Is it made by hand or mass-produced? Is it expensive, and presumably distinctive and perhaps made by hand rather than by robots and computers? A second factor is the way it is bought. Is the store anonymous or personal? Does buying require dealing with people in the store? How much? How well do I know them? Do the people at the store make it, prepare it or alter it just for me, or do I take it as it is? A third factor is what the object is for. Will I use and discard it quickly and privately, or will it last a long time in the living room? Is it for us at home or for me at work? Is it for my child or the office secretary? Each of the factors affects how urgent appropriation is and the forms it is likely to take. In Chapter 8 I describe the sort of appropriation that can occur on formal occasions when people give presents. While this appropriation is visible and familiar to people in Western societies, there are other appropriations that are equally important and often more common, if less self-evident.

For example, Miller (1988) describes the different ways tenants in a north London council housing estate confronted their housing as a commodity and appropriated it. This housing is not a commodity in the conventional sense. However, because it is allocated on impersonal criteria tenants are alienated from it. This impersonality is apparent when bureaucratic allocation is contrasted with Michael Young and Peter Willmott's description (1986) of private rental housing in Bethnal Green, in London's East End, which putatively was allocated by the impersonal mechanism of the market, though would-be renters in fact relied on kinship and other durable personal relationships to get housing.

Miller's immediate focus is the ways that tenants modified their kitchens, a key aspect of the social identity of their housing. He notes, first, that there was no obvious link between people's income and their kitchen modifications, which could be as simple and inexpensive as the decorative placement of towels, momentos and the like. There was, however, a clear association between modification and people's sense of alienation from the estate. Those who modified their kitchens tended to be those who were uneasy about the fact that they were in a council estate rather than in private housing. Modification, then, was associated with an attempt to transform what these tenants saw as impersonal and inappropriate council housing into something that embodied their social identity. Miller notes, however, that not all people in the estate saw council housing as equally alien. English and Irish tenants did so more than West Indians (1988: 360). Equally, people who appeared to have no significant social lives made the least effort to modify their kitchens (1988: 368).

Most of the objects in people's lives are less momentous than housing, and most of the ways that people appropriate these more mundane objects are less striking than redecorating a kitchen. Even so, appropriation can involve extensive physical work. For example, two American sociologists, Mihaly Csikszentmihalyi and Eugene Rochberg-Halton (1981: 61–2), report the words of a woman describing a chest that she inherited and particularly valued. She said it

> was bought by my mother and father when they were married, about 70 years ago. And they didn't buy it new, so it's practically an antique. My mother painted it different colors, used it in the bedroom. When I got it my husband sanded it down to the natural wood. It's beautiful.

Her mother appropriated the chest by painting it. Even though she and her husband did not acquire it as a commodity, they added their own identities to it by sanding it. Likewise, appropriation can come through sheer familiarity. Again, Csikszentmihalyi and Rochberg-Halton (1981: 108) provide an apt illustration, this time of a policeman describing his "working tools", his guns.

> [G]uns to a policeman are like a horse to a jockey, you got to get used to them, work them a lot, know what they are capable of, know their strength and weaknesses, how it does what it does, every gun is different. A gun is not just something that makes a loud noise. The policeman who knows his job, he knows his gun too, so with a new gun it takes a lot of breaking in.[2]

I said that the urgency and form of the work of appropriation can vary with a number of factors. One such factor is the setting in which the object is presented. By this I mean the physical setting where the would-be purchaser finds the object, the cultural symbolism of the setting, and the sort of relations that are involved in purchasing. For example, Sharon Zukin (1990) has noted how the object's setting can help bestow upon it an authenticity, a valuable historical and cultural identity, and so facilitate the buyer's appropriating it. However, while authenticity elevates the object beyond the mass of indifferent commodities by giving it a distinctive identity, some authentic identities can be abhorrent. To appropriate such an object it would be necessary to purify it. Something analogous to this is the way that people frequently purify their houses and belongings after they have been burgled, with compulsive washing and disinfecting (Leonini 1984: 136–41).

Perhaps the archetype of what Zukin describes is the reproduction item sold in a place like the restored area of Williamsburg or in the ubiquitous museum shop. Indeed, Zukin notes that in some circumstances there emerge special consumption spaces, such as "gentrified" urban areas, that provide a coherent identity for much of what is sold in them and so facilitate appropriation by those who live and buy there. Equally, as I speculated in Chapter 3, shopping malls can operate in this way. This would be most plausible where malls are designed and managed to attract only a narrow segment of the population. Such a mall would seem familiar to those likely to shop there, "their place . . . to shop in, to fool around, play games, be bored, be with friends, or do nothing alone comfortably" (Kowinski 1985: 123). As this quotation suggests, authenticity and familiarity can carry with them elements of entertainment, so that shopping, even without the intention of buying, can be a pleasurable leisure activity. The element of leisure and entertainment is explicit in Zukin's invocation of Disney World as a consumption space. Such spaces, then, are larger versions of the entertaining and alluring dream worlds that Rosalind Williams (1982) describes in Parisian department stores in the nineteenth century. Indeed, they echo a much older phenomenon, the sacred site where pilgrims would come, spend their money, and take home a relic or two of the local saint (Geary 1986).

In their different ways the mall, the gentrified area and Williamsburg provide a framework of identity that encourages the customer to see the object as familiar, and hence easier to appropriate. In the early general trade that I described in Chapter 3, it is the community of buyers and sellers who are likely to provide such a framework. The same is true in most specialist trade, as Charles Smith (1988) suggests in his analysis of auctions. An example of such specialist trade is oriental rugs. Brian Spooner (1986: 196–7) says that

> [b]esides being able to recognize a carpet as oriental, . . . [buyers] must be at least vaguely aware of a hierarchical taxonomy of types of oriental carpet, rationalized in terms of criteria such as age, provenience, materials, color, design, "handle" (that is, feel or pliability), condition, fineness, and evenness of weave.

Much of this communal knowledge defines these rugs as a class as distinctive, as it defines each rug in that class as more or less unique. In other words, the community of buyers and sellers assigns these rugs "special meaning through the construction of the social and cultural provenience of the artifact" (1986: 201).

Because they carry a history and personal identity, objects like oriental rugs are bad commodities. People are uncertain how to transact them and how to equate them with other commodities, which means how to price them. Highly personal objects or those with an extended or peculiar provenance are bad, whether they are family treasures, obviously made by hand (especially if sold by their makers), art works, antiques or exotica. Commonly they are traded at auctions rather than through the normal markets and practices of commodity transactions. This relationship between the goodness of the commodity and how it is sold reflects in part the assumption that normal, fixed-price marketing entails fair prices (Smith, C. 1988: 53). Conversely, abnormal selling means untrustworthy prices; even abnormally low prices often seem untrustworthy (Prus 1986). Used-car prices are notoriously negotiable and used-car sellers are notorious crooks; objects sold at auction are very difficult to price accurately, and the objects and their sellers are full of traps for the unwary. It is significant that an important aspect of being one of "the unwary" revolves around social relations – being an outsider, not being one of the community of buyers and sellers.

While Zukin's consumption spaces, like museum shops and Williamsburg reproductions, deny the anonymity of the objects for sale by giving them a cultural identity, this denial can occur in other ways. Sellers can stress the personality of the object and the relationship in which it is purchased. Some stores cloak their commodities in the symbolism of craft, rather than mass, manufacture, and have staff trained to treat customers in a friendly, person-able way. (In the next chapter I describe the way some catalogues present objects in such settings.)

However, people commonly buy objects in anonymous stores that sell anonymous commodities. The clearest example of this is supermarkets, though discount chain stores are similar. These stores are almost aggressively self-service, so that contact with humans in the store may occur – and, significantly, need occur – only as shoppers silently hand over their money and take their change, often enough from a machine. Equally, the objects supermarkets sell are almost aggressively anonymous. Aisles are heaped high with fungible commodities awaiting the shopper's selection, with the same good often displayed in five or six different brands, each in two or three different sizes. Of course brands confer social identities, but only the impersonal identities of public structures that I described in the Introduction, not the personal identities of possessions. In their stark impersonality, such stores present in most glaring form the consequences of the changes in retail trade that I described in Chapters 3 and 4.

Just as objects sold in consumption spaces acquire by association a distinctive identity, so objects sold in impersonal stores take on by association that impersonality. They tend to lose their distinctions and become mere commodities with no special claims on us, the retail equivalents of Miller's "manufactures". This loss is illustrated by a minor incident on the fourth of July in a Southern town. The report in the local newspaper captures the symbolism in a striking way.

One man's attempt to burn an American flag on the fourth of July on

Charlottesville's Downtown Mall was thwarted by a woman who snatched the flag from his hand just as he held a lighter to it . . . .

Dempsey McDaniels, a Greene County man who had been walking up and down the Downtown Mall carrying a sign that read "Down with Bush and Flag. Up with Liberation," stopped to make a statement to reporters and to set fire to the flag he had been swinging at his side and dragging along the ground with each step.

"I'm protesting," McDaniels said. "I'm saying, we have the freedom to burn the flag. If the flag is really precious, why do we sell it at K mart and at every store across the nation . . . when it was sold, that's when it lost its meaning."

(Wannamaker 1989: A1)

Supermarkets are extreme in their impersonality, but most people shop in them frequently because they buy food frequently, more frequently than they buy museum postcards or Williamsburg reproductions. The impersonality of the supermarket stands in marked contrast to the significance of what people buy there, for the meals that people prepare with the commodities they purchase are an important marker of family social relations. As I noted in Chapter 1, the family is generated and regenerated in important ways by its members' willingness to cook for each other and to accept the meal prepared. The contrast between the impersonality of the supermarket and the personality of home means that one would expect to find important but mundane acts of appropriation in the process of converting foodstuffs into meals.

The most obvious way that people appropriate purchased food is by cooking, a sort of transformation that is tangible and, indeed, usually necessary, but seldom straightforward (e.g. Lévi-Strauss 1966, or less grandly, Carsten 1989; Kerr and Charles 1986). In *The Hidden Persuaders* Vance Packard described what American motivational researchers found about the ways that housewives used and understood foodstuffs. His discussion of cake mixes illustrates both the need for and the processes of appropriation in the preparation of food for the family.

Housewives consistently report that one of the most pleasurable tasks of the home is making a cake . . . . A psychological consulting firm . . . found that "women experience making a cake as making a gift of themselves to their family" . . . .

In the early days the cake-mix packages instructed, "Do not add milk, just add water." Still many wives insisted on adding milk as their creative touch. . ., and often the cakes or muffins fell, and the wives would blame the cake mix . . . . [W]ives who were interviewed in depth studies would exclaim: "What kind of cake is it if you just need to add tap water!" Several different psychological firms wrestled with this problem and came up with essentially the same answer. The mix makers should always leave the housewife something to do. Thus Dr Dichter counselled General Mills that it should start telling the housewife that she and Bisquick together could do the job and not Bisquick alone. Swansdown White Cake Mix began telling wives in large type: "You Add Fresh Eggs. . ." Some mixes have the wife add both fresh eggs and fresh milk.

(Packard 1957: 77–8)[3]

Packard's description of cake mixes points to another important fact about the appropriation of food, that it is associated strongly with gender.

APPROPRIATION AND GENDER

Gender is important for understanding the processes and significance of appropriation, just as it is important for many other aspects of family life. However, more is involved in the distribution of the work of appropriation than public structures of gender identity and obligation, because more is involved than disembodied men and women acting in conformity to those structures. Rather, these men and women exist within a household. Likewise, within that household they are involved in patterns of interaction and obligation that have their own histories.

Consider first the fact that there is a household. The thrust of my argument in this chapter is that a household exists in part because its members appropriate the commodities that are circulated and consumed within it. This need is not universal or eternal, and at various points in this book I point to factors that affect it. None the less, in most Western capitalist societies it has to be met if the household is to maintain its integrity in the face of the impersonal economic sphere. But equally, in principle it does not matter who in the household performs which tasks of appropriation. In practice, of course, it may matter a great deal, and for a host of reasons, but these reasons are contingencies rather than necessities from the point of view of the household itself. To consider them necessities is to ignore the existence and efficacy of individual household arrangements, and thus to impose a conformity where none is necessary.

Consider second the fact that the members of any given household are in durable domestic relationships. That very durability means that members are likely to develop their own pattern of obligations to each other and to the household as a whole, shaped by their history together and their different personalities and idiosyncrasies. As a consequence, even though from the perspective of the household considered abstractly it does not matter who performs the different tasks of appropriation, the people in the household may come to see some among themselves as particularly competent at carrying out different of those tasks. But more is at stake than having the tasks performed by competent members. In addition, in most households the various tasks and responsibilities of the members operate as an exchange. Not only need each member perform his or her specialist tasks, but each member needs to perform his or her share. These shares need not be equal (Parry 1986: 454), but whether or not they are, they are relatively stable and people conceive of them as reciprocations. Members develop expectations of what they are owed by and what they owe to each other. Again I need to stress, however, that to speak of exchange and reciprocation is not necessarily to speak of equality among those involved. Durable bonds of obligation and expectation, maintained and regenerated by the give and take of daily life, can also be bonds of domination and subordination. (Morris [1990] describes many of the factors that affect, and theories that try to explain, power inequalities within the household.)

Thus it is that a woman who is cooking for her family may be conforming to public conceptions of what is feminine and to the pattern of obligation and structure of inequality in her particular household, at the same time that she is maintaining the integrity of the household by converting purchased commodities into a form suitable for use in household relations.

I have stressed the distinctiveness of three factors: public constructions of gender, the household considered abstractly, the pattern of obligations among members. The fact that they are distinct, however, does not mean that they are insulated from each other or from the patterns and changes that exist in the larger world. While households work out their own pattern of obligations, these patterns are themselves patterned because people in different households are likely to confront comparable external forces and constraints, just as they are likely to have absorbed comparable cultural expectations about how families and the people within them ought to be.

The interaction of these common factors with internal household relations is illustrated in the anomaly of housework. Ruth Schwartz Cowan (1983: especially ch. 4) has traced the shifting material activities of American households over the twentieth century, and she finds that though some that previously were carried out outside the household have moved into it (especially transport), the overwhelming change has been one of decrease. In purely technical terms housekeeping tasks have become fewer, and the development of household equipment like refrigerators and electric or gas stoves means that these tasks have become easier. The anomaly is that the amount of time that women who are housewives spend on housework has changed very little, as Joann Vanek (1974) reports in detail.

Cowan seeks to explain the anomaly in terms of changing cultural conceptions of what housework is about: no longer keeping things neat and tidy, but nurturing, marking status, expressing affection. She bases her argument in part on the changing orientation of advertisements in popular women's magazines in the period after World War I. These advertisements came to portray household equipment and tasks not in terms of technical efficiency but as reflections "of the housewife's personality and of her affection for her family" (Cowan 1976: 150). Cowan is not alone in describing this change. T. J. Jackson Lears (1983: 23) finds the same thing, and concludes that advertisers of household wares began to link them to "psychic security and fulfillment" and the promise of "domestic harmony". This stress on the symbolism of domesticity and personality seems appropriate in view of the likelihood that a growing number of people were beginning to think in terms of the sharp cultural distinction between home and work. Cloaking their commodities in domestic symbolism, firms masked the impersonality of their manufactured wares and so made them more appealing to customers, a point that I pursue in the next chapter.

I suggest that these changes in the presentation of objects in advertising are linked to the anomaly of the time housewives spend on their housework through the dynamics of relations within the household. Simply, with the technical simplification and mechanization of housework, housewives had less to do. However, as Mauss noted in his classic formulation, parties to a gift relationship are under an obligation to give. In the changing situation I have described, housewives would find it harder to fulfil that obligation, harder to contribute their "fair share" in domestic transactions. I suggest that this made them particularly receptive to a reconceptualization of housework that heightened its emotional intensity, just as it would motivate them to maintain the length of time they spent doing it. My argument here echoes a slightly different conclusion reached by Barbara Ehrenreich and Deirdre English (1978: ch. 5), who link the rising popularity of the American home economics movement in the early decades of the twentieth century to the technical simplification of housework.

Vanek's analysis of time spent on housework by homemakers who were and who were not in paid employment supports at least part of my argument. While those who were in paid employment could contribute both their wages and their housework to the household, those who were not in paid employment had only their housework to give. If I am correct, those not in paid employment would be more concerned to ensure that their housework was recognized by household members than would those who were in paid employment. This supposition is supported by Vanek's (1974: 120) finding that women who were not in paid employment spent more time on housework over the weekend, when their contribution is most visible, than did women in paid employment, even though many of the latter treated weekends as a time to get caught up on housekeeping tasks. (Analogous arguments about housework are in Valadez and Clignet 1984.)

Thus, as there is a symbolic dimension to the distinction between home and work, so there is a symbolic dimension to the things that household members transact with each other. The giving and getting have a material aspect, but they are defined and redefined in terms of the domestic relationship. This is illustrated by Anne Murcott's (1983b) point that many of the British women she studied saw cooking as a key contribution they make to the domestic relationship, even though she found (1983a) that the husbands of many of those women in fact prepared substantial amounts of food in the kitchen. However, she notes that routinely women did not define their husbands' food preparation as "cooking". This is not simply evidence of gender stereotyping. In addition, it shows how these women defined physical activities in a way that maintained the value of what they gave and so maintained their claim to be giving a fair share.

A similar symbolic manipulation is apparent in a form of appropriation that I turn to now, shopping. Usually this is considered as part of house-keeping, and thus culturally is women's work. And like housekeeping work, shopping carries a symbolic load beyond its material dimensions. Echoing my point that housewives may define housekeeping tasks as arduous in order to maintain their position as equitable contributors to the household, there is evidence that some housewives define shopping the same way. Cyril Sofer reports that when English housewives were speaking to male interviewers or were in group discussions led by men,

> organising the family's food was represented as a difficult job. House-work was said to revolve around food and many respondents com-plained that in their houses it was "food all the time". The housewife had to struggle to manage on her budget. Thinking about food, shopping for it and preparing meals kept her constantly busy.

However, when interviewed individually by women, a situation that calls for a somewhat different presentation of themselves, "the overwhelming major-ity, 88 per cent, felt that the task of providing food for the family was something they could take in their stride" (Sofer 1965: 193, 195).

But shopping is not noteworthy only because of its material aspects or even because it is a way of making a contribution to the household. In addition, it is a symbolic task that is important for the maintenance of the household in the face of the world of work. I want to illustrate this with reference to shopping for food, which usually takes places in stores that are extremely impersonal.

APPROPRIATION IN SHOPPING

I said that one way food is appropriated is in cooking. However, appropriation occurs as well before and during purchase, in the activities that usually come under the term "shopping". Indeed, it seems likely that shopping has taken on growing significance as a device for appropriation. This is because the growing simplification and mechanization of housework that I have de-scribed, together with the increasing use of foodstuffs that are already processed and even cooked, means that preparing meals has become simpler for a large portion of the population.

Purchasing food, like purchasing any other commodity, entails a rela-tionship between people in which objects are transacted, and the two forms of appropriation in shopping that I will describe focus on the two main aspects of purchasing: the object and the relationship. In the first form, the purchaser works directly, albeit symbolically, on the object. This work makes the object personal, appropriates it. In the second form, purchaser and seller work to redefine their relationship, making it personal. This redefinition of the purchasing relationship helps make the object transacted within it personal, and so helps the purchaser appropriate it.

One way of appropriating commodities in the face of anonymous mass retailing is to choose what to buy. The idea of consumer choice is important in capitalist economies. Stuart Ewen (esp. 1976) probably overstates the case when he says that touting consumer choice was a strategy American capitalists used to reconcile workers to alienation and loss of control in the workplace (see Schudson 1984: 175–6). However, Ewen does seem correct in linking consumer choice to mass and impersonal manufacturing and retail trade, and in fact a kind of reconciliation is involved, though not necessarily the kind he meant. Choosing is one of the few ways that people can, even if only partially, appropriate what they buy, transform things from being a part of the indifferent mass of objects to being the special things that the shopper selects. Daniel Miller (1987: 190) summarizes the core of this form of appropriation: "On purchase, the vast morass of possible goods is replaced by the specificity of the particular item . . . . Furthermore, this specificity is usually related to a person, either the purchaser or the intended user". In other words, when shoppers select an object, they do so in terms of the particular people who will use the object, their identities and relationships (see Davis, H. 1976).

Shopping inevitably involves selection, and thus all shopping entails this sort of appropriation to some degree. However, certain styles of shopping stress selection more than others. One such style is what I call "Wise Shopping", which stresses the sheer effort involved in selection. The Wise Shopper carefully compares price, quality and value, and so corresponds to what an American sociologist, Gregory Stone (1954), calls the "economical" category of shopping orientation. Although Stone presents this orientation in terms of economic rationality, that rationality can serve the very social task of helping to appropriate what is bought. This is because the investing of effort prior to and during the act of shopping by Wise Shoppers helps stamp the process of shopping with the shoppers' identity and so helps turn the product of shopping, the *mélange* of anonymous commodities that they buy, into their possessions in a way that unwise shopping cannot. Wise Shopping resembles consumer activism, and it seems reasonable to account in part for the rise of American consumer activism in the period after World War I (e.g. Baldwin, W. 1929), as well as for its durability, by noting that it too can serve as a means of appropriation.

I said that supermarkets are probably the most anonymous form of retail selling, and it is appropriate that Wise Shoppers usually are presented as food shoppers. An illustration is "When the Tough Go Shopping." For this article, in *The Washington Post*, Carole Sugarman observed three people who were especially skilled food shoppers: a Department of Agriculture home economist, a retired couple renowned for their wise shopping, a vice-president for consumer affairs of a supermarket chain. The article purports to be about "how to beat the high cost of shopping in Washington" (Sugarman 1987: E1). However, like Stone's focus on the rationality of the economic shopping orientation, this is too simplistic an explanation. Consider, for instance, the $24.91 shopping trip of the retired couple: This "began at Shoppers Food Warehouse .... From there, it was on to Dart Drug .... Then on to the co-op" (1987: E14). The cost, time and energy of the second and third stops are not likely to be justified by the savings; Sugarman never considered the question. Likewise, although the article is about how to cut food costs, we are not urged to eat differently or eat less, probably the surest ways to reduce costs in the place where food prices are "higher than in any other city in the continental U.S." (1987: E1). Instead, we are told to be "more aware", which means devote substantial effort to project the self onto the food shopping and so make possessions of the goods bought. This active mode is exemplified by one shopper, who "takes control of her shopping, remembering last week's prices, quickly scanning unit prices ... or running back to compare item prices in another aisle" (1987: E14).

Doubtless, aware shoppers pay less for what they get than do unaware shoppers. Equally doubtless, however, economism does not describe all that the article is about. Rather, it is also about the need to take shopping seriously. Indeed, we are urged to treat shopping as being very like work: Wise Shoppers plan and calculate, and of our three Wise Shoppers, two are involved with shopping for food professionally. It *is* work, though not the work of the clerk or factory hand, for these working shoppers are doing it for themselves, to satisfy their own needs and desires rather than those of an impersonal employer. And as work, it needs to be taken seriously, for the investment of large amounts of thought and energy, an investment of the self that pays off in a carefully selected food basket, may be the only way possible to appropriate the objects one buys in retail stores as anonymous as supermarkets.

My point is that Wise Shoppers are not simply those who rationally choose to make the best and most informed selection of commodities following utilitarian criteria and weighing cost and use value, though often they are described in this way. Instead, Wise Shopping is an avocation that is difficult to justify in terms of the utilitarian, economistic calculus put forward in cultural statements like "When the Tough Go Shopping". Such shopping is rational only if Wise Shoppers place no value on their time and energy, not to mention the monetary costs of shopping, a valuation that denies a key part of its overt justification. In failing to mention these costs, "When the Tough Go Shopping" resembles that bible of American Wise Shoppers, *Consumer*

Reports, which focuses on the cost and utility of objects while resolutely refusing to consider the costs of shopping itself. This is particularly notable in its attacks on fair trade, in which *Consumer Reports* never considers that the elimination of fair trade in many areas of commerce has arguably led to a fall in the number of stores and hence longer and more expensive shopping trips for buyers.

From what I said previously, however, this denial of the monetary and other costs of shopping should be no surprise. If a key part of shopping is the conversion of anonymous commodities into possessions, shopping is a cultural as much as an economic activity. It is a labor of love, for it is a part of the work that maintains and regenerates the relationships that unite families.

Whatever else it may be, then, Wise Shopping is a technique of appropriation. And because the world of "When the Tough Go Shopping" is one of abstract use and exchange values and impersonal retail establishments that command no loyalty (itself a cultural construction that is part of the imagery of the Wise Shopper), converting commodity into possession is arduous. The shopper takes possession of commodities through struggle and sweat – running back and forth between aisles, going to all those different stores in Washington's sticky August heat – almost in combat with the impersonal "system" to make a personal collection of goods.

The other form of appropriation in shopping that I said I would consider revolves around the relationship between buyer and seller. I call this form "Personal Shopping", which corresponds to Stone's "personalizing" orientation. (Only one of Stone's four categories, the "apathetic", seems to be a de-socialized approach to shopping.) In Personal Shopping the relationship between buyer and seller is redefined as social and personal, and this personality infects the objects transacted and so helps render them possessions. Thus, Personal Shopping entails establishing quasi-sociable relations with those who work in the store. In stressing these relations, Personal Shopping is, in a way, the antithesis of Wise Shopping. Less service and less human contact makes shopping easier for those who see themselves as wresting personal possessions from an impersonal system. The shop worker, after all, intrudes a disruptive and unwelcome personality in the Wise Shopper's impersonal and abstract world of use value and exchange value.

I said that the relations of Personal Shopping are quasi-sociable. This is because they depart in important ways from the personal relations of family and friendship in capitalist society, much less the sorts of relations that exist in societies dominated by the gift. They are embedded in commodity relations and the world of work. The only reason the customer comes into contact with the store worker in the first place is to purchase commodities. The customer is the worker's job and being friendly to customers is a way to be a good worker. As Arlie Hochschild (1989: 440) observes, many service workers are obliged to "create and maintain a relationship" with customers: "How she feels about these customers . . . is *part* of her job. If she is scornful, irritable or indifferent she's not doing her job well" (see also Hochschild 1983). In this sense these relations are an optional extra for shoppers, something that is a pleasant addition to the routine commodity relations of shopping, and many companies trade on this by advertising themselves as having amiable staff who desire long-term, personal relations with their customers, as I describe in the next chapter.

Opportunities for Personal Shopping are limited. Most obviously, it requires that there be another person with whom one can plausibly establish quasi-personal relations. Some food stores are distinguished by the relatively high level of social interaction possible or even required in shopping: Country Stores or Village Shops, Corner Stores and Gourmet Stores, or, more mundanely, the "deli" or bakery section of a supermarket. In each of these, at least in cultural imagery, most transactions require the intervention of a store worker, which presents the potential for the development of the sort of relationship that is the basis of Personal Shopping. Of course, up to about a century ago almost no stores allowed shoppers to select goods for themselves, so that amicable relations with store workers were more of a necessity than they are now.

Even a supermarket can become a vehicle for this sort of appropriation in the right circumstances. This is demonstrated by a columnist's complaint in *The Washington Post* of the consequences of an attempted hostile takeover of Safeway food stores. The columnist, Mary McGrory (1987), neatly opposes the inadequacies of her local Safeway with the anonymous efficiency of most large supermarkets. "It was nothing like those temples in the suburbs . . . . It was small, its narrow aisles leading to constant carriage gridlock . . . . Washingtonian magazine said it [was] 'the worst Safeway in the city.'" Certainly this is not where we would expect to find Wise Shoppers working away at their grocery lists.

However, in the midst of this inconvenience were warm personal relationships. The assistant manager "was kind of our host at the store, filling us in on local gossip and the comings and goings of our most prominent customers". McGrory herself explicitly juxtaposes cold efficiency and warm personality:

> Maybe you couldn't get everything you needed all the time, but you did get companionship. We had two Alices, one more amiable than the other, black-eyed Georgia and, of course, Wally [the assistant manager], so prized by his customers that they once took up a collection to send him to his Italian homeland.

This friendliness is distinct, in the author's mind, from the sort of rational, financial orientation that characterizes Wise Shoppers. Thus, the store was so cheery that "*[e]ven the Yuppies* yielded to the general good humor" (emphasis added).

The villain of the story is rapacious capitalism, in the shape of the Hafts, investors "who already owned enough companies to satisfy most people" and who indulged in "unbridled capitalist greed". As far as McGrory is concerned, the way the Hafts went about trying to increase their wealth by taking over Safeway was the sort of thing that, if it happened to a fruit stand, "we'd call the cops". As a result of the cost of repelling the takeover attempt, Safeway decided to close McGrory's local store. But the ending may yet be happy. The store was purchased by a company called "Brookville", no ordinary impersonal corporation: "Brookville is a family business, started by brothers. They have one other store." As yet the new store, operating so far for only a few weeks, is not very friendly: "No natterings at the registers. No happy greetings. Of course, we don't know each other, yet."

No doubt Personal Shopping, the sociality that McGrory presents in her complaint, is pleasurable in its own right, just as Wise Shopping no doubt makes for a cheaper basket of groceries. My point, however, is that there is more going on here than what appears at first glance. These are both forms of cultural work by which people can transform commodities into possessions suitable for transaction in the sociable relations of home and family.

APPROACHES TO SHOPPING

I have described shopping in terms of the appropriation of commodities, their transformation into possessions. Though I have treated these as arduous but straightforward processes, it is important to remember that they are problematic, which is another way of saying that people are frustrated shoppers much of the time. The objects we buy often are not really what we want, and often we are less than completely satisfied when we use them in gift relationships. As one might expect in societies that have such a significant process that is problematic, Americans and Britons have developed a ritual that sanctifies and makes potent the daily round of acquiring anonymous commodities and appropriating them. This is the ritual of Christmas shopping, which I describe in Chapter 8.

One of the reasons I have devoted this attention to shopping is that it has not attracted the scholarly interest it merits. Partly, no doubt, this is because most sociologists and anthropologists experience shopping as a minor, almost invisible part of domestic routine and hence are likely to think it too insignificant to merit serious attention. Those who are not so familiar with the mundane activities of capitalist life do not see shopping as so simple and unthinking an affair, but instead surround it with markers that indicate that it is problematic. The Cauca Valley peasants in Colombia that Michael Taussig (1977) describes, living at the geographical edge of capitalism, illustrate this. One practice there is the baptism of the bill. In this, a peasant would surreptitiously put a bit of paper money in the clothing of a child being baptized. Unknown to the priest and the child's relatives, the baptism would then apply to the money rather than the child. The peasant could then use this bill to pay for goods in a store, and with the appropriate invocation could recall the baptized bill from the cash till. With luck, the bill would be able to generate an increase for its owner by bringing several ordinary bills with it on its return. The association of commercial transaction and profit with a perversion of baptism and the damnation of the unbaptized child shows that, for these people, shopping is not just paying your money and making your choice.

I have described how shopping can be a means of appropriation as objects pass from the world of work to the world of home. In addition, shopping is an important point of intersection from the perspective of a number of social theorists and concerns. I will close this chapter by describing two of these briefly, in an effort to encourage attention to something that is too important to be ignored.

From a Marxist perspective, shopping is a key nexus where the two parts of the capitalist socio-economic system meet and regenerate each other. One is the process of consumptive production ("production"), the production of commodities, which requires the consumption of factors of production, including labor power. The other is the process of productive consumption ("reproduction"), the consumption of commodities, which not only produces consumer demand but also reproduces labor power. On the production side, shopping is where the exchange value of the commodity is finally realized. On the reproduction side, the object, now a use value, begins the process of conversion into labor power. In a sense, then, shopping is the inverse of hiring. One marks the onset of the production of commodities by the consumption of labor power, the other marks the onset of the consumption of use values in the production of labor power.

From a Weberian perspective, on the other hand, shopping is the point where class and status meet. Class is the realm of market economics, especially production and circulation. Alternatively, status is the realm of social identity and esteem, and as I noted in the Introduction, for Weber status groups are defined in part by patterns of consumption. Each realm is driven by different imperatives, and shopping is the point at which those different imperatives overlap and conflict. Particularly, the desire of powerful market actors to ensure the greatest demand for their products will conflict with the desire of powerful status groups to restrict the consumption of distinctive items.

6

PRESENTING COMMODITIES
IN CATALOGUES

I said in the preceding chapter that a number of factors affect the urgency and form of the appropriation of commodities for their use in personal relations. Drawing on Sharon Zukin's work, I said that one such factor was the setting in which the object is perceived – its cultural frame. Creating such frames is the work of advertising, much of which revolves around associating commodities with particular symbols. In this chapter I will describe some of those symbols that relate particularly to the problem of appropriation.

The most common sociological approach to advertising locates a key source of the meaning, and hence appeal, of objects in public structures of meaning and identity. Researchers using this approach have described how advertisements try to make objects attractive to people in particular segments of society by presenting them in a way that is pleasing to those people. This means, in effect, associating those objects with the badges or marks of particular status groups, so that the world of objects reflects and reinforces publicly recognized hierarchies of status and identity (e.g. Leiss, Kline and Jhally 1986). But this view of objects as markers in public structures of meaning ignores the issue that is important in this book – the unique personal relationship between individual and object. It is, thus, necessary to look at advertising from a slightly different perspective, to see not just how advertisements invoke symbols that reflect public status values and life-styles, but also how they invoke symbols that reflect the very notion of possession itself.

I argued in the preceding chapter that the spread of industrial capitalism has been associated with a growing cultural opposition between home and work. Daniel Miller's (1987: 115) observation about the cultural meaning of "manufacture" and "manufactured object" points to one manifestation of this opposition. To identify an object as "manufactured" is not to describe objectively the conditions in which it is produced. Instead, it is to invoke the world of work and typify the object in terms of the impersonality of that world as it is culturally constructed. What Miller points out is that imperson-ality has been elevated to the level of a cultural symbol, one that people can reflect upon self-consciously. The converse of this is that personality becomes elevated in the same way, "possession" being a cultural category that can stand in opposition to "manufacture". And because it is a cultural category rather than a technical description, it can be manipulated by advertisers, albeit within limits. The cultural marks of possession can be associated with objects that, considered objectively, are produced and transacted as commodities. After all, the farmer selling apples at a roadside stand does not simply embody values of freshness and wholesomeness, much less the chance to buy food cheaply. In addition, that farmer embodies possession, for those apples do not appear as impersonal commodities. Instead, they come, so to speak, bearing their maker's mark, even though the people who stop to buy have no knowledge of the actual social relations in which those apples were produced and even though when passers-by buy them they do so in a purely impersonal commodity transaction.

My argument, then, is that "possession" has become an identity that can be impressed on commodities and hence can be bought and sold in just the same way that the identity of status and life-style can be impressed, bought and sold. If the advertiser can associate goods with the symbolism of possession, and if the buyer accepts that association, then the commodities people confront will not appear uniformly impersonal and the task of appropriation will not be uniformly urgent or onerous. To repeat an observation I have already made, this is one implication of Kopytoff's point (1986: 68) that an object is "a culturally constructed entity endowed with culturally specific meanings and classified and reclassified into culturally constituted categories".

Harris Tweed is a good example of how this sort of imagery can be invoked even though it has only a tenuous relationship with reality. The cloth is presented as the product of cottage industry in the Outer Hebrides, with individual crofters weaving it by hand at home. The tweed is surrounded with the imagery of "the ancient as opposed to the modern, the traditional as opposed to the industrial, the folk as opposed to mass society", all embodied in the individual hand weaver who "is almost invariably invoked by the media representations" (Ennew 1982: 172, 174). In fact, and in contrast to the farmer's apples, the cloths come with a real maker's mark, for each one is stamped with the Orb Mark, the authenticating trademark of the Harris Tweed Association, and with each is a signed declaration that the weaver wove the cloth at home (1982: 170). While this imagery of the individual craft producer helps envelop the cloth with the symbolism of possession, the truth is rather different. Harris Tweed weavers may work in sheds near their houses, but their yarn is spun in textile mills and they receive their frames already warped, so they need no special weaving skills. Moreover, aside from the fact that they are narrower, the looms used most commonly are indistinguishable from industrial looms with one important exception: the power is provided by the weaver, who works a foot treadle. In other words, the main difference between the Harris Tweed weaver and the weaver employed in a textile mill is that the former "is the source of power *as well as* machine minder" (1982: 170).

CATALOGUES

The form of advertising that concerns me in this chapter is the mail-order catalogue. Catalogues are a particularly powerful device for sellers to present their wares. They are longer and more elaborate than single print or broadcast advertisements and so can offer a more complete presentation of objects. Moreover, they offer the seller greater control of visual and verbal elements than do store presentations, so that objects can always appear in the light that the company wants. These features mean that catalogues can be almost perfect representations of the objects and the identities that the company wants to sell. Because of this, catalogues allow us to see exemplified what often is partially obscured in the problematic interactions of the real world of buying and selling. They are, therefore, valuable for those interested in the way that commodities are presented for sale, the way that they are given a social identity.

These are not the only reasons why catalogues deserve detailed treatment by social scientists. In addition, they are a submerged form of communication that reaches more people and has more impact than much of the conventional mass media. Undoubtedly, they reflect and shape important cultural values. Unfortunately, the only social analysis of them that I know is of a highly abstract postmodern sort, ill-suited to the sort of issues raised in this chapter (e.g. Appadurai 1989; Smith, P. 1988).

Catalogues are not just advertising, they are also the mechanism by which the customer initiates the purchase transaction. If the customer buys by post rather than by telephone, the transaction in fact is more impersonal than what takes place in stores, where the customer usually has to deal directly with at least one person in the course of buying an object. This objective impersonality of catalogues as a form of selling may explain why some of them make such efforts to invoke the symbolism of possession. Equally, this mixture of personality and impersonality in catalogues also allows retail-trade companies to deal with a tension that is inherent in much modern shopping. That is the tension between the desire for sociality in goods and transactions, and at the same time the desire to avoid the intrusive sociality that can make people feel compelled to buy. Shopping in a catalogue is anonymous: there are no real humans there to make one uncomfortable or feel obligated to buy. Thus, for many shoppers the careful and polished symbolism of the catalogue may be more attractive than the more haphazard cheeriness of the live clerk.

However, it is important not to exaggerate the difference between catalogues and stores. As the semi-mythological status of the English Corner Shop and the American Country Store indicates, retail trade generally entails relatively impersonal transactions. In part this is because retailers assume that customers will be pre-sold by advertisers, will enter the store knowing what they want. Consonant with this, stores usually are self-service or have clerks whose job consists of no more than getting what the customer identifies and ringing up the sale, as I described in Chapter 4. Thus, although stores present the possibility of transaction within a personal relationship, this is realized relatively infrequently. Consequently, the symbolism of possession in the catalogues I describe need be no more or less tangential to the essentials of the buying transaction than is the friendly relationship between customer and store clerk that is part of Personal Shopping.

Not all catalogues frame their wares in the same way. While they differ in the class, culture and gender imagery that advertisers invoke in them, catalogues differ as well in the degree to which they stress these sorts of social images. Some restrict themselves more to the simple portrayal of their wares, their significant technical features and their prices, and avoid portraying the objects in use or in association with different sorts of people. This invocation of a no-nonsense concern for use value and thrift is itself cultural, and doubtless many companies invoke it consciously to appeal to certain sorts of customers. However, those catalogues that stress it do not overtly situate their wares in identifiable hierarchies of social identity.

The American catalogues I describe in this chapter illustrate different forms in which commodities are presented. I will describe first a catalogue that presents commodities without invoking the symbolism of possession or, indeed, much social identity at all. This will provide a point of reference for the catalogues that do invoke such symbolism. These catalogues invoke the symbolism of possession in three ways: they invoke the makers of the commodity, the people selling the commodity and the users of the commodity. In fact, of course, all commodities have makers, sellers and users; all have been thought up, designed and manufactured by particular people; all are sold by particular people to other particular people who use them in particular social relationships. It is when advertisements emphasize these particularities that they wrap the commodity in the symbolism of possession.

Invoking the makers, sellers or users of a commodity in an advertisement means giving the commodity a social identity based on these people. I need to distinguish, however, the sort of identity that concerns me from more general identities, though this distinction often is clearer at the conceptual level than it is in practice. One of these general identities is that of the brand name or company image. While these can bestow a social identity on a commodity and so rescue it from anonymity, that identity is likely to be abstract and impersonal. To call yourself the Bank that Cares is to invoke an identity for the corporation as a whole. This is different from stressing the individuals who are in the bank and their individual relations with individual customers. The other of these general identities is that of social strata and life-styles, public structures of meaning and identity. To invoke makers, sellers and users effectively is to invoke, or at least portray, particular people, whether they be real or imaginary. And particular people almost inevitably carry social identities in terms of those public structures. However, it is possible, again even if only in the abstract, to distinguish invocations that stress what sort of people these are from invocations that stress their individuality. It is the latter that stress the symbolism of possession.

RELIABLE – NEUTRAL PRESENTATION

I said I would begin with a neutral catalogue, one that does not invoke the symbolism of possession. The catalogue I use is published by Reliable, and I will describe the 1988 edition. This company sells a broad range of stationery and office supplies, from pencils and papers to desks and coat racks. The catalogue stresses the low price of the commodities. In this, and in its design and layout, the catalogue invokes the hard-headed symbolism of the bargain.

As with all the catalogues I describe in this chapter, the layout and illustrations of the Reliable catalogue are important vehicles for conveying imagery for the commodities that are advertised and the company that is selling them. This catalogue is slick and visually undistinguished. The photographs of the commodities advertised are uninspired and uniformly flat and frequently they appear slightly washed. Moreover, relatively few photographs show a commodity posed in a setting of any sort: the photograph illustrating three ball-point pens is of three ball-point pens, points extended, parallel to each other and to the bottom edge of the page, and nothing more.

The catalogue's layout is rigid, as the pages are grid-like. Where a page advertises more than one product, typically each is presented in a separate box. Usually this consists of a dark band across the top containing a general classification, such as "Refillable and retractable pocket pens" (Reliable 1988: 7), and a field of pale color on which are placed the photograph of the commodities and the text and stock information. A page of the Reliable catalogue consists of a set of these boxes, all with the same background color, arrayed as symmetrically as possible and separated by small gaps, all on a white background.

The catalogue is markedly serviceable. That is, it can be used by those who want to buy a particular class of commodity, and need only to know what varieties are for sale and what their prices are. The 200-page edition I am describing has no table of contents, but it does have an index of four pages, containing about 850 entries. Moreover, even though the catalogue is not divided into sections that are marked or headed clearly, it is apparent from a casual inspection that commodities are grouped in a systematic way. For instance, the first eight pages are writing implements – ball-point pens, markers, text liners and highlighters, china marking pencils, automatic pencils, regular pencils – and such implements appear only on these pages. Utility and organization are the dominant air of this catalogue.

As I have described it, the Reliable catalogue makes no effort to link the commodities it advertises with particular people or social relations. Instead, descriptions of the commodities and the company focus on value: high quality, low cost, quick and efficient service, free delivery.

The main display dealing with the company itself is a three-page layout at the front of the catalogue. It consists of pictures and text, but almost without exception these do not portray or describe people. For instance, the display includes nine key picture captions. Three advertise the speed and low cost of delivery, two advertise toll-free telephone numbers, two advertise the broad range of products the company sells, one advertises high discount rates and one advertises the company product guarantee.

The text in the commodity advertisements is equally anonymous, of a piece with the orderly layout and presentation. Frequently the majority of the text accompanying catalogue entries is technical information on stock numbers, color ranges and prices. The rest of the text is spare and impersonal. There is no one speaking or writing these neutral descriptions, and they are addressed to no one. Equally, the description of the commodities provides them with no identity. Further, while the catalogue often displays the brand name of the commodity being advertised, we are told nothing about the manufacturers that would remove them from the neutrality of their names and registered trade marks. An example of this anonymity is the text accompanying a photograph of pencils: "Finest cedarwood case / Extra strong, smooth writing lead / Self-cleaning pink pearl eraser tip / Leads won't break under normal writing pressure" (Reliable 1988: 11).

My description of the Reliable catalogue is brief, because from the perspective of this chapter there is nothing to describe. The catalogue is impersonal and orderly in its presentation of the company and the commodities it sells. There are no people here. Instead, we are presented with impassive, technical descriptions of commodities.

SMITH & HAWKEN – SYMBOLISM OF THE MAKER

Some catalogues invoke the symbolism of possession by associating commodities with their makers. Here, the catalogue provides the commodity with a history that describes the people involved in its design or manufacture. A good example of this is the *Smith & Hawken Catalog for Gardeners*, and I will describe the Spring, 1988, edition. Smith & Hawken is a company in California that sells gardening equipment. It was established in the late 1970s specifically to sell gardening tools. Although its catalogue retains this emphasis, it also advertises a range of other commodities, from garden furniture to seeds to dried flowers.

Unlike the utilitarian Reliable catalogue, the Smith & Hawken catalogue is informal. Its pages are not obviously divided into rows and columns or quadrants, and the catalogue's relatively large photographs are placed irregularly on the pages. The photographs themselves, all in color, are not neutral representations, but are appropriate to the cultural imagery of the objects portrayed. For example, the photographs of potting benches and cold frames are relatively dark, warm and brown, while the photograph of cut vegetables that accompanies an advertisement for seeds is dark and green. On the other hand, the photographs for a plastic hose and watering system generally are bright and flat.

The catalogue invites, and in fact demands, a leisurely, informal approach. It has neither a table of contents nor an index. Instead, small headings placed at the upper left corner of each pair of pages announce the themes around which the two-page layouts revolve, themes that are themselves not organized in any noticeable way. Though these headings do summarize the material displayed, generally they do so idiosyncratically, certainly not in any functional manner. Thus, for example, it is not clear why one spade appears under "Plant Care", one spade specifically for children appears under "Basic Tools" and no spades at all appear under "Yard Care". Equally, it is not clear why pruning shears appear under "Basic Tools" and "Romantic Garden", but not under "Plant Care". It would, in other words, be very difficult to use this catalogue if one wanted to see what sorts of spades, shears or other tools were for sale at what prices.

While the photographs create an overall tone for the catalogue, the text is the most important vehicle for socializing the commodities. And there is a lot of text. For example, the text accompanying a plant fertilizer contains 97 words; the text accompanying the advertisement of four different seed packets from a single manufacturer amounts to a miniature essay, being just over 400 words, and it is appropriate that 94 of these are devoted to a description and social identification of the manufacturer; the text accompanying a Panama hat is 155 words. (Contrast these examples with the 20 words in the description of a brand of pencils in the Reliable catalogue.) These words do a great deal of the symbolic work of the catalogue by providing commodities with a history that identifies who designed, suggested or made them.

The personal nature of these descriptions is matched by their general style. They are not neutral, third-person prose produced by a committee or a computer, in the style of the Reliable catalogue. Instead, the first and second person abound. For example, the text accompanying a spade begins: "We saw this tool on the Bulldog tool stand at the Chelsea Flower Show a few years ago and ordered it on the spot" (Smith & Hawken 1988: 5). Similarly, the text accompanying a photograph of a set of hand tools says: "If your trowel has ever fallen apart, bent or failed you, we suggest ours as a substitute" (1988: 10). Likewise, the description of a small greenhouse begins: "If you have limited space . . ." (1988: 8). Mr Smith and Mr Hawken are talking to the reader.[1]

Doubtless when catalogues were a new form of retail trade, advertisers needed to describe their wares and the companies that made them at length, as did early Sears, Roebuck catalogues (the 1908 catalogue is described in

Leiss, Kline and Jhally 1986). However, modern retailers do not have to identify the origins of what they sell, and it is significant that the Smith & Hawken catalogue does so at length. Perhaps the most striking example of this is the catalogue's centerpiece, two pages laid out as a single unit that present the core Smith & Hawken tools (Smith & Hawken 1988: 22–3). I intended to present this text in its entirety as it appears in the catalogue, together with a key text from the Lands' End (*sic*) catalogue, discussed below. I asked Smith & Hawken for permission to reproduce this text in its entirety as it appears in the catalogue, submitting an earlier version of this discussion of their catalogue and my reproduction of their text. I was told that Paul Hawken would not approve the reproduction, so I decided to omit the Lands' End text as well, though that company kindly granted the necessary permission. Readers will have to use their imaginations.

The central text in the Smith & Hawken catalogue does not describe this line of gardening tools in any straightforward way. Instead, it identifies the history of their invention and manufacture. The first paragraph presents the prehistory of the company that manufactures these hoes and rakes, Bulldog Tools, Ltd., of England. Bulldog Tools is "one of the oldest producers of hand tools in the world". Indeed, its origins "can be traced back" to a monastic forge early in the thirteenth century. The manufacturer is, thus, identified as being exotic in time as well as in space (remember that this is an American catalogue). This is enhanced and overlaid with a curious modernity when we are told that, after the forge closed in the eighteenth century, it was re-opened by a woman, a Mrs Elizabeth Beecroft, using borrowed money. Her company later merged into a company run by a family named Parkes, personified by a Mr Francis Parkes, though it seems he flourished at least a half-century after the Parkes firm acquired the Beecroft interest.

The middle two paragraphs trace the inventiveness and technological improvements of Mr Francis Parkes in his effort to produce a better digging tool. Along the way, he is associated with the industrial revolution, the 1851 Great Exhibition at the Crystal Palace, and Henry Bessemer. Through these two paragraphs, the commodities that Bulldog Tools manufactures are stamped with their historical association with the genius of one man, struggling to develop the perfect spade. And his struggle was a success: "When Parkes' spade was finally perfected, it had the right temper, hardness, handling and balance."

This text illustrates in detail the way that the company wraps its commodities in the symbolism of possession. As one might imagine, this is not accidental. Rather, as Hawken has written elsewhere,

all the early products we sold were so exceedingly commonplace they were ignored and unattended to by vendors and manufacturers .... We noticed that hand tools such as forks, spades, and trowels were so prosaic that people were beginning not even to understand them. So we began to inform them about style, weight, design, and usage. Our catalogs described just how they were invented and by whom – easy to do because our vendor in England literally invented the steel fork and spade.

(Hawken 1987: 74)

Interestingly, Hawken does not argue that the presentation is effective in large part because of the cultural work it performs. Instead, he focuses on the technical descriptions of the use values of the commodities that it provides.[2]

This way of invoking the symbolism of possession is a constant theme in the catalogue. The description of a device for forming small cubes of soil for starting seeds includes: "We carry the original soil-blocking system created by Michael Ladbrooke, a British engineer and gardener. His system..." (Smith & Hawken 1988: 3). The description of a line of plant sprayers begins: "Made by the Berthoud family of France, these are the finest sprayers on the market .... Known for making agricultural equipment in France for three generations, the Berthoud family designed..." (1988: 4). The description of a line of black iron pot-stands and holders begins: "The blacksmiths at Stone County Ironworks in the hills of Arkansas are dedicated to high-quality, hand-forged metalwork" (1988: 30). The catalogue advertises the Rothenberg Rake: "Alan Rothenberg, an old customer, suggested we take a hacksaw to our Wizard Rake and cut it down to size so it could be used around shrubs, beds and borders. We did. He was right. So we named it after him" (1988: 12).

The Smith & Hawken catalogue invokes a broad range of imagery, including a clear elite class-cultural imagery that I have ignored. But what is striking about this catalogue is the way that it persistently stresses the people who design and make what it sells. By its detailed presentation of the history of its objects, the recurrent identification of objects with specific people in specific times and places, this catalogue denies the impersonality of the alienated manufactured objects that it sells by endowing them with a cluster of attributes that symbolize possession. The association between object and producer is so intimate as to suggest that the purchaser is almost getting a personal possession of Mr Parkes or Berthoud *père* or Mr Rothenberg. With this presentation, then, the catalogue seeks to remove these objects symbolically from the realm of commodities and put them in the realm of possessions. I shall demonstrate this point further by describing two other catalogues that invoke the symbolism of possession in a different way.

LANDS' END – SYMBOLISM OF THE SELLER

Not all companies sell commodities that have attractive histories and makers. Many of the things that we want and need to buy are produced under mundane circumstances in uninteresting places by anonymous people working for humdrum companies. A company selling such undistinguished commodities must use other tactics to invest what it sells with the symbolism of possession. One such tactic is to stress the identities of the people who do the selling. When this happens, the commodity acquires an identity based on the company's workers and on the relationship between those workers and the buyer. I want to illustrate this using a 1988 catalogue of Lands' End, Inc., a company that sells primarily men's and women's leisure outer clothing.

This catalogue differs from that of Smith & Hawken in a number of ways. The photographs do not convey mood through tone but use the sort of bright colors and flat lighting that appeared only rarely in the Smith & Hawken catalogue. Further, while the Lands' End catalogue has no index or table of contents, it is relatively orderly. The first nine pages of commodities deal with varieties of shirts and sweaters. The last four interior pages advertise men's semi-dress shirts, neckties and belts. In between is a section of six pages advertising pants and trousers for men and women. While the order is not absolute, the catalogue creates an impression of orderliness that is very different from the spades scattered with abandon through the Smith & Hawken catalogue.

The text of this catalogue is different from Smith & Hawken too. To begin with, there is much less of it. Instead, the pages are dominated by large, color photographs. Furthermore, the text describes the attributes and qualities of the commodities as use values, rather than the invention and production histories that feature so strongly in the Smith & Hawken catalogue. Perhaps because its orientation is less romantic, the text itself is less romantic. An illustration of this is the slightly breathless text advertising men's and women's shorts and sport pants (Lands' End 1988: 15). It begins: "You may have seen bottoms like these before. Just pull 'em on and go. Great for after work, weekends, vacations, whatever." It goes on to advertise their durability ("'Bulldog tough' fabric") and useful features ("Waistband won't sag", "Lots of pockets"), ending with a stress on value ("That's a lot for $19.50 and $13.00").

I said that the orientation of this catalogue is different from Smith & Hawken. Indeed, Lands' End goes out of its way to avoid identifying the people who actually make what the customer buys. While commodities frequently are identified by origin – United States vs "imported" – there is nothing more than this. The closest we get to knowing who makes what we are being asked to buy is in an advertisement for denim trousers: "The same manufacturers that make the famous brands make our Square Riggers" (Lands' End 1988: 13). How, then, does this catalogue exemplify endowing commodities with the symbolism of the seller?

The answer lies in the first thing the reader sees. In describing the Lands' End catalogue I referred to pages that had commodities on them. This is because the front cover and the first two pages of the edition I describe do not advertise commodities. Instead, they advertise the people who work at Lands' End. This is a common feature of Lands' End catalogues, but not ubiquitous. Some of the catalogues without this arrive together with a small booklet with photographs, all in black and white, of company employees, their children and pets, and rustic scenes. In portraying the people who work for the company, these pages convert the anonymous transaction of buying into a social relationship with individual people, and they convert the anonymous commodities that Lands' End buys from its anonymous suppliers into objects that have been through the hands of the individuals who selected them, packed them, inspected them, modified them.

The front cover is almost completely filled with three photographs of different, unnamed employees of Lands' End. Under each is a brief quote. The smiling man in the top photograph is saying "I make sure our Lands' End shirts give you your money's worth." The smiling woman in the middle is saying "One thing that should ease your mind: we'll <u>always</u> accept your return!" The smiling woman at the bottom is saying "Each time I finish hemming a pair of pants, I ask the question: would I wear it myself?" (Lands' End 1988: 1). These photographs are repeated on the spread of the first two inside pages. And these photographs are different from those of Lands' End commodities. They are not high-resolution and glossy-looking in flat colors, they are grainy and informal-looking in black and white. They are, if you will, snapshots to the commodities' portraits.

The first two inside pages of the catalogue are laid out as a single spread. They are the core of the identification of Lands' End commodities with the individuals who work there, and it is worth describing them in some detail. The advertisement of the collection of individuals who are presented as constituting Lands' End begins with a quotation that runs across the top of the layout: "At Lands' End, we treat our customers the way we like to be treated. And here are just some of our people who take pride in making this happen." Below its bottom right corner is a signature, below which in turn is printed "Gary Comer / President, Lands' End" (Lands' End 1988: 2–3). Immediately, then, the relationship between buyer and company is cast in terms of a personal relationship between individuals, not a commodity relationship between customer and company. This is because Lands' End is not an anonymous corporation. It is a set of people who, taking pride in their work and following the Golden Rule, are fully suitable to enter into relations of exchange with the buyer.

These two pages are divided into a total of four columns of equal width. The right-most column (Lands' End 1988: 3) contains general text advertising the virtues of Lands' End, virtues dominated by the sociality of the people who make up the corporation. Like the description of the origin of the Smith & Hawken tools, this text sets the tone of the image that the Lands' End catalogue presents. According to the text, Lands' End is "not out to make a quick sale". Instead, it wants "to build a relationship with you. A long-term relationship", a relationship based on "trust". It is, the text concludes, "[a] company with people that care. A company you can trust." This is not, in other words, a company of anonymous wage laborers. And just as the company is not anonymous, so the transaction that the buyer enters into is not the anonymous exchange of money for commodity.

The rest of the material in this two-page layout complements this presentation and distinguishes it from advertising that tries to create the uniform company image of caring that I mentioned earlier in this chapter. The first three columns of the layout consist of three photographs each. Each is of an individual employee, seemingly looking up or around from his or her work to be photographed. Each photograph has a few lines of quotation below it, together with the name and job of the person photographed. Thus, at the top of the middle column is a photograph of a woman standing between two dress dummies. The text below the photograph is,

> I'm responsible for the fit and construction of the blouses, skirts and dresses you order from Lands' End. I work with the manufacturers to make sure you get consistent sizing, and the quality you've come to equate with the Lands' End name. – Amy Queram, Quality Assurance.
> (Lands' End 1988: 2)

Uniformly, the people in these family snapshots are smiling and friendly. Equally uniformly, none is presented as having an insignificant or anonymous job. Instead, each has an identifiable, individual-seeming job, and each is photographed surrounded by the paraphernalia of that job, making it even more individual and identifiable: customer sales, buyer, customer returns, quality assurance, specialty shopper, luggage maker, computer specialist, inseaming, order packer. Lands' End does not present its janitors, clerk-typists or gophers.

Just as each of these individuals has a name, an identifiable job and a smiling face, so each has something to say. And what they have to say is important. Each speaks briefly about his or her work and its relationship to the transaction the customer has initiated, and many personalize that work beyond the straightforward "This is what I do." Thus, Julie Halverson, in Customer Returns, says: "I know how it is when I return something to a company. I always wonder, 'Will they act on it?' Well, at Lands' End we process returns as quickly as possible." Dan Raisbeck, Luggage Maker, says that "if you ever find a 'kink' in your luggage, we'd like to see it. It can help make that piece better at the next go-round" (Lands' End 1988: 2). (Luggage is the only product presented in this catalogue that has an identifiable maker, and it is significant that it is made by Lands' End.)

The sociality that pervades these texts, then, defines the employees of Lands' End as people with whom one enters a social relationship, one based on the exchange of your desire and money for their care and concern and the company's commodities. In an important sense, this Lands' End catalogue is not just advertising commodities, it is advertising gift exchange. And it is the construction of this transaction as a gift relationship that endows the things that Lands' End sells with the symbolism of possession.

By this logic, the customer of Lands' End is not simply an anonymous buyer, any more than the employees of Lands' End are anonymous wage laborers. Instead, each has obligations toward the other, customer as well as Lands' End employee, for it is this mutual obligation that is the core of gift exchange. It is, then, not surprising that some of the texts that accompany the pictures of employees point out the obligations of the customer, point out that buying from Lands' End is not simply a matter of pay your money and you're quits. Of course these obligations are not particularly onerous, and they are presented as being in the customer's own interest, for the purpose is to attract customers, not repel them. They are, however, obligations that the customer has, a reciprocation for the obligations of the people at Lands' End. I have already quoted Dan Raisbeck, Luggage Maker, who wants the buyer to tell him if the luggage has problems. Similarly, Dave Barbian, Computer Specialist, says that "if something we've given you to read could be clearer – from the packing slips to the cards that tell you where your order is – please let us know." Phyllis Toay, Inseaming, is concerned that customers give her exact measurements: "[H]ere's a piece of advice: measure a pair of pants you're comfortable in, and give us the exact measurement down to ¼ inch." Even Charlene Dodge, Order Packer, wants the customer to transact properly: "I check the packing slip against what's in the box to make sure everything you ordered is in it. So, when you get your order, check it out, would you? Just to make sure I didn't slip up" (Lands' End 1988: 3).

This catalogue ignores the people and companies that manufacture what it sells, and so does things very differently from Smith & Hawken. Here the people have a story to tell, not the objects. But it accomplishes a similar result by identifying the specific individuals with whom the buyer transacts, so that the company itself is dissolved into a welter of individuals, each with a face and a name and a personal relationship with the customer, a relationship that transforms "commodities" into "possessions".

More than Smith & Hawken, Lands' End demonstrates sheer personalization as a force in itself. These people do not have the history or genius of those in Smith & Hawken. Instead, they are ordinary, doing ordinary things. But what they may lack in attractiveness they make up in presence, the fact that they are named, identifiable people whom we can see. More than some of those in Smith & Hawken, they are real people, here and now, whose relationship to us and to the objects that we are asked to buy is more immediate, and thus in its own way more powerful, than what exists between the long-dead Mr Parkes, us and Bulldog tools.

COMFORTABLY YOURS – SYMBOLISM OF THE USER

The two forms of the symbolism of possession that I have described link anonymous commodities with specific people involved in their production and circulation. The third mode that I will discuss operates in a different register. It presents no inventors, makers, packers or inseamers as the people in the past of these objects. Instead, this third form identifies a world of users who transact these commodities in a set of durable social relationships of their own. It is these relationships and transactions that identify the objects as being possessions.

I will illustrate this form of the symbolism of possession with the catalogue of the company Comfortably Yours. The company sells a range of items that defies any simple description, such as electric kettles, sugarless candies, foundation cream, wooly bed socks, exercise equipment, adjustable shower heads. While the commodities range broadly, generally they are intended to make life easier for the infirm, especially the old and infirm. The appliances are presented as being especially safe or especially easy to use, the foods are touted as suited to those who are no longer young and slim or who are diabetic, the cosmetics are to cover age spots, the socks are for those with poor circulation, the exercise equipment is for especially easy and un-energetic exercising, and so on.

The catalogue itself is unassuming. The photographs are simple portraits of the commodities, either by themselves against a plain background or in a simple setting. Thus, some items of clothing are photographed on the bodies of models, bed lamps are affixed to or next to beds, tool racks are mounted on walls and full of tools. The text itself is simple as well, with a slightly fussy and old-fashioned air. The catalogue has no index or table of contents. Instead, it has a headline at the top of each layout of two facing pages, which is supposed to indicate the general nature of the commodities advertised on those pages. However, like the Smith & Hawken headlines, these do not provide any reliable guide to the contents. A number of the categories overlap, and frequently the placement of items in the different categories appears arbitrary.

This catalogue presents its commodities as anonymous objects, because it ignores their origin, either the people who designed them or the people who manufactured them. Equally, company workers do not appear in the cata-logue. The only people associated with the company are an older woman named Elaine Adler and her adult son, named Jim. This identification takes place on the cover and in a letter to customers on the first inside page. Though the implication is that Elaine Adler runs Comfortably Yours, she is never identified as manager or president, and all the firm information we are given is that customers can write to her: "Peruse the pages and if you don't see what you want or need, please write to my son Jim or me" (Comfortably Yours 1988: 2). This letter is anonymous and flavorless.

This disembodied, smiling face of Elaine Adler is appropriate given the way that Comfortably Yours associates the commodities it advertises with the symbolism of possession. Freeing Elaine Adler from the impediments of company life facilitates the creation of a fictional world of Mrs Adler (one is sure she is not Ms), her son Jim and an array of relatives and friends who transact and use the commodities the company sells.

Many of Elaine Adler's friends and relatives have troubles: their physical frailties, spreading midriffs and deteriorating skins are making their lives more difficult. Elaine Adler herself, Jim and a few younger friends and relatives are fortunate in being able to find commodities that will ease the difficulties and discomforts of this cohort of the slowly failing.

Mrs Adler herself is still busy and energetic. But even she has problems, the solution to which may help those whose difficulties spring more from old age, less energy and perhaps a return to living alone after years of marriage. An advertisement for spice bags illustrates this.

> For years I enjoyed cooking elaborate gourmet meals, but lately, a hectic schedule doesn't allow me that luxury. Recently, I discovered these "short cut" garni bags, (like tea bags) that allow me to add subtle flavor to beef, fish, poultry and vegetables . . . as they cook . . . in no time at all!
>
> (Comfortably Yours 1988: 5, ellipses in original)

The tone of this advertisement is typical. Routinely, Elaine Adler is talking to us personally about herself and her various friends and relations. And as in this text we are told how, for one reason or another, someone is no longer able to do what he or she had done before. And again as in this text, we are told how Elaine Adler herself, or one of her coterie, has found a commodity that makes life easier.

These helpful friends appear throughout the catalogue. One appears in a description of strip lighting: "Roz saw this new concept in strip lighting in a restaurant. So *thin*, it was used under steps for safety and over mirrors for decor" (Comfortably Yours 1988: 18). Another appears in a description of automobile sun deflectors: "Louisa discovered these practical sun deflectors in her rented car in hot Aruba" (1988: 32). Even Elaine Adler's husband is pressed into service: "Our doctor gave my husband, Mike, this knee support for relief of pain when he twisted his knee badly . . . . Helpful to arthritics and those with painful joints" (1988: 12). He also appears as the person who shares house with Elaine Adler in a description of a water detector: "Mike and I avoided disaster recently when this smart little WATER BUG detected a leak in our hot water heater and sounded a piercing alarm!" (1988: 18).

While Elaine Adler and her husband may have problems that require solutions, they are not frail. Mike needs this support because he twisted his knee, not because he has the arthritis or chronically painful joints of the genuinely frail, just as Elaine needs packaged *bouquet garni* because she is busy. Most of the other people in this fictional world, however, are less fortunate. They are more like two of Elaine's cousins, Annette and Bob:

> My mother called one day asking for my help. Two cousins of mine, Annette who suffers from lupus, and Bob who has spurs on his spine, were unable to sleep. Because they were experiencing so much dis-

comfort in their beds, I sent them each a convoluted foam bed pad . . . .
P.S. Annette is now resting well, and Bob is off the floor and getting a
good night's sleep.

(Comfortably Yours 1988: 9)

The world created in these texts, then, associates the commodities with
specific problems that Elaine Adler's friends and relatives have, or with the
people in her world who brought the products to her attention. In doing so,
the catalogue identifies these commodities as helpful gifts that Elaine Adler
gives to friends and relations who in their turn are forever better and happier
and grateful for what she does. Annette and Bob are sleeping better, and "My
friend Sam thanked me a million times when I gave him this cane/umbrella.
It solved the problem of having to juggle both his cane AND umbrella on
cloudy days" (Comfortably Yours 1988: 3). This is a world of people
transacting gifts and gratitude. In effect, we are being told that these
commodities have been tested in gift relations, and that they work.

In this, Comfortably Yours is the most explicit of the catalogues I describe.
We are not presented with simple utilities. We are not even presented with
objects bearing the identities of their makers or of the social relationships in
which we acquire them. Instead, we are presented with objects that mediate
and embody complex and enduring personal relationships.

INVOKING POSSESSION

These catalogues show how advertisements can present commodities in terms
of images that echo Mauss's description of the nature of the gift, and so cloak
them with the symbolism of possession. Just as the gift is inalienably
associated with the giver, so Smith & Hawken invests their commodities with
the identities of those who have thought up or made them, and Lands' End
invests them with the identity of their employees. Just as the gift is transacted
as part of a personal relationship, so Lands' End points to the people at Lands'
End and their relationship with the buyer and the object, and so Comfortably
Yours portrays objects in the context of enduring personal relationships of
mutual assistance and gratitude. These presentations illustrate in concrete
ways a point that I made at the beginning of this chapter. This was that
"possession" has become a distinct symbol that is partly independent of the
actual social relations in which the object is produced and transacted. And
because "possession" is a symbol, it can be manipulated, as indeed it is
manipulated by advertisers to try to make what they are selling attractive to
people.

My discussion of the different ways these different catalogues invoke the
symbolism of possession implies that each catalogue relies primarily on such
symbolism for its advertising appeal, and that each exhibits only one mode
of invocation in a perfect form. Neither of these is the case. Each of the

catalogues invokes a complex set of imagery in the effort to get people to buy, including class-cultural imagery and aspects of the symbolism of possession other than what I described. I have selected these catalogues not because they are pure types, but because they contain particularly interesting examples of different forms of the symbolism of possession in the advertisement of commodities. Equally, of course, outside advertising there are other examples of the use of the symbolism of possession in commodity relations and transactions. A particularly interesting one is the way that personality is treated as a commodity in the emotional work of airline cabin staff. Arlie Hochschild (1983) describes how staff are directed to act as hosts and hostesses serving guests, hiding their personal moods and the resentment they may feel toward more obnoxious passengers, and so to present their commodity relationship with passengers as one of personality and gift transaction. A much older, women's profession presents a marked potential for the same sort of conjunction of commodity transaction and gift symbolism.

These catalogues are, of course, symbolic presentations of objects, and no one would argue seriously that analyzing them will reveal how their readers respond to them and how their readers interpret these objects. However, no one should argue seriously that the producers of the catalogues are ignorant of and indifferent to these blatant images and their effects. The words and images are not minor features that might have slipped into these catalogues unintentionally, nor are they whimsical expressions of the self-indulgence of corporate managers. They are intentional representations that are supposed to make people buy. Of course, this need not be all they are. For instance, they may also be aimed at the firm's employees, intended to make them feel better about their work and hence more productive or tractable. But persuading people to buy is one important purpose that they are intended to serve, not likely to be sacrificed to other purposes. And it is almost certain that these firms have studied carefully the ways that people respond to their presentations, although anyone interested in more detail than is offered in magazines like *American Demographics* finds that such studies are proprietary, usually secret and ephemeral or costly to acquire. Hence, it is hard to assess their quality, but impressionistic evidence suggests that at least some are sound and imaginative. A reasonable working assumption, then, is that these catalogues are pieces of applied cultural analysis, collections of images that professional image-makers have found to appeal to people.

The images in these catalogues suggest that these image-makers have arrived at the same conclusion as has Igor Kopytoff (1986: 80), that in a society in which many areas of life are dominated by anonymous commodities, there "is clearly a yearning" for the personal, for objects that bear the marks of possession. That is an important element of what these catalogues advertise. And they demonstrate that, once "possession" becomes a symbol, it can be bought and sold in commodity transactions, used to cloak objects that are produced as commodities and sold in commodity relations.

The juxtaposition in these catalogues of a symbolism of possession with objects that are commodities may be important when considering appropriation. People buy commodities and turn them into possessions almost every day, but the need they feel to appropriate the commodities and the ways that they do this are likely to vary. From a perspective that considers only the real status of objects as commodities or possessions, the fact that people take different measures to appropriate them is relatively invisible and insignificant, for a commodity is a commodity is a commodity. Further, when that variance is noticed, it is likely to be attributed without much thought to personal factors or other *ad hoc* causes. But a perspective that considers both the real status and the symbolic representation of the object helps make this variance visible and explain its significance, for the need to appropriate commodities and the means of their appropriation likely will reflect both the status and the representation. If the imagery of possession in these catalogues does make the objects advertised seem less impersonal, then those who buy will be acquiring things that fit their notion of "possession" more closely than would things that were not wrapped in this symbolism. Consequently these objects would appear to require less effort to appropriate them and turn them into possessions. In that sense, the spade designed by Mr Parkes and the shirt packed by Charlene Dodge are easier to possess than these objects would be if they were presented and acquired in more anonymous circumstances.

The fact that "possession" is a symbolic value that can be applied to objects leads to a further point. That is that the need to appropriate an object and the work required to appropriate it will be shaped by a host of symbols attached to it, not just the symbols of possession or commodity. Mr Parkes's spade and Charlene Dodge's shirt are not attractive and easy to possess only because they are cloaked with the symbolism of possession. They are so as well because Mr Parkes and Charlene Dodge are attractive to those for whom these catalogues are intended, though again I am assuming that catalogue designers would not include such obvious images if they were not shown to appeal to intended customers. Mauss's point (1990: 33) that objects transacted as gifts "are never completely detached from those carrying out the exchange" means that the communion of person and object in possession is also a communion of the person who possesses it and those who possessed it in the past. Consequently, when advertisers invoke the symbolism of possession, these past people become part of one's understanding of the object, as are the symbolic meanings that those past people carry. If they are unappealing, their symbolic possession will make the object unappealing.

Here the Maussian concern with possession intersects with the more conventional concern with the place of objects in public structures of meaning and identity. The people who are presented as possessing objects, such as exist in these catalogues, do not only remove those objects symbolically from the realm of commodities by stamping them with personality. They also stamp them with particular social sorts of personality, that are more or less pleasing

143

and congenial. Thus, the objects presented in these catalogues carry symbolic identities that have two distinct dimensions. They are "possessions", and they are associated with certain sorts of people. Each of these dimensions can be expected to influence how and why the purchaser acts to appropriate the object.

In noting the importance of the sort of person with whom the object is associated, I raise a point that has been implicit in much of what I have said about appropriation. Any invocation of cultural imagery can make the object seem more familiar, and so can facilitate appropriation, if that imagery links the object to what purchasers see as their personal identities. Suppose, for example, that I were to see Italian descent as a salient and inalienable part of myself. In that case, any object that I identified as Italian, or any object that I was persuaded was Italian, would be relatively easy to appropriate, for to a degree it and I would already share identity. "Italian descent" is a more abstract identity than those that concern me in this book, identities based on extended interaction with specific other people, such as exist in the family and among friends. However, more general identities – whether Italian descent, male, academic or any of the other ways people might think of themselves – can be expected to have some effect on appropriation, though the degree of that effect is likely to vary according to the degree to which those identities are important in daily life and interactions. The ways that such identities can be important and the ways that they can affect people's perception of consumer objects is illustrated in Millie Creighton's (1991) discussion of the ways that large Japanese department stores evoke and invoke the identity of things foreign.

7

THE IDEOLOGY OF THE GIFT

In previous chapters I have described some of the ways that economic life has come to be distinct from social life. However, as I noted in Chapter 5, people construe these areas in ways that exaggerate the differences between economy and society, work and home. In this chapter I investigate one element of the cultural construction of social, as distinct from economic, relationships. This is the ideology of the gift. Although it reflects basic beliefs about gift relations, it does so in terms of presents, ceremonious and self-conscious gifts. The ideology of the gift expresses the cultural image of the perfect giving of the perfect present.

Social scientists are not really interested in gifts in Western societies. Periodically there is a discovery, often presented in faintly shocked or sardonic tones, of the fact that presents are not spontaneous expressions of sentiment but are recurrent, predictable and socially regulated (e.g. Caplow 1984; Cronk 1989; Shurmer 1971). But these discoveries usually are lost and have to be made again. Such repetitive lapses of memory suggest not simple forgetfulness, but motivated inattention, an uneasiness about the message we are given. There is good reason for this. These periodic rediscoveries challenge important elements of British and American understandings of gifts, understandings that reflect central notions of how people ought to transact objects with each other, the different sorts of objects that they ought to transact, and the different social identities and relationships that ought to exist among transactors.

THE PERFECT PRESENT

We give different sorts of presents to different sorts of people on different sorts of occasions for different sorts of reasons, and there are different expectations and ideals against which these are judged. The presents that primary-school pupils give each other as part of class Christmas celebrations are judged according to criteria that are different from those applied to the birthday presents that middle-aged parents give their growing children. Underlying these differences, however, is an ideology that defines ideal

145

actions by ideal actors in ideal relations. This ideology defines a pure state of giving, and so defines one end of the dimensions along which people locate less pure presents and giving.

An excellent statement of this ideology of the perfect present comes at the end of *Bribes*, by the historian John Noonan, a book that traces the changing attitudes toward presents to office-holders. It deserves to be quoted at length.

> A gift . . . is meant as an expression of personal affection, of some degree of love. It is given in a context created by personal relations to convey a personal feeling. The more it reflects the donee's interests and the donor's tastes the better. The more completely it is a gift the more completely it declares an identification of the giver with the recipient . . . . The size of what is given is irrelevant. What counts is how much the donor expresses identification with the recipient. The gift once given is wholly the donee's and no one else's – it is with this donee and not someone else that the donor identifies . . . .
>
> The donor . . . does not give by way of compensation or by way of purchase. No equivalence exists between what the donee has done and what is given. No obligation is imposed which the donee must fulfill. The donee's thanks are but the ghost of a reciprocal bond. That the gift should operate coercively is indeed repugnant and painful to the donor, destructive of the liberality that is intended. Freely given, the gift leaves the donee free. When the love that gift conveys is total, donor and donee are one, so the donee has no one to whom to respond. Every gift tries to approximate this ideal case. A present of any amount is a gift when it conveys love.
>
> (Noonan 1984: 695)

Noonan presents a description of the perfect present. But underlying this description and reflected in it are two central tensions that exist in the way people give and take in personal relations. Noonan says that the perfect present is immaterial. Its material form and, especially, its monetary worth themselves are beside the point, because they are transcended in the sentiment the present contains. This reflects the tension between the need to have the object express the giver's identity, and the fact that the objects that are available for giving are impersonal mass commodities. I will refer to this as the tension between gifts and commodities. Noonan says that the perfect present is unconstrained and unconstraining, that it is a pure expression from the heart, freely given, that does not bind giver and recipient. This reflects the tension between the desire to be self-reliant and independent, and the mutual dependence and obligation, and even the merging of identities, that people desire when they give. I will refer to this as the tension between freedom and obligation.

It is appropriate that Noonan offers this definition of the perfect present in a book on bribery, for the bribe is the converse of the present. People disapprove of bribes, but that disapproval is not simply a dislike of the intended consequence of bribery, that decisions that should be rendered on impersonal, bureaucratic criteria are instead rendered on personal and calculating criteria. After all, people are much less upset when the same subversion of bureaucratic rationality occurs in nepotism. Instead, at least part of the reason the bribe repels is that it is a prostitution of the present. In bribes people transact presents, but the transaction, the things transacted and the relationship created are sordid. The object given is the opposite of the embodiment of immaterial and personal expression that exists in the ideal present, for it is the embodiment of material value, particularly money, anonymous and impersonal. The purpose is the opposite of the spontaneous expression with no thought of return that exists in the ideal present, for it is purely calculated to bind the recipient and ensure a return. Bribery, then, points out to us what people view with distaste and deny in the ideology of the gift: presents have monetary value and once given they bind the recipient and the giver.

The ideology that Noonan expresses is not new. About a century-and-a-half ago, Ralph Waldo Emerson wrote "Gifts", a brief discussion of two sorts of presents that points out the dangers of the two tensions that the ideology of the gift seeks to transcend. Emerson calls the first sort of present the "common gift", which is best when guided by the material needs of the recipient: "[I]f the man at the door have no shoes, you have not to consider whether you could procure him a paint-box" (Emerson, R.W. 1983: 94). However, such presents are dangerous, for they obligate the recipient: "It is not the office of a man to receive gifts. How dare you bestow them? We wish to be self-sustained. We do not quite forgive a giver" (1983: 94). Emerson resolves this tension between freedom and obligation by mystifying the recipient, making him even more magnanimous than the giver: "The service a man renders his friend is trivial and selfish, compared with the service he knows his friend stood in readiness to yield him, alike before he had begun to serve his friend, and now also" (1983: 95–6).[1]

The second sort of present is that of affection, of "compliment and love". Of these, Emerson (1983: 94) decrees:

> The only gift is a portion of thyself. Thou must bleed for me. Therefore the poet brings his poem; the shepherd, his lamb; the farmer, corn; the miner, a gem; the sailor, coral and shells; the painter, his picture; the girl, a handkerchief of her own sewing. This is right and pleasing, for it restores societies in so far to its primary basis, when a man's biography is conveyed in a gift.

Thus, gifts of affection bear the identity of the giver. Here arises the tension between the need to give a personal possession and the fact that most things that people have are anonymous commodities. Emerson contrasts these presents to bought presents, which in the modern West are all people really have to give: "[I]t is a cold, lifeless business when you go to the shops to buy me something, which does not represent your life and talent, but a gold-smith's" (1983: 94) (nowadays, of course, the things people buy in the shops seldom represent anything so personal as that). Emerson resolves this tension by mystifying the work that people do. He ignores the existence of wage labor and commodities: the shepherd's lambs are his employer's, just as the farmer's corn and the miner's gems are claimed by those who pay the one to farm and the other to dig. And he ignores the fact that the clerk and the factory hand do not really seem to make anything at all.

These tensions are transcended in a favorite American Christmas story of an earlier generation, O. Henry's "The Gift of the Magi". Della, a poor, young and loving wife, sells her hair, her proudest possession. It was hair that fell "rippling and shining like a cascade of brown waters. It reached below her knee and made itself almost a garment for her" (Henry, O. 1917: 19). She made this sacrifice to get money to buy a Christmas present for Jim, her poor, young and loving husband. Jim's proudest possession was his "gold watch that had been his father's and his grandfather's" (1917: 18). The present she wanted to buy on that Christmas Eve was a fob chain for Jim's watch. "It was like him. Quietness and value – the description applied to both . . . . With that chain on his watch Jim might be properly anxious about the time in any company" (1917: 20). But just as Della had sold her most valued possession to buy an adornment for Jim's most valued possession, so Jim had done the same for her. He sold his watch to buy "The Combs – the set of combs, side and back, that Della had worshipped for long in a Broadway window. Beautiful combs, pure tortoise shell, with jewelled rims – just the shade to wear in the beautiful vanished hair" (1917: 23–4). The self-sacrifice of each failed. But note how O. Henry (1917: 25) ends his story:

> The magi, as you know, were wise men – wonderfully wise men – who brought gifts to the Babe in the manger. They invented the art of giving Christmas presents. Being wise, their gifts were no doubt wise ones, possibly bearing the privilege of exchange in case of duplication. And here I have lamely related to you the uneventful chronicle of two foolish children in a flat who most unwisely sacrificed for each other the greatest treasures of their house. But in a last word to the wise of these days let it be said that of all who give gifts these two were the wisest. Of all who give and receive gifts, such as they are wisest. Everywhere they are wisest. They are the magi.

This story evokes the perfect present of love. Each gave their most precious thing to buy the thing most perfectly suited to adorn the most precious thing of the other: Jim his watch for Della's hair; Della her hair for Jim's watch. And for each the present once given was useless. But the very futility of their presents points out the foolishness of thinking of these presents as commod-ities or even as material objects to be judged by their utility. Instead, these two people were the wisest because they gave the best present there is, the self given wholly for love.

On less exalted occasions givers and recipients may attend more to mundane matters (see Cheal 1987). Is the present useful? Does it say something nice about the recipient? About the giver? Does it cost too little? Too much? Is it appropriate to the relationship between giver and recipient, and to the occasion of the giving? These considerations have a vaguely calculating air, especially in the face of the purity of Jim's watch and Della's hair. But even so, they reflect the same tensions as the perfect present: how can the giver freely give in a relationship of mutual obligation? How can the giver express and define social identities and relationships with impersonal objects? In the United States these tensions appear even in the ritualized giving of Secretary's Day. The bosses who give have to express the right degree of personality with impersonal commodities, just as they have to express the right degree of spontaneity in a work relationship. The relative impersonality of the relationship makes the boss's task easier – florists sell masses of standard bouquets at this time – but the job is there none the less; and it is even harder for the secretary, who has to play the right supporting part by being appropriately surprised and flattered.

In the purity and intensity of their statements, Noonan, Emerson and O. Henry illustrate in heightened form the two elements of the ideology of the gift that concern me. The first element is that the perfect present is priceless, that its material expression is immaterial. For these writers, the object, so soon as it steps forth as a gift, is changed into something transcendent. Noonan says that for giver and recipient the perfect present is an embodiment of sentiment rather than of monetary value or even utility. For Emerson, the gift of compliment and love is valued not because of its material nature, but because it is the biography of the giver. O. Henry carries out the transcendence that Noonan and Emerson only describe: the combs and the fob chain are expensive: but this is only a vehicle for a more important point, that Della and Jim sacrifice "the greatest treasures of their house" to acquire these objects. Exchange value is transcended when it is subsumed under the sacrifice of the self. Even utility is transcended, because the hair and the watch are gone.

The second element is that the perfect present is free, unconstrained and unconstraining. Noonan makes this point explicitly, as when he says the recipient's "thanks are but the ghost of a reciprocal bond". For Emerson, even the common gift is free because we would be so indebted to our friends were we to need their help that any present we may give to them is insignificant in comparison. This point is contained more obliquely in O. Henry. The presents of these foolish children do not bind because, though totally different, they are perfectly equal. And they are the most valued possession of each, a sacrifice that only the free can make. As a result, Della and Jim are not beholden to each other.

This is a powerful ideology, one that is able to disembody objects, divest them of their material aspect and transmute them into pure, spontaneous expressions of being and love. Not only can it do away with the material nature of presents, it can create a wholly new form of relationship, in which people can be related but independent, joined but separate, linked fundamentally but in no way bound to or restricted by each other. We give the thing which is not, and so are joined but free.

GIFT AND COMMODITY

The first element of the ideology is that the perfect present is priceless, transcending its material expression and economic worth. Of course people do worry about price, but uneasily, especially with presents to and from those who are close. For such presents in particular, but for all presents in general, crowing over the cheap price of the expensive-seeming present, like openly comparing costs of presents given and received, is to cross a line that is important, the line that separates people from an open recognition of the contradiction between commodities and gifts.

Cast in the terms of this book, the good present, and the good gift more generally, is an object that is a possession, and if it is too clearly a commodity it is anomalous, a "bad" gift. It is an embarrassment that needs conversion into a possession, a conversion signaled in O. Henry by the personal sacrifices Jim and Della made to get their presents for each other. This is a matter of degree, of course. At times of high ceremony presents need to conform to the ideal more than at less significant ceremonies, and the mundane objects used in the gift transactions of daily life will need to conform least of all. The present from boss to typist can be more commodity-like than the present from lover to lover. Indeed, for most bosses and their secretaries it needs to be more commodity-like lest it redefine their work relationship as one that is more personal. Similarly, the meal served to a family on a weekday evening can be more commodity-like than the more intense Sunday Dinner, not to mention holiday meals. But however mild its sociality, Tuesday-night supper is not the same as a commodity purchased and eaten in isolation.

People deal with the contradiction between gift and commodity in different ways. One way is the work of appropriation, which, as I said in Chapter 5, stamps the commodity with the personal identity of the appropriator, and so converts it into a possession. Equally, the ideology of the gift itself helps transcend the contradiction. The denial of the material value of presents, the insistence that it is the thought, and only the thought, that *really* counts, signals to people not to think about gift relationships, especially with those close to them, in terms of the material object transacted, and even more it tells them not to think about the object in monetary terms. To a degree, of course, the ideology is correct. It *is* the thought that counts, or perhaps it is the act of giving in which the thought is expressed. It is true that the identity of the object colors the identity of the relationship in which it is transacted: a commodity transacted in a personal relationship can make that relationship more impersonal, which is one of the reasons why I have attended so closely to appropriation in this book. However, the reverse is also true, for the link between the object and the relationship is reciprocal: the identity of the object is colored by the relationship in which it is transacted. Consequently, giving tends to make the object a possession: "[O]nce it has been given – and *because* of this – it is *this* object and not another. The gift is unique, specified by the people exchanging it and the unique moment of the exchange" (Baudrillard 1981: 64).

While formal presents doubtless have special meanings in all societies, the ideological statement that the perfect gift is disembodied and immaterial does not reflect some fundamental aspect of human sociality. Instead, it springs from people's concrete circumstances. The anthropologist Erik Schwimmer (1973: 49) points to this in a book on exchange in a Melanesian society, the Orokaiva in Papua New Guinea:

> Westerners often criticise Melanesians for being too grasping and mean in gift exchange. Absurd though this criticism may seem, it arises from a real cultural difference: Westerners depend on institutions other than gift exchange for the acquisition of desired scarce resources. Hence the institution of exchanging Christmas presents need serve no other end but the fostering of social exchange relations. For the Melanesians . . . gift exchange must serve economic as well as social ends.

Schwimmer's point is that in some societies the main way that people get the things they need to survive is through personal relationships. In the trans-actions that occur within these relationships, whether informal give and take or the ceremonial exchange that Schwimmer mentions, the value of what people give and get is important. It may not always be uppermost in people's minds, but it is never far down the list. For such people, then, it would be silly to claim that it is the thought that counts.

This same conjunction of gift and utility, the social and the economic, appears in an English treatise on estate management, Walter of Henley's "Husbandry", from about 1285 (chapters 12–14 in their entirety, from Oschinsky 1971: 311; the material in brackets with modern spelling is Oschinsky's collation of variants). Indeed, the conjunction is so strong that it is not clear whether the writer is referring to gifts or payments.

> The goodes that God hathe lent youe, wiselye dispende theim. Concern-ing charges and expenses you must understand foure things [: when you ought to give presents, how this ought to be done, to whom you ought to make presents, and how much you ought to give].
>
> The furst, that youe give before that you have neede [because two shilling in good time will be worth ten when you are forced to do it].

The second that if you must give or bee at charge, then doe it with a good wylle and then that one thing shalbe allowed unto you as twayne.

The thyrd that you give to him which may doe you eyther good or harme; the fourthe lyeth in this, how muche you ought to give, truely, neyther to muche nor to little but according as the parsone is and according as the cause is, eyther little or greate that you have to doe with him.

The situation of people in rural, self-reliant British and American households in the past resembles that of the Orokaiva and of the medieval English estate manager in important ways, for there too the social and economic spheres overlapped markedly (e.g. Ulrich 1990: 75–90). This was the way most people lived in the eighteenth century and the way many lived in the nineteenth. Christopher Clark describes the existence, and decay, of this pattern in the Connecticut Valley of Massachusetts. While there were local manufacturers and merchants in the area in the last decades of the eighteenth century, most households and communities were oriented toward the sort of self-reliance that I described for much of England in Chapter 3.

In rural areas of the Valley, many households survived primarily by producing their own needs. These households and communities may not have been self-sufficient (Pruitt 1984; Shammas 1982; Walsh, L. 1983), but they did not acquire what they lacked primarily through transactions in an impersonal market. Instead, they entered "into complex networks of exchange relationships with their neighbors and relatives" (Clark 1979: 173). In other words, economic and social relations overlapped to form a fairly integrated whole. People acquired the bulk of their subsistence through work coordinated with, and through transactions between, members of their own households, and they got most of the rest through transactions that took place within durable relationships with kin or neighbors.

This pattern survived even when the household became dependent upon money and market transactions to acquire subsistence. In Chapter 3, for instance, I showed how English merchants in urban areas up to about 1800 did not distinguish household and business, so that relations within the shop were not distinct from family relations. Equally, in Chapter 2 I showed that prior to the spread of the modern factory system, family and household relations overlapped with production relations in English textile manufacture. This was most obvious in the systems of cottage industry and putting out, but it was true as well, albeit in somewhat different form, in artisanal production, for skilled workers commonly belonged to craft communities in which members were linked in durable, personal relationships. Even in early factory production, which did not take place in the household, economy and society overlapped in the case of patriarchal production, where, remember, contractors commonly employed their own children or the children of relatives as their assistants. But even in firms that did not use contractors, family and work could overlap. Tamara Hareven (1982: 62), describing Amoskeag Mills, in Manchester, New Hampshire, at the end of the nineteenth century, says the company

> recruited its workers through family and kinship ties and encouraged their placement in the workrooms in family clusters. It often relied on relatives to socialize and discipline family members in the factory setting and to assist them in learning work processes.

In fact, Margaret Grieco (1987) argues on British data that kin links remain important in the workplace for many areas of manufacturing.

While many of these forms of production survived into the twentieth century, for many people the passage of the nineteenth century meant a growing differentiation of economic and social relationships. More and more people produced their subsistence indirectly, through wage work outside of the household and outside of relations of family and friends. As a consequence, the household was becoming a realm of domestic affection distinct from an outside world that was, characteristically, a world of commerce (Matthews 1987; van de Wetering 1984). Jonathan Parry (1986: 466, 467) indicates the consequences of this sort of change for the ways people think about their transactions with each other: "As the economy becomes increasingly disembedded from society, as economic relations become increasingly differentiated from other types of social relationship, ... [g]ifts can ... be given the sole objective of cementing social relations."

I linked the ways people think about transactions to the ways that they generate their basic subsistence, either directly through production or indirectly through wage labor. Securing subsistence is important, but attending only to it can limit unduly our understanding of the ways that economy and society can overlap in people's experience. Even a household that depended on the wage labor or commercial activities of some of its members depended as well on the cooperation of household members to produce a significant part of what it consumed. Families routinely, if decreasingly, made their own candles, soap and butter, and if they no longer wove their own cloth, they sewed their own clothing through much of the nineteenth century (Ehrenreich and English 1978: 129). Further, it was not until the first decade of the twentieth century that households gave up substantial work in the growing, preserving and preparing of foodstuffs. Except in the most densely populated areas, urban working-class families continued to grow significant quantities of fruit and vegetables, chickens, rabbits and even pigs (Smuts 1971, in Braverman 1974: 273–4).

Indeed, even a concern with who makes what within and without the household misses the point that there is more at issue than the objective degree of overlap between durable household relations and the ways people secure their subsistence. Also at issue is the way people think about their economic activities. Stephen Gudeman and Alberto Rivera (1991) address this issue in their anthropological description of what they call the "house economy". For my purposes, the core of their complex discussion is that the house economy is not just a set of economic activities. It is as well a way of thinking about those activities, an orientation that sees the household itself as the focus of economic action and that subordinates the economic pursuits of its members to the survival of the house as a social unit (for an illustration of this pattern of thought in medieval England, see Postles 1986; for its decay on the borders of capitalism, see Heyman 1994). Though it is far beyond the Colombian peasant households that Gudeman and Rivera describe, it is reasonable to look for traces of the house economy even in settings where householders are enmeshed closely in commodity relations and wage labor. If such householders constituted a house economy, the appearance of a separation of the family from the economic activities that take place outside could be belied by the orientation of family members. In this circumstance, members would see themselves as dependent upon, and responsible for the existence of, the household. Consequently, for such people economy and society would overlap in important ways, as economic activities would be infused with social identities.

The idea of the house economy casts an interesting light on David Schneider's distinction between home and work. As he describes that distinction it centers on how people see work identities and relations as transient and distinct from home identities and relations. However, Schneider's concern with the conceptual opposition of these two realms diverts attention from the ways that they, and people's identities in them, may be linked. Most obviously, it diverts attention from the possibility that people are motivated to enter the world of work because of their identity at home. In this case, their work identities would be expressions of their family identities. Likewise, their family identities would be an expression of their work identities for two reasons. First, the contribution they make to the family would affect their identities within it. Second, it is through their work that the family and, hence, their identities as family members can survive. Leonore Davidoff and Catherine Hall (1987: part 2) describe these issues at length in their study of English middle-class families in the first half of the nineteenth century, as Lydia Morris (1990: esp. ch. 2) describes them in the present day.

In suggesting the existence of a house economy and its attendant orientations I do not mean that people's perspectives on life and work are independent of their material and social situations or that the analyst is free to infer whatever perspective seems most satisfactory. In the absence of careful study of how people actually conceive of their situations, the house economy can be no more than a sensitizing concept. It suggests that in certain situations members may have a house-economy orientation, even though their household relies primarily on market activities and relations. Further, it suggests that the house-economy orientation can exist well after the more obvious economic activities move out of the household and into the capitalist sphere.

154

John Modell provides an example of the situation I mean. He makes the point (1979: 119) that, at least through the 1920s, American families confronted "widespread externally-imposed uncertainty" that threatened their subsistence, especially urban families in the working class. Such uncertainties included the death of the husband and father and, less spectacularly but routinely, unemployment through illness, dislike of the job, inability to get to work, layoffs and the like (1979: 125). Because private insurance cost more than many could afford and because public welfare schemes were insignificant, death and unemployment posed a serious threat to the survival of the family.

Modell (1979: 128) argues that families coped with this uncertainty by adopting a "'defensive' mode of family economic cooperation". (Bose 1984 describes the strength of this mode nationally around 1900.) A key feature of the defensive mode is that the family did not rely on the income of a single wage earner. Instead, children, and to a lesser extent wives, went out to work and most of their pay was appropriated by the family. This appropriation was not endless. Modell's evidence (1979: 130–1) indicates that families were aiming at an overall level of income for the household as a unit distinct from the individuals within it. As household income reached that level, the amount of children's wages that was left to them and not claimed by the household increased. Equally, families sought to save, and especially to buy a large house. While these both brought security in the face of uncertainty, the house served other purposes as well. A family that owned one was in a good position to induce older children to remain in and contribute to the household, even in the early years of their marriages. Equally, when the children did leave, the house could be a source of income if the family took in lodgers.

Hareven's description of Amoskeag Mills, also from the period around 1900, reinforces the points Modell makes. Like him, she describes how children were expected to go to work to help support the family, and she points out some of the complexities of this process. For instance (Hareven 1982: 100), when families worked together in the mill, younger members were expected to do the tasks that were more demanding physically. This helped the family because it allowed older members to stay on the job longer than they could if they had to perform those tasks themselves. Also like Modell, she (1982: 109) links much of this familial orientation to the uncertainties that people faced: "In a regime of insecurity ... kin assistance was the only continuing source of support". She says (1982: 108) that the resulting orientation "entailed not only a commitment to the well-being ... of the family but one that took priority over individual needs and personal happiness".

Others describe a similar state of affairs. Leslie Tentler studied American families of the urban working class, again in the period around 1900. She found that parents "stressed aid in family support as a natural, normal, and important element of filial loyalty", and apparently with effect, for "more than 85% of the 347 New York City department store employees interviewed in 1910 were surrendering their entire earnings to their families" (Tentler 1979: 92, see 89–93). And, of course, R. E. Pahl argues that this reliance on a combination of the wages and efforts of a number of household members has, historically, been the rule rather than the exception. As he puts it: "The notion that there should be, in general, one waged worker or 'breadwinner' in a household who, typically, should be male is, in historical terms, a very odd idea" (1984: 41; for a discussion of just how odd, see Myles 1990).

Thus, well into the first decades of the twentieth century many people saw themselves, their families and their economic activities in ways that resemble the house-economy orientation. For them, economic and social relations overlapped in significant ways. To point to this overlap is not to imply that home and work were not separate for these people. They were, because most paid work took place outside the household in commodity relations with employers. Equally, the existence of this overlap does not mean people did not distinguish home and work and try to keep them separate. Indeed, Hareven (1982: 63) says that Amoskeag workers sought to maintain the separation and resisted efforts by their employer to interfere with their domestic lives. However, the separation of home and work need not mean the autonomy of domestic and economic relationships. Instead, people went out to work because of their position in the family, and though I have not described what these authors say on the issue (e.g. Modell, John 1979: 132–5; Tentler 1979: 89), people's position in the family was affected by their ability to go out and work. Home and work may have been distinct, but economic and social relations and identities were not.

Although this conjunction of economic and social relations continued for sections of the lower class well into the twentieth century, it had begun to disappear in other parts of society in the nineteenth century. With that disappearance the distinction between home and work came more nearly to match the distinction between economy and society. As that conjunction of economy and society weakened and disappeared for more and more of the population, so for more and more people gifts and gift relationships lost their material dimension and came to stand instead in opposition to calculating and material commodity relations.

What I have described in these paragraphs is the complement of the changes in production and retail trade relations that I described in earlier chapters. With changes in production, the objects that people confronted became more impersonal commodities. With changes in retail trade, the processes through which people acquired those objects became more impersonal. With the changes that I have described here, the basis of people's ability to acquire those goods became more impersonal. Together, these changes made for "home" in Schneider's sense, a beleaguered personal sphere. These are the historical conditions that have led to the emergence of the disembodied and immaterial present, "altruistic, moral and loaded with emotion" (Parry 1986: 466). It is under these conditions that it became the thought that counts.

FREEDOM AND OBLIGATION

The second element of the ideology is that the perfect present is given freely, purely as an expression of sentiment that binds neither giver nor recipient. Parry (1986: 466) calls this notion that presents are "free and unconstrained" the "elaborated ideology of the 'pure gift'". Underlying this notion is the idea of the free, independent individual who is motivated by internal will and who is neither bound to give nor bound by the giving. Indeed, were people not to conceive of transactors this way there would be no "thought that counts". But the fact that people place a cultural stress on the free present does not mean there is no obligation. At the level of articulated cultural values the perfect present may be free. At the level of structured cultural expectation and everyday behavior the obligation that giving generates can be strong and the obligation to give can be overwhelming.

This second element of the ideology of the perfect present is not different from the first only in its content. I argued that the idea that the present is immaterial emerges from the growing differentiation of economy and society and stresses the distinctiveness of social, and especially familial, relations as they are seen to oppose the commodity relations of the economy. However, the idea of the free present appears to deny the distinctiveness of the family and celebrates instead the individuality and freedom, the other side of impersonality, of the world of commodity relationships.

The individuality and freedom of the giver is not just a part of public culture. Though I said that social scientists have shown little interest in gift transactions in the West, those who have tend to follow a student of marketing, Russell Belk. Speaking of the gift, rather than the narrower category of the present, he says (1979: 100) "that (a) it is something voluntarily given, and that (b) there is no expectation of compensation". That is, gifts reflect the second element of the ideology, which defines giving as a voluntary act by independent individuals. Thus, David Cheal (1988: 12) says that gift-giving occurs when "the incumbents of roles go beyond their recognized obligations and perform gratuitous favors". This idea of the free and independent actor is, of course, a central element of Western liberal tradition (for a particularly nice discussion see Ouroussoff 1993) and is a staple in formal economics and in the work of those who seek to apply economistic models to social life (see Friedland and Robertson 1990). In addition, it appears in the classic sociological descriptions of social exchange, a term meant to cover all transactions between individuals outside the commercial sphere. Richard Emerson (1976: 337) observes that these descriptions revolve around a core set of concepts: "resource, reward, reinforcement, cost, utility, opportunity, profit, outcome, transaction, payoff, etc." (see also Davis, J. 1992: 73–4). These concepts reflect the voluntaristic assumption that if the calculator decides that a transaction is not profitable, it will not be made. For these writers, then, "exchange" does not consist of a range of sorts of transactions, as it does for Mauss. Instead, it is all of one sort, mimicking commodity exchange and explicable in terms of classic, individualist calculation of gains and losses. This model portrays exchange "as essentially *dyadic* transactions between *self-interested individuals*, and as premissed on some kind of *balance*" (Parry 1986: 454).

This economic individualism is most obvious when George C. Homans (1958: 603) seeks to explain social exchange behavior by invoking the equation "Profit = Reward – Cost." Alvin Gouldner (1960: 164) says the same thing less concisely when he argues that understanding a social exchange relationship "requires investigation of the mutually contingent benefits rendered and of the manner in which the mutual contingency is sustained". Similarly, Peter Blau (1964: 91) defines these sorts of transactions as "voluntary actions of individuals that are motivated by the returns they are expected to bring and typically do in fact bring from others". This view persists in Marcia Millman's (1991) presentation of an economistic and individualistic calculus for personal relationships, as much as it does in Francesca Cancian's rejection (1987) of the common assumption that such a calculus is adequate for describing those relationships. What Marx says of bourgeois economy, then, applies as well to the way many writers construe social exchange, for in each there rules

> Freedom, Equality, Property and Bentham. Freedom, because ... [they] are constrained only by their free will .... Equality, because ... they exchange equivalent for equivalent. Property, because each disposes only of what is his own. And Bentham, because each looks only to himself.
>
> (from *Capital*, ch. 6, in Tucker 1978: 343)

Of course, some scholars see givers as more constrained. For them, the free gift exists primarily when people are creating a new relationship or modifying an old one. For example, the sociologist Georg Simmel (1950: 392) says that the first present given "has a voluntary character which no return present can have. For to return the benefit we are obliged ethically; we operate under a coercion". Mauss himself (1990: 27) describes this same freedom in the preliminary present that, the giver hopes, will lead to a *kula* exchange relationship among Trobriand Islanders of eastern Melanesia. He says the *kula* partnership

> begins with a first gift, the *vaga*, that is solicited with all one's might by means of "inducements". For this first gift the future partner, still a free agent, can be wooed, and he is rewarded, so to speak, by a preliminary series of gifts .... [O]ne is not sure that the *vaga* will be given, or even that the "inducements" will be accepted.

In spite of these qualifications, the predominant sociological view seems to be little more than a simple reflection of the liberal view of gifts in popular ideology.

Even though the ideology asserts that the perfect present and the perfect giver are free, people recognize that giving is important for creating and recreating social relations and the obligations they entail. As I described in Chapter 1, in gift relations people are not free, autonomous individuals, but moral persons, identified and bound by the relations in which they exist. A man from a middle-class London suburb pointed to these bonds when he explained to Peter Willmott and Michael Young why he looked after his aged parents: "'When they've brought you up', said Mr Burgess, 'you feel you've got a certain amount of moral obligation to them'" (Willmott and Young 1960: 50). A housewife made the same point when she explained why she took in her aged uncle: "He's an awful nuisance sometimes, but I *can't* turn him out, can I? After all, he's my father's brother and there's no one else he could go to" (1960: 58).

In the face of this, we can see how the assertion that the perfect present is unconstrained and unconstraining is as much a denial as is the assertion that the present is immaterial. The world is not one of free and freely transacting individuals any more than it is of disembodied expressions of sentiment. Though we may stress individual freedom, people *are* constrained in their social relationships and they *do* act as moral persons, however ambivalent they may be about their relatives and their obligations to them.

One factor that may account in part for the ideological assertion of the freedom of the giver is that the constraints people bear in gift relations appear insignificant compared to what they experience in the world of work. Although capitalist labor may be free, it is so only until work starts. Then people are constrained, and they identify and interact with others in the company in terms of their positions in an over-arching corporate structure. Moreover, because people enter a job abruptly, the constraints it imposes are likely to be more noticeable than those that people experience in the social realm. People develop social relationships and identities slowly, often over the course of years, and these identities emerge through implicit negotiation and adjustment among those involved. Perhaps because of this, people tend to think of the obligations that these relations entail as chosen freely, rather than imposed externally.

The result is a curious state of affairs. Because different people in their different families confront many situations in common, and because they are likely to interpret those situations using common cultural resources, their actions are likely to be routine and predictable. However, because of the assumption that personal relations are voluntary, those people will tend to see themselves as thinking up on their own courses of action to deal with the situations that they confront. Thus, people have to struggle to reinvent the wheel, to think up anew for themselves just what all those others in the same situation have struggled to think up for themselves.

But what I have said does not explain why the ideology of the perfect present includes the idea of the free individual at all. As I said was the case

159

with the ideology's stress on disembodied sentiment, it will not do to see this as an expression of some human universal. It, too, is a result of historical circumstances. Mauss (1985) has argued that the notion of the self underwent a marked change in the seventeenth and eighteenth centuries in Western Europe, the time of the rapid spread of capitalism. In particular, he argues that it was around this time and among some intellectuals that the modern idea of the individual began to appear. I need to explain briefly how I interpret Mauss's elliptical discussion of this change. In essence, it is a change from a conception of the self appropriate to gift relations to one appropriate to commodity relations.

The argument is not that people previously were thought to be without a self. Rather, it is that prior to this time people commonly thought of the self as situated, defined by and springing from the relationships in which it exists.[2] To translate this into the terminology of social science, the self was a location in a structure or web of relationships. Consequently, people's motives, or perhaps their only valid motives, sprang from their locations. With this understanding of the self, people identify each other in terms of their respective positions in the social frame, and each is concerned that the other be "sincere", in the way that Lionel Trilling (1972) uses the term – not hide or be misleading about that position.

Gradually, however, a different view became more powerful. Under this view, the self was individual consciousness as an autonomous and irreducible being. To construe the self as autonomous asserts that each is individual and self-contained, "equal, identical and separate monads" (Barnett and Silverman 1979: 73). Consequently, the individual was the source, or perhaps the only valid source, of motivation. With this understanding of the self, people identify each other in terms of their respective individual wills and pre-dispositions, and each is concerned that the other, again in Trilling's terms, be "authentic" – not hide or be misleading about that will. Although the importance of this new view increased, it did not do so uniformly. Nicholas Abercrombie, Stephen Hill and Bryan Turner (1986: 104–10) say that before 1800 in England it was important primarily among larger land-owners and capitalists.

Alan Macfarlane's *The Origins of English Individualism* seems to contradict what I have said of the nature and timing of this change. This is because he argues, largely on the basis of legal and demographic evidence, that since the thirteenth century England has exhibited a distinct individualistic orientation. (Critical evaluations of Macfarlane are in Abercrombie, Hill and Turner 1986: 99–102; Sabean 1990: 410–12.) However, Macfarlane is comparing England to peasant societies of Eastern Europe, where the individual is subordinated to strong household units that almost take the form of lineages. Further, Macfarlane generally focuses on individual behavior and legal form, rather than on the understanding of the individual self that was behaving or invoking the law.

The two conceptions of the self that I describe, the autonomous and the situated, resemble what an American sociologist, Ralph Turner, calls the impulsive and the institutional selves. Turner's impulsive self resembles closely the autonomous self. While Turner (1976: 992) echoes Freud when he says that the locus of the impulsive self is "deep, unsocialized, inner impulses", what is important is that he locates this self in the individual rather than in social relationships, so that the legitimate source of motive is the independent will. However, the match between the situated self and Turner's institutional self is somewhat less clear. For Turner (1976: 991), the institutional self "is recognized . . . in the pursuit of institutional goals and not in the satisfaction of impulses outside institutional frameworks". Turner's institutional self, then, resembles William Whyte's *Organization Man*, resisting "serious temptation to fall away" (Turner 1976: 992) from the duties of the post. Turner, however, portrays the institutional self in terms that speak of constraint imposed on the self as much as they speak of the identity of the self. Any social conception of the self is constraining to a degree. Children have to be socialized and disciplined to adopt it; adults have to be monitored for compliance and exhorted to adhere to it, urged not to be "insincere" or "inauthentic" as the case may be. But in attending to this constraint only in terms of the institutional self, Turner implies that within the institutional framework there is a real self already in existence that is being constrained. My point is somewhat different, for it sees the situated self as generated by and conceived in terms of a web of relationships, rather than trapped by it.

While the older view of the self identifies people in terms of their location in a web of social relations, it does not deny that selves are individual. They can be individual in the sense that each person can be unique, though they are not individual in the sense of being self-contained. Equally, the autonomous construction of the self does not require that each person be unique, though it provides no ready mechanisms that would produce commonality. It is, perhaps, appropriate that at about the same time that the view of the self was changing there emerged as well a concern with describing commonalities of people. This was the period that marked the development of national surveys and censuses.

Here, however, the commonality that is investigated and described is not the commonality of being that is implicit in the idea that people are founded on their relationships with others. Instead, it is the commonality of individuals' attributes within a territorial entity, typically the state. Derek Sayer points to this connection in the case of England. He says that prior to the period that concerns me, the relatively weak English state "was nationally projected and locally administered as a patriarchal family writ large" (Sayer 1992: 1409), and hence one that conceived people in terms of their relationships (here Sayer echoes some of the arguments in Thompson 1971). However, with the growth of state power, the state's subjects became instead individual citizens, "endowed with private rights and public representation" (Sayer 1992: 1399).

Colin Campbell, a sociologist, describes aspects of the emergence in England of the idea that the main legitimate source of motive is the individual, internal will. He says that early in the 1700s the idea began to spread that people had an intuitive moral sense of what is right and wrong, good and bad, and a natural desire to do the good and avoid the bad. Although Francis Hutcheson, one of Adam Smith's teachers, held this view (Myers 1983: 68), a prime example of it is Shaftesbury's *Characteristics of Man, Manners, Opinions, Times*, which appeared in 1711. Campbell summarizes Shaftesbury's argument, saying that because of this inherent moral sense and the way it operated, "virtuous behaviour can only be conduct which is freely chosen, arising directly out of one's very being" (Campbell, C. 1987: 150). Thus, Shaftesbury says of the good man:

He never deliberates . . . or considers the matter by prudential rules of self-interest and advantage. He acts from his nature, in a manner necessarily, and without reflection; and if he did not, it were impossible for him to answer his character, or be found that truly well-bred man of every occasion.

(in Campbell, C. 1987: 150)

Moral behavior, then, springs from the free and unconstrained will, for it is in freedom that the moral sense is best able to operate. And from this it is only a small step to the argument that free and unconstrained acts are good, as well as to the inverse argument, that constraint, external regulation, is bad. (Garry Wills 1978: chs 13, 16, 21 describes this moral philosophy and its influence on Thomas Jefferson and American thought.) This positive valuation of the independent self was elaborated in the eighteenth century in the notion of the social and moral virtues of individual economic independence exhibited by the gentleman "patriot" living off his landed estate (Pocock 1975: ch. 13; 1979) and more recently by those living off their capital (Hirschman 1977: 127–8).

An aspect of this view is that external criteria of judgement, such as public standards of taste, are suspect. One recognized the beautiful, the good and the true because they were pleasurable, as one recognized the ugly, the bad and the false because they were displeasing, not because they conformed to or violated esthetic, ethical or logical criteria (Campbell, C. 1987: 154–60). To put it another way, Campbell is arguing that personal feelings became valid moral judgements rather than mere idiosyncratic reactions.

If Campbell's arguments are correct, the assertion that the perfect present is given freely reflects a fundamental conception of what it means to be human and good. The good present is the spontaneous, unfettered expression of the real inner self and inner feeling. In this way the notion of the "good present" has two meanings. The good present is one that reflects or expresses the giver, and if it is good in that sense the present is also morally good. Conversely, the present that is constrained and interested is repulsive, because constraint and interest conflict with the source of goodness, which is spontaneous expression.[3]

Allan Silver points out another appearance of this changing conception of the self, in the Scottish Enlightenment of the later eighteenth century, especially in the writings of Ferguson, Hume and Smith. For these writers, in the old order people existed in terms of their position in structures of faction or patronage, such as existed, but was decaying, in areas of English commerce in the eighteenth century (see Chapter 3; McKendrick, Brewer and Plumb 1982: ch. 5). People's positions in these structures both gave them an identity and shaped expectations of their behavior. In other words, it was the source of their motive. Furthermore, these structures were exhaustive, in the sense that everyone was a member of one faction or another, so that in principle strangers were not neutral. Instead, they were only potential allies or potential enemies, depending upon their structural location relative to one's own.

The writers Silver describes, however, saw another form of sociality and social identity emerging, that of the independent individual. For them, strangers were "authentically indifferent co-citizens" (Silver 1990: 1482). These strangers could become enemies or friends, or indeed remain indifferent, but they were not bound to become one or another because of their position in a structure. Instead, they became so through the operation of "natural sympathy". In basing personal relations on such a mechanism, these writers were, like Shaftesbury, denying that they spring from the history of the interaction that constitutes the relationship. Instead, they are asserting that these relations spring from the timeless beings or selves of those involved. This attitude – that close personal relationships are discovered in the self, if you will, rather than constructed in interaction – is expressed by the modern, middle-class American women that Helen Gouldner and Mary Symons Strong (1987) describe. In *The Theory of Moral Sentiments*, Adam Smith (in Silver 1990: 1481) says this is "an involuntary feeling that the persons to whom we attach ourselves are the natural and proper objects of esteem and approbation". Here is Shaftesbury's "good man" meeting new people and finding new friends.

Mark Girouard says that these people met in what the English of the Georgian period called "polite society". Such people sought to do away with the factions and interests that, they thought, disfigured the preceding era. In its place they wanted "polish" (cf Hirschman 1977: 56–63). "A polite man was someone polished, in the sense that he had no angularities which limited his contact with other people" (Girouard 1990: 76). In this society, said John Toland in 1711, "A Tory does not stare and leer when a Whig comes in, nor a Whig look sour and whisper at the sight of a Tory. These distinctions are laid by" (in Girouard 1990: 78). The view of themselves and of their social lives that members of polite society espoused was embodied in the architectural unity and spaciousness of the public promenades, assembly rooms, theaters and coffee-houses that were so important in Georgian architecture and town design. For Girouard (1990: 77–8), the quintessential polite Georgian place was a resort town like Bath. Such towns attracted people from many different occupations and places, though all were, of course, genteel. Furthermore, when these polite people traveled to their resorts they freed themselves of the normal obligations of trade or profession. The result was a heightened opportunity to see and be seen, and to let the sentiments play in the greeting of old friends and the meeting of new.

According to the writers of the Scottish Enlightenment, one of the things that allowed the appearance of the disinterested stranger was the differentiation of economy and society. For Adam Ferguson, in the old order people's relationships with each other were guided by their desire for gain.[4] This was because the absence of an impersonal market meant that it was only through personal relationships that people could acquire wealth. The result, says Silver (1990: 1484), was that "one has no choice but to be, in Ferguson's disapproving phrase, 'interested and sordid' in all interactions, concerned only with whether they 'empty [or] fill the pocket'". However, with the appearance of the impersonal market, matters of the pocket acquired their own, independent sphere, leaving the social sphere free to be ruled by matters of the heart.

I noted earlier, drawing on Derek Sayer, that one factor shaping the emerging conception of the autonomous self in England was the growing power and changing nature of the state. From Silver, it is clear that another factor was changes in the economic realm, especially the emergence of the impersonal retail market, which I described in Chapter 3, and the emergence of the notion of free labor, or the impersonal labor market, which I mentioned in Chapter 2. But the separation of economy and society did not, for these writers, mean that people were different in these two realms in any fundamental way. Rather, populating each was the same, emerging autonomous individual. The autonomous self endowed with sentiment of the Scottish Enlightenment was not just the actor of the social sphere, but was also the actor in the market of classical economics (for a Marxist analysis of the emerging conception of the market actor see Taussig 1977: 141–4). As Parry (1986: 466) summarizes the relationship of market and social life, "free and unconstrained contracts in the market also make free and unconstrained gifts outside it." Market actors are possessed of personal resources to trade, as they are possessed of an internal will that motivates them to enter the market in order to trade. The autonomy of the selves of these market atoms meant, however, that they could only be described in the aggregate, just as censuses and surveys were beginning to chart the attributes of the citizens of the state. In the aggregate, these atoms constituted the economists' "demand", but as the source of that lay in autonomous selves, it could not be understood in economic terms (see Baudrillard 1981; Douglas and Isherwood 1978; Sahlins 1976).

Shaftesbury, Toland and the writers of the Scottish Enlightenment talked of the spontaneous judgements of the autonomous self, rejecting the older notion of the situated self and the relationships that it entailed. But however much they may have thought they were doing so, they were not describing a society made of autonomous individuals devoid of constraining structures. The "good" that Shaftesbury says we sense spontaneously, like the operation of Adam Smith's "involuntary feeling", is not free and unconstrained. Whigs may not have looked sour at the sight of a Tory, but both were quite ready to "distinguish the polite Gentleman from the rude Rustick" (1737 etiquette manual, in Girouard 1990: 77).[5] The sentiments are shaped by social and economic circumstance, so that society is differentiated. This is not the personal differentiation of faction or family, but the impersonal differentiation of taste and class, for polite society "was made up of the people who owned and ran the country" (1990: 77).

This sort of differentiation took different forms. For instance, William Creech, an Edinburgh bookseller of the time, noted a number of signs of the emerging segregation of the different classes between 1763 and 1783. He said that over this period families ceased bringing their household servants to church with them, and apprentices no longer lived with their masters (Chitnis 1976: 34, 35). Further, this period saw the building of Edinburgh New Town, which had a marked impact. As Anand Chitnis (1976: 31) summarizes Creech's observations, a result

> was the end of the old town pattern of residence whereby representatives of all classes of society might be found living in apartments off a common stair in the closes and wynds of the High Street. Such shoulder rubbing of peer, preacher and pauper gave way to the more modern pattern of residential segregation by class, income, or occupation.

In the case of people's relationships with servants within their household, the change was profound. Where Samuel Pepys, late in the seventeenth century, lived in close social and physical contact with the servants in his household, by the early part of the nineteenth century the elite were designing their houses in a way that nearly eliminated contact between the family and the servants who supported it, even visual contact (Franklin 1981: 88; for contact with servants in France see Maza 1981: esp. 14–18).

However, while the notion of the autonomous individual may have encouraged the investigation of people in the aggregate, whether to survey a country's strength or a market's demand, it made it difficult to understand how external factors could shape the autonomous self. This difficulty is illustrated by the somewhat anomalous status of Emile Durkheim's *Suicide*. This book differed from much of the sociological work done earlier in the nineteenth century. It did not seek to analyze the properties of social systems, but instead selected for study an act that "must seemingly depend exclusively on internal factors" (Durkheim 1951: 46), and it sought to show how external factors shape that most private and terminal of acts. It thus seeks to address a core question, how social forces exterior to the individual affect individual decisions and actions. Analytically, this question seems inherent in the construction of the autonomous self, but at the same time it contradicts that very autonomy. This contradiction may account for why *Suicide* appeared only in 1897, and why commentators commonly describe the book as a treatise on method or a discussion of the systemic attributes of social integration.

I have described a set of changes in the way that people conceived of the self in order to explain why the perfect present is given and received freely. But discerning these changes is easier than assessing their significance, for the autonomous self that people described had a circumscribed existence. The polite Georgians at Bath lost their disinterest when their holiday ended and they went back home. Adam Smith's indifferent strangers may have been numerous, but they were also transient, for once met they tended to become friend or enemy, with the obligations of amity and enmity that ensue. And, of course, relationships within the household continued to be mixtures of sentiment and interest.

These qualifications do not mean that the autonomous individual was just a fairy tale. Rather, to some degree I think it marked a growing cultural construction of public and private life as entailing distinct sorts of relationships, a distinction that echoes the disengagement from public life described in different ways by Richard Sennett (1976) and by Robert Bellah and his colleagues (Bellah *et al.* 1985). This distinction is contained in a contradiction of Georgian architecture, for at the same time that grand and orderly public spaces were appearing, people were devoting more of their effort to creating comfortable private spaces. The Georgian era was not, after all, distinguished only by its public buildings and spaces, but also by its domestic architecture, within which people lived more and more of their lives (see Rybczynski 1988: esp. 105–21). Perhaps one attraction of polite society and the indifferent stranger was that they marked not a stable thing, but an exhilarating point of transition and potential, the first stage in the transformation of public strangers and acquaintances into private friends.

In this chapter I have described and analyzed what I call the ideology of the gift. In this ideology, when objects are presents they are transubstantiated in a kind of reverse fetishism of commodities. They become disembodied – they lose their past as commodities and even as material things, instead becoming subordinated to the individual emotions of the giver. In doing so, they are seen to entail no taint of obligation or interest on the part of either the giver or the recipient.

This ideology is not a reflection of some fundamental human aspiration. On the contrary, it is held by people who live their lives in particular ways, and in this chapter I have related the ideology to the socio-economic situation in which people who espouse the ideology find themselves. Thus, this ideology is not merely a curio, an aspect of a highly stylized, perhaps colorful, but ultimately insignificant aspect of social customs of interest only for itself. Instead, this ideological understanding of presents deserves more than the cursory consideration it usually receives. This is because it is related to, and thus is a way of discovering, conceptions of people, objects and social relations: what people are, how they interact with each other, how objects are part of those interactions.

Jonathan Parry (1986: 458) summarizes briefly the argument I have made in this chapter at length. He observes that presents occur both in the archaic societies that Mauss describes as well as in industrial capitalist societies. However,

> in our kind of society gifts come to *represent* something entirely different. *Gift-exchange* [in archaic societies] – in which persons and things, interest and disinterest are merged – has been fractured, leaving gifts *opposed* to exchange, persons *opposed* to things and interest to disinterest.

In other words, as economy and society become distinguished, so "the transactions appropriate to each become more polarised in terms of their symbolism and ideology" (Parry 1986: 466).

8

CHRISTMAS AND THE
CEREMONY OF THE GIFT

People give to and receive from each other in social relations every day. They give each other formal presents several times a year. But it is at Christmas that they all give at once. If there is a national industry on Christmas eve and Christmas morning, it is the production of used wrapping paper and ribbon. At Christmas both Britons and Americans attend most closely to gifts and gift relations, and it is the one time of the year when they talk to each other, collectively and publicly, about what it means to give. Christmas is appropriate as the topic for this final, substantive chapter of a book on gifts and commodities, because the patterns of the giving and the taking illustrate many of the arguments I have made about how people see themselves, others, objects, and the relations and transactions that link them all. In this chapter I will attend primarily to Christmas in the United States. The points I make apply generally to Christmas in Britain, though there are important differences in the ways people think about and celebrate the holiday in the two countries.

Perhaps the first lesson to draw from Christmas is its very ubiquity and uniformity. We may like to see ourselves as free and autonomous individuals, but as I said in Chapter 7, often we find ourselves in similar situations, which we interpret by way of similar cultural frameworks. The result is that, however much we may see ourselves as acting freely and spontaneously, we do similar things. In his analysis of Christmas in Middletown, Theodore Caplow (1984: 1308) pointed to this mix of freedom and uniformity. "There are no enforcement agents and little indignation against violators. Nevertheless, the level of participation is very high." Here we are in the realm of what Pierre Bourdieu (1977: 164) calls "doxa", the taken-for-granted set of beliefs and perceptions, "seen as self-evident and undisputed", that lead to "the reconciliation of subjective demand and objective (i.e. collective) necessity". The rules of Christmas are nowhere written, and yet the degree of conformity to them is remarkable.

CHRISTMAS GIVING

The heart of Christmas is affectionate giving, which is a celebration of personal social relations. In American society, as in Britain (Bennett 1981), those are the relations that characterize the nuclear family. Festivities in general and affectionate giving in particular are more intense within the family than outside it. Further, compared to giving outside the family, giving within the family is more concerned with the expression of sentiment and less concerned with the reciprocation of equivalents that characterizes commodity transactions.

The fact that Christmas is a celebration of gift relations, however, does not mean that it is always easy or harmonious. Just as I said in Chapter 5 that appropriation is problematic, that people are dissatisfied shoppers much of the time, so Christmas has its sour side, for its celebrations are problematic too. The lament of an Englishwoman, Janet Hadley (1986: 36), expresses this:

> I look forward to Christmas, especially the rituals of cooking and hospitality. I love making the puddings and mince pies and decorating the tree. I enjoy planning the presents and the food. I just wish it didn't all have to be so much a question of "who are we going to have to offend this year?", for there always seems to be someone. The simple enquiry about your whereabouts and the company you'll be keeping on 25 December oozes with sour layers of family history.

But whether they go well or ill, giving and other key features of Christmas are centered on the immediate family. Thus, Caplow (1984: 1308–9) found that having a Christmas tree was not ubiquitous in Middletown. It was the norm for married couples with children, but rare among the unmarried and the childless. Likewise, while giving presents was common, the vast majority of presents went to those within the nuclear family rather than elsewhere (1984: table 2). People gave presents to their fathers, mothers, children and children's spouses in over 90 percent of cases, regardless of whether the relative lived in Middletown or was distant from it. However, gifts to relatives outside the core family were less common and more conditional. For grandparents and grandchildren, people gave presents in over 90 percent of the cases where those relatives were within fifty miles of Middletown, but in only half to three-quarters of the cases where those relatives were more distant. For collaterals – siblings, siblings' spouses, siblings' children and parents' siblings – giving was less frequent yet. Regardless of where these relatives lived, less than one-third of them got presents from Middletown residents. In other words, at least in modern Middletown, Christmas is not simply a time of home and family, it is almost exclusively so.

The centrality of the family household for Christmas can create problems for those who want to study the giving of presents purely in economic terms. An instance of this is a report on presents by Thesia Garner and Janet Wagner for the Bureau of Labor Statistics of the U.S. Department of Labor. Echoing elements of the ideology of the perfect gift, the authors were concerned to exclude transactions where the giver might have benefited from the utility of the object, which led them to ignore presents given within the household. Their argument is this: "From the perspective of the household as an economic unit, the gift given within the household may not be a real gift, because the entire household, and not just the recipient, may derive utility." From this they conclude that "the only true gifts are those given outside the household" (Garner and Wagner 1988: 2). Their concern with the utility of the object illustrates Jean Baudrillard's point (1981: 53–7) about the alibi of use value. Thus, while they rule out gifts where the giver receives a material utility, they do not rule out those where the giver receives an immaterial benefit, even though they are aware (1988: 18) that such benefits exist: "[A] tangible gift from a parent or grandparent may be exchanged for an intangible return from a child or grandchild". Indeed, their orientation requires that they separate the utility of the object from the other pleasures it brings, which in turn requires them to distinguish the pleasure the recipient gets from a new necktie, from the giver's pleasure at the gratitude of the recipient. In thus focusing on utility, they define the object as a material bearer of use value that is divorced from the giver, recipient and their relationship. While their reasoning may be impeccable from an economic standpoint, it is almost breathtaking in its denial of how people think about presents, how and why they give them, and their rewards for giving.

I pointed out in Chapter 1 that a characteristic that distinguishes people in gift relations from those in commodity relations is that they are relatively unconcerned with direct reciprocity, because their transactions are part of a durable relationship between people rather than activities that define or express equivalence between things. Appropriately, lack of concern that the giver receive an equivalent in return is most pronounced in giving between parents and children in the household. Caplow (1984: 1316) found that parents and young children exchange presents unequally "in both quantity and value. Respondents gave 946 gifts to persons under 18 and received 145 in return; 84 of these were of substantial value and six of the return gifts were."

One might argue, as does Michael Schudson (1984: 134), that this imbalance springs from the fact that children have few resources that they can use to acquire objects to give. However, if it were important for them to give presents equally with parents, then parents would give presents in their children's names, just as parents do so much else in their children's names. That parents do not do so indicates that the reciprocation of equivalents is not a concern. The fact that the ability to reciprocate does not account for the imbalance, is illustrated by the transaction of presents between parents and their adult children, who are likely to have the resources to give as good as they get. Caplow (1984: 1316) found that "[p]arents expected to give more valuable and more numerous gifts to ... their adult children living at home than they receive in return." While presents within the core family in the household are given without the expectation of equivalent return, Caplow found a growing concern for reciprocation with the realm of collaterals and their spouses. Not only were presents to those relatives less frequent, but it is in presents to them that there appears "active concern that the gifts exchanged be of approximately equal value" (1984: 1316).

There are other studies that address the distinction between presents in the core family and presents to more distant kin. David Cheal studied the giving of presents in Winnipeg, Canada, and found a similar pattern. He looked at largest presents given rather than imbalances in transactions, but his data show the same break between presents to core family members and to collaterals. Children received the largest Christmas present from about 30 percent of Cheal's subjects, spouses accounted for another 30 percent and parents 15 percent. Every other sort of recipient was below 10 percent (Cheal 1986: table 6). Similarly, J. Bussey and his colleagues studied presents given in Bradford, England, and like Cheal they present data on most expensive Christmas presents given: over three-quarters went to spouses and children (Bussey et al. 1967: 10). And although there is little demographic data in this report, it seems that not all of their respondents were married or had children, suggesting that three-quarters is an underestimate for those who did in fact have a spouse and child.[1] Finally, Adrian Ryans (1977), studying how people buy presents, found an analogous distinction between presents intended for those within the household and for those without. Those buying presents for people within the household were likely to spend more time considering what to buy and were less likely to have fixed in advance an approximate amount of money they were prepared to spend (see also Heeler et al. 1979). Ryans's study suggests that presents to fellow household members were more likely to reflect the giver's understanding of the needs and desires of the recipient, and were less likely to be concerned with reciprocation.

When we move beyond the circle of kin, giving becomes less intense and its nature changes. In Middletown, at least, the concern with reciprocation disappears once more. This does not, however, connote a return to personality, but a greater degree of disengagement from the relationships involved. This giving includes presents at club meetings and office parties, where "each recipient gives and receives some small gift, but there is no direct exchange between giver and receiver" (Caplow 1984: 1316). Beyond the circle of fellow workers and club members there is yet another and even less convivial form of giving, where even the echo of reciprocation found in the office party disappears. This is presents to those who provide services, whether they are of menial status (letter carriers, garbage collectors, apartment-house door-men) or more elevated (the family physician or the teacher of the family's child). Although people give these presents at Christmas, they might better be called *douceurs*. This sort of present "keeps the wheels greased. It's a recognition of good service, and hope that the service will continue" (in

171

Streitfeld 1987; see Snyder 1985: ch. 5). People depend upon those linked to them only through commodity relations, particularly those whose jobs contain significant elements of discretion. Refuse collectors can spill the dustbins and leave the gate open (Mars 1982: 89–100); secretaries can spoil their bosses' front or let slip their secrets (Kanter 1977: ch. 4); almost anyone can be rude and unhelpful. To echo Marshall Sahlins (1974a: 201), Christmas presents in such relationships are preemptive strikes, attempts to secure the goodwill of those on whom the giver depends, and so forestall chicanery.

Thus it is that the pattern of Christmas giving echoes the common anthropological finding that reciprocity and generosity reign at home, while relations at the margins of the group are more impersonal and calculating (e.g. Godelier 1977; Sahlins 1974a). Transactions within the nuclear family household are most likely to conform to the model of affectionate Christmas giving, and it is in these relationships that the objects transacted most need to be expressions of the personality of the transactors and their relationships. As we move away from this core the nature of the relationship changes, and with it the nature of transactions and of what are transacted. As the relationship becomes more distant, transactions become less the expression of affection and more the calculated concern for tit-for-tat or the formulaic and relatively alienated giving that marks relationships that are fairly impersonal or utilitarian. The office-party present is hardly spontaneous; the *douceur* is almost coerced. Paralleling this, the presents given are less personal and more stereotyped, for here too the present must express the relationship between transactors. The office-party present is more impersonal than the family present because it expresses impersonal office relations rather than mutual affection. The annual *douceur* to the doorman is the most impersonal object of all, money.

The use of money as a present is intriguing. People usually see money as anonymous, and it requires substantial effort to identify money with those who transact it or to give it a social history (Parry and Bloch 1989; Zelizer 1989). For most people, money appears to be indifferent to the social relationships with which it is implicated. David Cheal, in his Winnipeg study, found an informant who explained this nicely: "Money is kind of cold. It's spent usually on nothing in particular, and when it's gone the memory's gone" (1987: 165). Further, when people are urged to contemplate giving money in close relationships in its naked state, not transformed into something like a gift certificate, they say they would give much more in monetary terms than they would if they could give an object instead (Webley, Lea and Portalska 1983).

Even though money is so awkward, people do give it. Appropriately, its use as a present is ambiguous. In Christmas *douceurs* it is given to those of more menial status, like garbage collectors and letter carriers, but not to those of higher status, like teachers and physicians (Caplow 1982: 386). Here the impersonality of the object expresses the impersonality of the routine interactions between giver and recipient. Within the family, parents can give money to their children, but children cannot give it to their parents, except in extraordinary circumstances that are likely to redefine fundamental elements of their relationship. Further, when parents do give money to their children, at least in England, usually they do so only on birthdays (Bussey *et al.* 1967: 57). In Middletown, only 5 percent of Christmas presents were of money, over 90 percent of them between people of different generations (Caplow 1984: 1315). Money is also given to friends and kin outside the household, but usually in the guise of help for major purchases or for setting up a new household (e.g. Bell 1969: 92–3; Cheal 1988: ch. 7). Thus, money appears to be undesirable as a present in close relationships outside that between parents and children unless it is likely to be memorialized in a durable object that embodies the relationship between transactors.

CHRISTMAS GIFTS AND COMMODITIES

I have argued that people see the family as the place of gift relations. Yet their understanding of and experience with the objects that are commonly available for use as presents means that those objects are inappropriate. They are Daniel Miller's "manufactures", impersonal commodities manufactured in the world of work. This is not to deny that they have social meaning. They do – the impersonal meaning that derives from their association with abstract categories or sorts of people, as I described in the Introduction.

This meaning can be important at Christmas, as families define themselves socially in part by the sort of presents that they give. This meaning also can be important to recipients personally, for they are likely to see in the presents they get a reflection of how the giver thinks of them. This is especially noticeable when people are given presents of the "wrong" social meaning. Caplow observed this in Middletown. His description of the ways that recipients were dissatisfied with their presents indicates that they were dissatisfied with the identification that was imposed on them by what they received:

> The standard disappointing gift is an article of clothing in the wrong size. Women are particularly resentful of oversized items that seem to say that the giver perceives them as "fat". Children are often insulted by inattentive relatives who give them toys that are too "young".
>
> (Caplow 1984: 1314)

While the purchased commodity has an abstract social meaning, it lacks the personality that is necessary for the good present, and in previous chapters I have described a number of the ways that people cope with the unsuitability of commodities in gift relationships. In mundane circumstances the ways that people cope typically are automatic, as in appropriation through shopping, and people seldom comment upon them. At ceremonious times like Christmas, however, this coping is more urgent and visible, and people are more articulate about it. For example, Christmas brings a heightening of the sense that presents need to express relationships rather than be utilitarian, that they need to be Emerson's gift of compliment and love rather than his common gift. This is translated into the belief that a present should not really be very utilitarian, should not be the sort of thing that recipients would buy themselves. By having presents be frivolous, luxurious or otherwise special, they are distinguished from the concern for ordinary utilities that leads people to purchase commodities more routinely.

As well, the ways that people present and treat presents help to overlay their commodity identity with sentiment and festivity, and so cope with the distinction between the objects at hand and the uses to which they are put. Once again, Caplow's study of Middletown is illuminating. Among the unspoken rules about Christmas that he describes, there is one that produces "exceedingly high" conformity, the Wrapping Rule: "Christmas gifts must be wrapped before they are presented" (Caplow 1984: 1310). (Lévi-Strauss 1969a: 56 sees a similar purpose in wrapping.) The ubiquitous Christmas wrapping is complemented by unspoken rules about display, particularly display that is captured in Christmas photographs. Caplow says

> the pile of wrapped gifts was photographed; and individual participants were photographed opening a gift, ideally at the moment of "surprise". Although the pile of wrapped gifts is almost invariably photographed, a heap of unwrapped gifts is not a suitable subject for the Christmas photographer.
>
> (Caplow 1984: 1311)

The heap of loot is too obviously a pile of useful commodities rather than special presents.

Caplow provides only one class of exception to the Wrapping Rule: "Difficult-to-wrap Christmas gifts, like a pony or a piano, are wrapped symbolically by adding a ribbon or bow or card and are hidden until presentation" (Caplow 1984: 1310). In other words, awkward presents are wrapped less than others. However, the two examples Caplow gives are distinguished not only by their awkwardness, but also by their price. Ponies and pianos do pose a puzzle for anyone who wants to wrap them. But equally, as I said in Chapter 5, their very price means that people are likely to think of them as different from the average anonymous manufacture. Price elevates them to the level of the special, perhaps made by artisans but certainly not made by robots. Because of this identity, such objects are less in need of wrapping.

Caplow does not mention another class of items that is also relatively unwrapped: presents made by the giver, especially sweet foodstuffs. At least in cultural imagery, homemade jams and sweet breads are wrapped simply. The breads are wrapped in aluminum foil with a simple card. This foil is less than wrapping because it is not wrapping paper and because it is considered necessary to keep the food fresh. Equally, the foil is associated strongly with the kitchen, where people make only possessions. The jam is likely to have only a bow and a card. These are not hard to wrap, they just do not need wrapping. And they do not need wrapping because they have the personal identity that commodities do not.

In asserting that wrapping is a way people cope with the contradiction between gifts and commodities, I am not arguing that this is the only reason to wrap presents. If they were not wrapped there would be little anticipation and surprise in the pile of presents beneath the tree. It is closer to my concern in this book that if presents were not wrapped, Christmas gift transactions would resemble immediate reciprocal exchange of the sort that characterizes commodity transactions (see Belk 1979: 100); but because they are wrapped, each party is under an obligation to reciprocate next year the present received this year. In this way, the exchange regenerates webs of long-term obligation and hence helps to create anew the gift relationship that it expresses. I do not deny the importance of these other aspects of wrapping. I mean only to point out an additional significance.

I said in Chapter 5 that women commonly have the primary responsibility for much of the mundane appropriation that goes on in families. Likewise, in Middletown they had the primary responsibility for wrapping presents (Caplow 1984: 1311), just as culturally they are associated closely with the presents from the kitchen that do not need wrapping. Equally, women in Middletown, as elsewhere, are central to a range of other Christmas activities that celebrate family relationships (Caplow, Bahr and Chadwick 1983: 188–92; Benney et al. 1959: 239–40). Among these is Christmas dinner, which is exceeded in the United States only by Thanksgiving dinner as the most important meal of the year. Caplow reports that almost two-thirds of the Middletown people he studied had been at a Christmas dinner, and that preparing the meal was exclusively a woman's task: "There was not a single reported instance in this survey of a traditional Christmas dinner prepared by a man" (Caplow 1984: 1313). On the other hand, in less-developed countries like Mexico, where the separation of economic and social life is likely to be less pronounced culturally, men have more of a role in making important decisions about Christmas activities (Jolibert and Fernandez-Moreno 1982). However, I need to repeat a point I made in Chapter 5. To say that women predominate in various aspects of Christmas in the United States is to relate who does what at Christmas solely to public gender structures, while ignoring the histories of the individual relations that result in different tasks being the work of different household members, and indeed the significance of the tasks themselves. Structures, histories and significances are related closely in practice, but need to be distinguished analytically.

CHRISTMAS SHOPPING AND CHRISTMAS GIVING

At Christmas we celebrate family relationships within the household. I have said that the objects people acquire to give in these relationships carry an inappropriate identity as commodities, and that people attempt to deal with that awkward identity through various beliefs and acts that deny the material significance of objects and that transform them into possessions. However, to describe how commodities are inappropriate and how people appropriate them leaves unanswered, and even unposed, a central question. Why do people give objects at all, much less commodities? There is no material need to give objects. Though we give each other many presents at Christmas, most people are sufficiently secure financially that they do not need the presents to make it through another year. Further, according to the ideology of the gift the material nature of the object is there only to be transcended by the sentiment that it embodies. To give a material object, especially a commodity, is to question the relationship in which it is given, to imply that it is one suited to commodity transactions.

It may be true, as Cheal (1987: 157) says, that people buy most Christmas presents

> for the same reason that most goods consumed in an industrial society are purchased. A much wider range of objects, of superior quality and hence greater utility, is available in the marketplace than any family would be able to produce on its own.

But Cheal's point does not explain why people give presents at all. In the face of all the dangers that objects pose at Christmas, why not say "I am glad we are a family"? The less articulate could give cards or make small tokens that really would convey their biography and identity within the family.

To begin to answer this question, it is necessary to consider what may seem just a functional prerequisite of the season, Christmas shopping.

Christmas shopping and the cultural responses to it are important for understanding Christmas. After all, people do not just casually go and buy the odd item. Instead, they shop for Christmas presents intensely. As Caplow notes for Middletown, Christmas "mobilizes almost the entire population for several weeks, accounts for about 4% of its total annual expenditure, and takes precedence over ordinary forms of work and leisure" (Caplow 1984: 1306–7; see also Davis, J. 1972). The impact of this expenditure is particularly marked in the area of retail sales. One American economist (in Mayer 1987) estimated that about one-third of annual retail sales come in November and December, twice what would be expected if retail sales occurred evenly throughout the year, and that Christmas accounts for the bulge. In other words, one-sixth of all retail sales is brought about by Christmas shopping and related activities. Moreover, this pattern is not particularly new. For some time, people have done much of their shopping for Christmas presents in department stores, and reliable data on department store sales exist from the mid-1920s in the U.S. Department of Commerce Survey of Current Business. The proportion of annual department store sales accounted for by November and December has remained stable from 1925 to the present, ranging from about 23 to about 26 percent.

Not only is Christmas a time of intense shopping, it is a time of abnormal shopping. Stores have special festive decorations, displays are reorganized and in many stores special seasonal items are offered for sale. People respond in an ambivalent way. On the one hand, Christmas shopping is agreeable: store staff are friendly and helpful, customers are cheery and the celebratory nature of the goods being bought is exhilarating. On the other hand, it is disagreeable: shops are crowded and the temporary staff hired for the crush are ignorant and over-worked, customers crowd and shove to get what they want, the goods being bought are shockingly expensive and finding suitable objects, much less the perfect choice, is frustrating and almost impossible. If people are frustrated shoppers much of the time in everyday life, they are frustrated shoppers even more of the time at Christmas. They regale each other with stories about how hard it is and they resolve to start earlier next year, though regularly they fail to do so: an American survey in 1988 found that half of those questioned did not begin until after Thanksgiving (Daily Progress 1988).

Inconvenience is not the only reason that people complain about Christmas shopping. Another is the materialism and commercialism that is so apparent in the rush to buy that is Christmas shopping. The stores that put up their decorations earlier and earlier, the advertising, the Christmas sales, the need to buy more and more, all drown out the familial values that were supposed to exist in the Christmases of our youth and before. The title of a column by William Raspberry (1988) in *The Washington Post* sums it up: "Christmas Run Amok: Our Gift-Giving Has Gotten Out of Hand." Who can maintain the spirit of Christmas when merchants tell them that the store Santa Claus is not "part of economic reality today" (in *The Economist* 1983: 23)? Further, the majority of Americans are practicing Christians, and the materialistic, commercial air of Christmas conflicts with important religious values bearing on the birth of Christ in particular and the glorification of material wealth more generally.

Just as Christmas shopping is not particularly new, neither are these complaints. Indeed, they are not even distinctly American: *The Times* complained about commercialization in its lead editorial of Christmas Day, 1912 (Golby and Purdue 1986: 10). In the United States, when Franklin Roosevelt moved Thanksgiving one week earlier in November to extend the period of Christmas shopping during the Depression, people complained about commerce defeating spirituality (Sickel 1940: 87–8). Earlier yet, in 1890 *The Ladies' Home Journal* complained about commercialism in American Christmas (Belk 1989: 116).

In the face of this bother and complaint, why do Americans, even devout Christians, spend so much effort in Christmas shopping to buy objects that are not suited culturally to use as presents? It is true that the giving of purchased presents reflects a number of motives, ranging from displays of affluence to a desire to shower a loved one with things lovelier than one can make. However, these more commonly recognized motives do not explain the intensity of Christmas shopping and the ambivalence that people feel about it.

An additional, and important, reason to buy and give lies below the surface. This reason becomes more apparent if we expand the meaning of "Christmas" to include the arduous shopping that goes with the activities that the word normally denotes. This expanded view sees shopping as an integral part of Christmas, rather than as an unfortunate commercial accretion on a real ritual and familial core. Taking the shopping and giving as parts of a single, complex ritual helps make sense of a number of the tensions that exist in people's conception of Christmas.

I described in Chapter 5 how shopping is one of the mundane ways that people transform things from a part of the indifferent mass of commodities in the store to the special things that reflect the shopper and the social relations in which the shopper is located. Christmas shopping is a heightened version of this activity. The volume of items to be purchased, and the range and intensity of the social relations that are taken into consideration – all are greater than normal. Because the heightening of sociality at Christmas heightens the importance of the giving and the presents, it heightens the importance of appropriation, which is reflected in the common feeling that Christmas shopping is especially hard work. In this sense, then, Christmas shopping is an annual ritual activity through which we convert commodities into gifts. In performing this activity people demonstrate to themselves that they can celebrate and recreate personal relations with the anonymous objects available to them, and this demonstration serves to strengthen and reassure them as they undertake the work of appropriation in everyday life during the rest of the year.

This is what makes shopping an integral part of Christmas. It is a mistake to construe Christmas in isolation, to see it only as a celebration and recreation of family and friendship. Rather, it is a celebration and recreation that needs to be seen in its social context. Family and friendship are surrounded by the impersonal world "out there", the world of work and alienated commodities. It is the Christmas shopping that proves to people that they can, in Schneider's terms, create a sphere of love in the face of a world of money. Shopping is a key part of Christmas.

With this enlarged view of Christmas some things that had been anomalous begin to make sense. For instance, it begins to make sense that people complain about the hard work of shopping and resolve each year to do things differently next year. The sense of hard work and the complaints about growing commercialization help affirm and heighten the impersonality of the commercial world, and so heighten the cultural opposition of home and work. Again, the complaints and the sense of hard work help affirm that people are, at this heightened time of the year, really able to wrest family values from recalcitrant raw materials. It is work – it has to be hard work – but they can do it. Equally, this enlarged view suggests that children give few presents not simply because they have little money, but because they do not normally undertake the daily round of shopping, appropriating and giving objects. The ritual of Christmas shopping is, therefore, inappropriate to them, and the few presents they give are usually only markers of family relationships. Finally, this view helps make sense of the status of objects made by the giver. Though they are possessions, they are not satisfactory, except perhaps as embellishments to a core of purchased presents. In Middletown, for instance, givers made less than 2 percent of the presents given – mostly, and appropriately, young children (Caplow 1982: 386). Such presents are unsatisfactory because they deny the ritual of Christmas shopping.

The argument I have laid out about American Christmas is a broad one. It relies on common cultural conceptions of the sort of relations proper to family and economy and of the place of objects in each of those realms. But precisely because it relies on common cultural conceptions it is limited in important ways. Though probably everyone in American society knows these common conceptions, there is no reason to assume that everyone responds to them in the same way. For instance, people for whom time is an especially scarce resource are likely to interpret presents made by the giver differently from those with time on their hands.

There are as well, of course, more profound, systemic factors that affect how much people are likely to respond to the symbolism of Christmas shopping and giving. First of all, the model I have laid out would be less likely to reflect the position of the relatively poor. Though they may confront the same problem of appropriation as those who are wealthier, they may very well see in Christmas presents the sheer ability to buy. Their presents would likely carry a strong message of economic security, a message probably more muted, though hardly absent, among the wealthier. Second, my model would be less likely to reflect the position of those whose experience with objects and with the economic sphere more generally departs from the common cultural assumption of alienation. Like those who have a house-economy orientation, those who produce and transact in relatively personal and less alienated relations would seem less likely to feel the need to celebrate their ability to appropriate commodities.

My argument is that Christmas shopping and giving are cultural activities that spring in large part from the perception of an alienated realm of work. Support for this argument exists in the giving of presents in Japan. It is a commonplace that economic relations there are less impersonal than in the West (Abercrombie, Hill and Turner 1986: 121–31). In idealized terms, this means that employees have a durable relationship with the firm that employs them; that employees subordinate themselves to the firm and its interests; that relations within the firm have a strong social, as distinct from just utilitarian, element; that employees derive their social identity from the firm rather than the specific work that they do (Nakane 1986; Rohlen 1973; see also Dore 1983). While this situation may exist primarily for core employees in larger firms, it reflects a widespread set of assumptions about how real work ought to be, which reflects in turn a widespread set of assumptions about what people are and how they ought to relate to each other (Moeran 1984). Because real work ought to be unalienated, at least as compared to work in the West, in Japan there is less likelihood that people will see the economic world as one of impersonal relations and things, surrounding and differing radically from the household world of personal relations and things. In saying this I do not claim that the Japanese do not distinguish between the household in which they live and the corporations in which they earn and spend money. I do claim, however, that they do not distinguish these realms in terms of the personality and impersonality that underlie the American cultural distinction between home and work.

Consequently, the Japanese would be unlikely to share the orientation toward Christmas giving that I have described for the West. This absence is manifest in the ways that the Japanese give presents (see generally Befu 1968; Creighton 1991; for a different sort of Japanese giving, see Graburn 1987). There is extensive giving at year's end in Japan, as well as at mid-year. However, the bulk of it is to those outside the household. Particularly important are gift transactions between superiors and inferiors within the firm. Further, generally the presents given do not appear to be seen as expressions of individual sentiment or relationship, though the Japanese do identify such a kind of giving. Instead, the presents are formulaic, expressing in standardized form the degree of inequality between giver and recipient. Millie Creighton (1991: 679–80) puts it succinctly:

> Personal sentiment – affection, intimacy, friendship – have no place in choosing gifts or who is to receive them. The price of the gift should be clearly discernable. There are no mutual exchanges; gifts flow one-way from inferiors to superiors .... Most important among these in contemporary Japan is a man's company.

I have over-simplified the complex Japanese process of selecting and giving presents, just as I have ignored the distinctive place of the household in Japanese giving and the growing interest in giving presents as part of the adaptation of Western holidays, including Christmas, all of which Creighton describes. However, the formulaic nature of core Japanese giving shows that in a society where the economy is not regarded as distinctively impersonal, giving presents does not revolve around the appropriation of commodities in the way that I have said it does in the United States.

My discussion of the variability of people's experience of alienation and the cultural separation of home and work raises perhaps the most important qualification to my argument, an historical one. Modern Christmas, centered on the buying of commodities and the giving of them within the nuclear family, should emerge with the spread of industrial and commercial capitalism.

THE SPIRIT OF CHRISTMAS PAST

In Chapter 7 I described some of the historical processes that changed the relationship between economic and social identities, and between home and work, in many people's lives. The history of Christmas echoes those patterns. It does not echo them perfectly, of course. The historical processes I described affected different sectors of society in different ways at different times. Thus, a ceremony like Christmas may have made sense to people in some sectors while being pointless to people in others. Equally, even if such a ceremony would have made sense to some people, it had to be available to them. People had to confront the existence of such a ceremony, or at least the elements from which they could plausibly construct one. Sheer historical accident, then, was important and need not have occurred as soon as people were receptive. Furthermore, while the giving and the shopping are now part of a unified whole, they need not have emerged together. The growing impersonality of wage work and retail trade were part of the same broad process, but they occurred at different times. Consequently, the growing cultural opposition of home and work might make a celebration of familial relations attractive, even though the persistence of personal relations between shopkeeper and customer would not make buying Christmas presents particularly significant culturally. Finally, different sections of society differed in their ability to propagate more widely a ceremony that appealed to them, to so institutionalize Christmas that it became a common celebration. For all these reasons, the most that one can look for is a rough fit between socio-economic change and the appearance of Christmas giving and shopping.

Although modern Christmas emerged relatively late, as I will show, it had its precursor. That was the English end-of-year festivities that took place indifferently around New Year rather than at Christmas itself. While England was not the only foreign influence on the emerging American Christmas, it was important, and of course it was the cultural ancestor of much of early America. There is substantial variation across time and space in the ways that the English marked year's end prior to the end of the eighteenth century, and evidence is sketchy. However, it is possible to draw out what appear to be two important themes that differentiate these festivities sharply from the modern Christmas. Appropriately, these themes resemble Japanese giving. One is the importance of the quantity or value of the gift, the other is the stress on hierarchy.

An important gift was food, in the form of feasts (see Golby and Purdue

1986: ch. 2). Commonly feasts were put on by superiors for their dependants, and in rural areas often they used foodstuffs that the dependants themselves provided (Pimlott 1978: 20). Feasts and presents celebrate social relations in different ways. A feast is more evanescent than a necktie, scarf or toy, and it stresses collective identity more clearly than does the giving of presents from individual to individual. Furthermore, sheer quantity is important in feasting in a way that is much less true for modern Christmas presents, with their stress on sentiment and fitness.

While the feast was important at all levels of society, presents seem to have been more the preserve of the gentry and nobility. However, like feasts, presents generally were not given within the household in familial relations. Instead, they moved between individuals, and hence the households of which they were a part, in ways that celebrated hierarchical structures of faction, patronage and allegiance. The celebration of vertical relationships may be antithetical to modern American Christmas, but it is an ancient form of ritualized giving. It was, after all, the offering to the gods and ancestors. And like this ancient form, the net flow of these presents apparently was upward. Equally, while they were intended to express or foster bonds of allegiance, one important way that people understood them was as monetary value, the value of the present reflecting the social positions of giver and recipient. These two aspects of presents appear at the end of the sixteenth century in the existence of a standard present from nobles to the monarch: a purse of £20 or the equivalent in plate (Davis, D. 1966: 131). Nobles and state officials, in turn, received presents from their subordinates (Pimlott 1978: 41–3). Both feasts and presents, then, illustrate the themes of hierarchy and quantity.

Hierarchy was important in many activities at year's end. The Lord of Misrule, the Boy Bishop and Boy Abbot – ceremonies in which humble people, especially children, were selected to act important borough and ecclesiastical roles – stressed the importance of hierarchy by inverting it (Jones, C. 1978: 303–6; Pimlott 1978: 24–7). As well, presents from burghers to borough employees and menials, from merchants to their more substantial customers (Davis, D. 1966: 209) and from householders to servants and merchants (Hervey 1845: 184; Hood 1991: 241–2; Pimlott 1978: 63–4, 72) celebrated hierarchical relations outside the household.

While hierarchy and quantity were important at year's end, the seasonal celebrations themselves were threatened repeatedly. There were sporadic attempts to suppress seasonal festivities, especially in northern Europe following the Reformation and in England under Cromwell, though in England, at least, these attempts were desultory and had little success (Pimlott 1978: 56). The main objections were that the festivities were idolatrous and bacchanalian (Golby and Purdue 1986: 35; Jones, C. 1978: 305–6, 321). In the colonies that became the United States, Southerners followed the pattern of seasonal feasting and the giving of presents to menials, including slaves (Richards 1971: 56; Snyder 1985: 59), while Puritan New Englanders suppressed Christmas.

Further, at least in rural New England at the end of the eighteenth century, there seems to have been little giving of presents at any time (e.g. Ulrich 1990: 138–41). Generally, however, and in contrast to England, where there were seasonal celebrations, they occurred in urban rather than rural areas (Golby and Purdue 1986: 37).

One distinctive and significant variation on year-end festivities centered on New York City. There, by the 1770s, people were celebrating the sixth of December. That was the day of St Nicholas, precursor to Santa Claus. That celebration is one of the sheer historical accidents that influenced the appearance of modern American Christmas. Although St Nicholas begat Santa Claus, St Nicholas Day in New York in the last quarter of the eighteenth century was not a celebration of familial relations. Instead, it was a celebration of anti-colonialism. Like much else at the time, festivities at year's end were political, and St Nicholas was drafted to fight for the revolutionaries.

St Nicholas was something of an invented tradition, an imaginative reconstruction of supposed Dutch custom, and things Dutch became popular in New York near the end of the period of British colonial mastery. The saint's proclaimed Dutch ancestry placed him in a past when New York was not British, but Dutch New Amsterdam, and so helped to legitimate opposition to British rule (Jones, C. 1978: 338–9). In fact, St Nicholas Day was an anti-Christmas, because Christmas itself was British. It was British because it was a holy day in the calendar of the Church of England. That made it suspect for many, and doubly offensive to Puritan New Englanders, so much so that the governor of the Massachusetts colony required an armed escort to protect him when he attended Christmas service in the 1760s. Christmas was British as well because it was an official British holiday. In New York, it was one of 21 proclaimed in 1775. These included St George's Day and nine others celebrating the king's birthday and other significant monarchical events. For revolutionaries this colored Christmas with the tones of monarchy that those holidays sported (Jones, C. 1978: 335).

Disaffected New Yorkers may have resurrected and refurbished a moribund Dutch custom for political purposes, but once recreated, the central character began to take on a life of his own, indicating that he appealed to more than partisan political interest. As Charles Jones (1978: 345) puts it, "Santa Claus was a local joke with an anti-British sting until 1809; after 1809 the spritely SC spread like the plague." What happened in 1809, in fact on St Nicholas Day, was that Washington Irving published *Knickerbocker History*, larded heavily with reference to the saint.

Even so, St Nick only slowly became recognizable as Santa Claus bringing presents to children. Until the 1820s in New York he was likely to bring little more than seasonal sweets, as he had done in Holland. This is illustrated by a poem addressed to St Nicholas published in the New York *Spectator* in 1810 (in Jones, C. 1978: 346–7). In its 69 words, it asks him to bring oranges, almonds, raisins, waffles, doughnuts, crullers, oley-cooks and cookies, ending: "Or if in your hurry one thing you mislay, / Let that be the Rod – and oh! keep it away." By the 1820s, St Nicholas abandoned his own day and moved to year's end, helped along in 1823 by the publication of Clement Moore's "A Visit from St Nicholas". In that decade children in New York City, the seat of industrial and commercial capital in the United States, were likely to be getting toys as well as sweets. However, festivities were still held indifferently on Christmas and New Year's Eve, and they centered on adult conviviality (Jones, C. 1978: 350–1).

In sum, by the end of the first quarter of the nineteenth century there were no marked signs of modern Christmas in the United States. Seasonal customs varied and frequently centered on adult feasting. Gifts to children were only beginning to appear, predominantly in New York City. The next forty years, until the end of the Civil War in 1865, marked the clear emergence of capitalism in large areas of the United States. During this period, production and circulation increasingly moved out of the household and into an independent commercial sphere. A concomitant was a growing sense of the household as a realm of domestic affection distinct from the outside world. And appropriately, it is during this period that the family and its relationships became the subject of seasonal celebration.

The vagaries of New York rebel politics were not the only historical accident shaping modern American Christmas. Another was a growing German influence in the United States (and in England as well, embodied in Prince Albert). During the 1840s and 1850s there was a wave of German immigration, and Germany was popular among the American intellectual elite, many of whom visited the area. The result was the introduction of elements of German end-of-year festivities, most notably the Christmas tree (Richards 1971: 97–102).

Also influential was Charles Dickens's *A Christmas Carol*. While the appearance of this book at this time may have been fortuitous, its impact was formative in the way that the appearance of the Christmas tree was not. *A Christmas Carol* appeared in the United States in 1843, just a year before Ralph Waldo Emerson finished his essay "Gifts". It was wildly popular, and Dickens read from the work on long American tours, where many people reported being strongly affected by the sentiments he expressed. Because *A Christmas Carol* was so important at the time, because it is so often evoked in modern Christmas entertainment and because often it is said to mark the onset of the modern Christmas (Belk 1989), it is worth devoting some attention to it. Doing so will show that if indeed it did mark the onset of modern Christmas, it did so only obliquely. Modern understandings of the work as a Christmas tale tend to focus on Tiny Tim and Bob Cratchit, who embody modern values of familial affection, and their moral victory over Scrooge, who embodies the self-interested impersonality of the world of work. However, these are by no means the only important themes in the book.

A central theme in *A Christmas Carol* is the old one of hierarchical relations outside the household, stressed by a number of English writers at the time (Pimlott 1978: 87). For instance, when the Ghost of Christmas Past takes him to revisit the Fezziwig Christmas ball, Scrooge explains why the ball was so important to Fezziwig's employees:

> He has the power to render us happy or unhappy; to make our service light or burdensome; a pleasure or a toil. Say that his power lies in words and looks; in things so slight and insignificant that it is impossible to add and count 'em up – what then? The happiness he gives is quite as great as if it cost a fortune.
>
> (Dickens 1918: 78)

More striking, perhaps, are the words of Scrooge's nephew on the meaning of Christmas. He says that it is the only time of the year

> when men and women seem by one consent to open their shut-up hearts freely, and to think of people below them as if they really were fellow-passengers to the grave, and not another race of creatures bound on other journeys.
>
> (Dickens 1918: 14)

This theme of hierarchical relations had two important aspects. One was that Christmas was a time of impersonal charity towards inferiors. This is a noteworthy theme in the book, expressed in the laments of Marley's ghost and in Scrooge's vision after the ghost departs (Dickens 1918: 43, 47–8). Such charity embodies an aspect of the appearance of the autonomous, impersonal individual that I described in Chapter 7. At the same time, however, it reflects old Christian virtues, and carries a clear, hierarchical tone in *A Christmas Carol*. While modern Christmas is still a season marked with charity and concern for the poor, this element is now clearly secondary to the concern for family relationships. Equally, but less obviously, Christmas fellowship of the sort Dickens evoked was a device by which people sought to transcend the class differences and tensions that were of growing importance in England at the time. The British historian Hugh Cunningham argues that the desire to transcend these differences underlay some of the more spectacular efforts to resurrect what some imagined to be the old-style Christmas, "a romantic attempt to re-create a socially-harmonious medieval past" (Cunningham 1980: 101).

Likewise, the older stress on sheer quantity and feasting is strong in the book. Consider the description of a room prepared for the Ghost of Christmas Present:

> Heaped up on the floor, to form a kind of throne, were turkeys, geese, game, poultry, brawn, great joints of meat, suckling-pigs, long wreaths of sausages, mince-pies, plum puddings, barrels of oysters, red-hot

chestnuts, cherry-cheeked apples, juicy oranges, luscious pears, immense twelfth-cakes, and seething bowls of punch, that made the chamber dim with their delicious steam.

(Dickens 1918: 94)

Such sybaritic imagery is reflected in English representations of Father Christmas at the time, for he is commonly portrayed surrounded by great quantities of food and drink (see Golby and Purdue 1986: figs 3.40, 3.41).

Food to the point of sensual, even erotic, excess appears frequently in the book, as when Scrooge is led around to see people spending Christmas:

The poulterers' shops were still half open, and the fruiterers' were radiant in their glory. There were great, round, pot-bellied baskets of chestnuts, shaped like the waistcoats of jolly old gentlemen, lolling at the doors, and tumbling out into the street in their apoplectic opulence. There were ruddy, brown-faced broad-girthed Spanish Onions, shining in the fatness of their growth like Spanish Friars; and winking from their shelves in wanton slyness at the girls as they went by, and glanced demurely at the hung-up mistletoe. There were pears and apples, clustered high in blooming pyramids; there were bunches of grapes, made, in the shopkeeper's benevolence, to dangle from conspicuous hooks, that people's mouths might water gratis as they passed; there were piles of filberts, mossy and brown, recalling, in their fragrance, ancient walks among the woods, and pleasant shufflings ankle deep through withered leaves; there were Norfolk Biffins, squab, and swarthy, setting off the yellow of the oranges and lemons, and, in the great compactness of their juicy persons, urgently entreating and beseeching to be carried home in paper bags and eaten after dinner.

(Dickens 1918: 99–100)

These passages demonstrate the strength of older themes of year-end celebrations in *A Christmas Carol*. The most that can be said is that Dickens marked, not the onset of the modern Christmas, but something more modest, the onset of a transition.

Even so, the transition was rapid. For instance, Christmas Day quickly became a public holiday in the United States – as it did in Britain in 1834, even though some workers preferred New Year (Golby and Purdue 1986: 76). The first state to declare Christmas a holiday did so in 1836. Between 1845 and 1865 twenty-eight states declared it a holiday, even Puritan Massachusetts in 1855 (Golby and Purdue 1986: 76). In 1865 Christmas was declared a national holiday (Jones, C. 1978: 354). Further, it was during the Civil War that the modern image of Santa appeared, from drawings by Thomas Nast published in *Harper's Weekly*. The first of these appeared in 1862 ("Christmas in Camp") and 1863 ("A Christmas Furlough"). Both included Santa Claus and presents, and the latter included the family and a Christmas tree (Jones, C. 1978: 354; see Belk 1987).

What John Golby describes of England in the 1830s supports my general argument about the link between the emergence of familial Christmas and broader social changes. He says that in that decade only two groups had marked Christmas celebrations. One was the gentry, who celebrated Christmas in what I have identified as the old style, with a church service, a feast and small presents to dependants and retainers. The other group was the growing urban bourgeoisie, "the professional, clerical and shopkeeping classes" (Golby 1981: 16). This group was strongly exposed to the growing impersonal commercial sphere. Golby says that it was the members of this group who were the enthusiastic readers of Dickens and celebrants of familial Christmas (see also Pimlott 1978: chs 7, 8).

The cultural influences that I have described were significant because they attracted attention and helped shape modern Christmas symbolism. It is important to remember, however, that the attraction was not Christmas itself. Instead, Christmas was the historical accident around which influential groups of people could construct a festival that celebrated relations within the family that are distinct from relations in the outside world. Evidence that it was the push of motive that was important, rather than the pull of decorated trees and resuscitated Dutch customs, is found in the emergence of a related American celebration, Thanksgiving.

Like Christmas, Thanksgiving is a festival whose history is much shallower than is commonly assumed. And like Christmas, Thanksgiving emerged by the end of the Civil War. Prior to the 1860s there had been thanksgiving days in the United States. However, these were distinctly religious days, proclaimed whenever an event had occurred that called for national prayer and the giving of thanks to God. Prior to the Civil War, the last day of thanksgiving was during the War of 1812 (Sickel 1940: 30). However, in the 1860s Thanksgiving Day became established as an annual holiday not associated with any particular event. During the Civil War days of thanksgiving were resurrected and pressed into political service, just as had happened earlier to St Nicholas, for thanksgiving was linked closely to the Union effort. This is clear in Abraham Lincoln's 1864 proclamation, which enjoined

> all loyal and law abiding people, to assemble at their usual places of worship or wherever they may be: To confess and to repent of their manifold sins; to implore compassion and forgiveness, of the Almighty, that the existing Rebellion may be suppressed and the supremacy of the Constitution and the Laws of the United States may be established throughout all the states; that we as a people may not be destroyed.
>
> (in Sickel 1940: 34)

While these days of thanksgiving may have expressed sorrow at the losses brought by the Civil War, by the end of that war the day had become an anodyne national holiday, fixed at the last Thursday in November, as is illustrated by the beginning of Andrew Johnson's proclamation of 1867: "In conformity with a recent custom that may now be regarded as established on National consent and approval" (in Sickel 1940: 40). Quickly it became particularly identified as a family event, "a reunion of families sanctified and chastened by tender memories and associations; and let the social intercourse of friends, with pleasant reminiscence, renew the ties of affection and strengthen the bonds of kindly feeling" (Grover Cleveland, in Sickel 1940: 40). The emergence of Thanksgiving that I have sketched is an event parallel with the emergence of modern Christmas, both oriented toward a celebration of family relationships in what was increasingly a world of work.

By the end of the 1860s, then, familial Christmas was established in the United States, as well as in Britain (Pimlott 1978: 94). While Christmas was marked by the giving of purchased commodities, especially toys given by parents to children, the appearance of the mass ritual of Christmas shopping was somewhat slower to appear. By the 1870s Christmas shopping appears to have become a marked event in New York City, and stores were beginning to set up special Christmas window displays (Belk 1989: 116; Snyder 1985: 63–70), though as late as the 1880s, presents that people made far out-numbered presents that they purchased (Snyder 1985: 96–8). As I mentioned already, in 1890 *The Ladies' Home Journal* was complaining about the commercialism of Christmas, though in many parts of the country it remained true that "Christmas trade in the 1880s was nothing to get excited about" (Scull 1967: 115). Even department stores in Paris were mounting store-wide Christmas displays by about 1890 (Miller, M. 1981: 169; for England see Pimlott 1978: ch. 11).

There are a number of factors that can help account for the gap between the emergence of familial Christmas and Christmas shopping. One is that social relations in retail trade remained relatively personal for many people through most of the nineteenth century, as I described in Chapter 4. The growing impersonality of the trade around 1900, especially in urban areas, was matched by the growth of suburbs. Modern suburbs began to appear in the second half of the nineteenth century in England and the United States, but became ubiquitous in the first decades of the twentieth century. Not only did they mark a further, clear spatial and cultural separation of home and work (Girouard 1990: ch. 7; Hayden 1980), increasingly they marked the disappearance of the local store and its familiar people and relationships. Thus, at the same time that retail trade was becoming more impersonal, a growing number of people in urban areas were exposed to its more im-personal forms. The spread of this impersonal trade meant that, in novel ways, shopping itself became an important point of contact between the familial and the impersonal worlds, and Christmas shopping became an important way that people constructed and dealt with the distinction between gifts and commodities.

THE SPIRIT OF CHRISTMAS PRESENTS

Christmas is the focal point of the American ritual calendar. Not only is it the time of most intense celebration, it is a time that celebrates the institution that, it seems, lies closest to people's hearts – the family. Everyone goes home for the holidays, even the 24-hour service stations and supermarkets are closed, and no one can be as alone as someone at Christmas with no family to go to.

But as I have shown, there is more to Christmas than the primeval urge to gather around the hearth. The holiday is not the celebration of a thing, the family. Instead, it is a celebration of a relationship, the family in the world beyond. That outside world is part of Christmas, for its existence provides the foil against which people define the family as something distinctive and worth celebrating. In essence, then, Christmas is a celebration of the opposition between the world of the family and the world of work. While Christmas marks and celebrates that opposition, however, it is not a passive reflection of it. Instead, Christmas also heightens that opposition. Family life is not always one of close and enduring affection, any more than economic life is always one of calculating impersonality and transience. At Christmas people simplify the world they face, purify their images of the two realms they inhabit. It is the time of year when people tell each other how warm the family is and how cold is the world outside – for much of the country even the weather conspires to reinforce the message.

Just as the presents that family members give each other around the tree are a central part of Christmas, so those presents are a central part of how Americans celebrate the opposition of Christmas, and even transcend it. These presents are not things people gather casually. Instead, people work hard to pick them out in the crush of Christmas shopping. The result of all that work is the transfiguration of what people buy. The objects cease to be commodities of concern only to stock clerks, advertisers and accountants. Instead, they become gifts, selected to embody the ties between family members. In this transfiguration, people prove to themselves that the world outside may be cold, but it is one that they can keep at bay as they recreate the loving family in the face of a heartless world.

CONCLUSION
Oppositions of Gifts and Commodities

In *The Gift*, Marcel Mauss describes archaic societies, societies of the gift and modern Western societies. His descriptions are animated by a model that links changing ways that people organize and live their lives to changing ways that people understand themselves, others, objects and the relations among them. From Mauss's description of different kinds of society I have drawn a distinction between different kinds of selves, relations, transactions and objects, the distinction between gifts and commodities. I used that distinction in the preceding chapters to guide my presentation of historical changes in production and circulation to describe the important features of modern British and American societies.

In the course of this presentation I introduced terms and concepts from other writers to elaborate and apply the core Maussian perspective. Perhaps unavoidably, the result is a degree of muddle, with "gift", "commodity", "home", "work", "society" and "economy" circling around and against each other in different ways. I want now to impose some terminological order. Doing so will help bring to the fore certain analytical distinctions that these terms mark, but that were obscured in the empirical analysis in this book. These distinctions are not necessarily those intended by the writers whose terms I have borrowed, for they reflect as much the issues raised in my historical presentations as they do the works in which those terms appear.

OPPOSITIONS

As I introduced "gift" and "commodity" in Chapter 1, the pure gift and the pure commodity, like the pure gift relationship and the pure commodity relationship, are polar terms that define a continuum along which one can place existing transactions and relationships. I need to stress the analytical nature of these terms. Because he presents them in the context of empirical descriptions of different societies at different places and times, Mauss roots them in concrete phenomena. However, I have preferred to treat them as ideal types and to assume that their applicability to concrete cases is problematic.

My reservations about the terms spring in part from the very neatness of the opposition they define. As Nicholas Thomas (1991: 15) observed, the gift looks too much like a simple inversion of the commodity, rather than an adequate description of a distinct form of relationship. The main source of my reservations, however, is the context in which Mauss presents them. "Gift" and "commodity" get their meanings from the presentation of different types of societies, a presentation that does not consider the complexities of what goes on within them. Thus, Mauss construes the societies of Eastern Melanesia in terms of an essence that pervades and defines them, "gift", in which "all kinds of institutions are given expression at one and the same time – religious, judicial, and moral, . . . likewise economic" (Mauss 1990: 3). Whatever Mauss's intentions, the implication is that, for these societies, the gift transaction is of such overwhelming importance that nothing else demands our attention. To be fair, however, I must admit that my concern springs as much from the overwhelming stress on gifts in modern Melanesian anthropology as it does from the work of Mauss himself (see Carrier 1992a, 1992c).

This essentialist approach, moreover, also colors Mauss's presentation of the modern West, though obliquely because it is not the main focus of his work. The essence of the West is alienation and autonomous individuals. People are alienated from each other and from the objects around them. Not only are transactors alienated from each other, but the realm in which transaction takes place is itself alienated from other areas of life. Modern Western society is one "of purely individual contract, of the market where money circulates, of sale proper, and above all of the notion of price reckoned in coinage," of the "strict distinction" between "things and persons" (Mauss 1990: 46, 47). Here I caricature Mauss to a degree, for he is uncertain about the nature of the West. In the introduction to *The Gift* he says that gift relations "still function in our own societies, in unchanging fashion", although these relations are "hidden, below the surface" (1990: 4). This uncertainty recurs, as when he says that "societies immediately preceding our own" have "traces" of gift systems (1990: 47), implying that we do not. Likewise, he refers to the "victory of rationalism and mercantilism" in the West (1990: 76; but also see the contrary points he makes on the same page). Mauss describes the existence of gifts in the West at greatest length in the book's conclusion. However, many of his illustrations are reports of decaying practices among French peasantry or of laws that are not enforced (1990: 66–7, 154 n. 5). Where he asserts the existence of gift relations in more central parts of modern society, the uncertainty is clearest and most poignant. Often he seems to be straining to see signs of a resurgence of gift relations in reforms that are always "laboriously in gestation" but have not yet borne fruit (for example 1990: 67–8, 78).

My reservations about the way that Mauss constructs, opposes and uses "gift" and "commodity" do not lead me to reject these terms and the distinctions they express. They are useful and I have applied them throughout

191

this book. However, my reservations do lead me to think that their applicability has to be investigated rather than assumed. In other words, to repeat my point, these terms are analytical tools rather than empirical descriptions.

The second pair of terms is "economy" and "society", which I borrowed and adapted from Jonathan Parry's discussion of Mauss. These terms too are analytical, but they are not so problematic as "gift" and "commodity". I take "economy" to refer to the activities in which people produce and circulate the objects and services that provide the utilities that satisfy their wants, regardless of whether those wants "spring from the stomach or from fancy" (Marx, *Capital*, in Tucker 1978: 303). The realm of the economy is simply the sum of these activities in a given social unit, and economic relations are simply the relationships within which people carry out these activities. "Society", on the other hand, is all other social activities, and, *mutatis mutandis*, the realm of society is the sum of these activities, just as social relations are the relationships within which people carry out those activities.

While "economy" and "society" in the abstract present no particular difficulties, the same cannot be said of efforts to apply them and, particularly, to distinguish between them in real societies. Here, some of the cautions that I mentioned regarding gifts and commodities pertain as well. Parry (1986: 466) is correct to say that Mauss was concerned with the consequences of the progressive disembedding of economy from society, the progressive differentiation of economic from social relationships. In being concerned with disembedding, Mauss was echoing the concern with the differentiation of social institutions that is part of classic social thought, notably in the work of Emile Durkheim. But just what does that differentiation mean in practice? I point to some of what it means in this book: the historical transfer of substantial activities of production and circulation out of the household, the realm of society *par excellence*, into separate commercial institutions. Disembedding and differentiation have occurred, but as I noted repeatedly, they have not been as complete or as uniform as the model and conventional wisdom suggest. This observation leads me to the final pair of terms, "home" and "work".

As I noted in Chapter 5, David Schneider says explicitly that these terms are his summarizing names for the ways that Americans think of two distinctive realms in their lives. Schneider's point is that these terms do not simply name objectively a reality that people confront. Instead, they name people's interpretations, their cultural constructions, of their lives. While Schneider presents "home" and "work" as derivations from modern America, the constructions and the opposition they summarize echo the writers of the Scottish Enlightenment, who distinguished impersonal utilitarian and personal affective relationships.

The purity of home and work, like the strict separation of society and economy, is undercut when we attempt to relate these categories to how people actually live. As I described in Chapter 7, during the nineteenth century a significant amount of economic activity took place within the household using family labor even after more conventional production had moved into a distinct commercial realm. Moreover, it appears that many households, well into the twentieth century, were organized as socio-economic, rather than purely social, units in the manner of the house economy. Consequently, economic and social relations overlapped in them in significant ways, as did people's home and work identities. This pattern is widespread in industrial societies. Carlo Trigilia (1990) describes it for parts of northern Italy, and R. E. Pahl (1984) suggests that in Britain, if not in the modern West as a whole, it is becoming more common. Equally, as Lydia Morris (1990) argues, the identities of men and women within the household are shaped by their work identity, especially whether they are in work or unemployed. Likewise, I have already described how social relationships can carry significant economic loads, as people help their friends, kin and neighbors in various ways.

The cultural construction of home and work, then, resembles the idea that economy and society have become differentiated in modern Western societies. Both make it difficult to see the degree to which the core of the social realm, the household, involves relationships that are both social and economic, and indeed the degree to which many social relationships have a real economic significance. In the second half of this book I described in various ways how the household has continued to contain elements of economic life. However, because of the specific historical issues I addressed in the first half of this book, I did not attend as closely to the corresponding phenomenon, how economy has continued to contain significant elements of social life. I want to do so now, albeit only briefly.

The permeation of the economic realm by social relations is apparent, and perhaps to be anticipated, at the margins of reputable commercial transactions, where the black economy is pervasive. An example is the petty dealing of stolen goods in London's East End. Here, transactions are not impersonal exchanges of material equivalents. Instead, according to Gerald Mars, the giving of a thing is frequently seen as a "favor", one that "has to be repaid, but only when the opportunity arises and only with whatever comes to hand. And 'whatever is at hand' may not be material at all." These transactions, then, entail diffuse, open-ended personal obligations of the sort that characterize home and social relations, with the consequence that the "goods that . . . [are] given have been dematerialized and the transaction has been personalized" (Mars 1982: 173; see also Henry, S. 1976).

These transactions are economic in that they are an important source of the material objects and money that the transactors need. However, transactors often do not act in ways that reflect the logic of the world of work. They do not seek maximum economic advantage, and in fact "money is only a part, and rarely the most important part", of these deals (Mars 1982: 171). Furthermore, such dealings are not between the anonymous transactors linked only fleetingly that characterize the market, but usually involve people who are linked in important ways through ties of kinship, neighborhood, and extensive personal experience, people for whom these transactions are part of the development and maintenance of durable social relations with others. It is these ties that make these transactions obligatory in a way that pure economic transactions are not. People need to offer to transact in order to maintain their social reputations as fully competent members of the community. Indeed, one of the points that Dick Hobbs makes in his study of the East End is that people there who are entrepreneurs, ready to buy and sell anything, cannot be understood in terms of commodity logic, as rational actors in an impersonal market. Instead, they are enacting a moral value:

> For example, when Barry was approached by Vince and offered several hundred yards of high-quality stolen carpet, Barry was not interested, but promised to attempt to find a buyer. Barry could have refused to buy the carpet and left it at that; however it was important that Vince's entrepreneurial abilities be acknowledged, thereby reaffirming the mechanisms and language of exchange as a core organizational device of the indigenous order.

> (Hobbs 1989: 142)

Here, commodity logic is not some residual propensity to truck and barter that finds expression when it is liberated from social constraint. Rather, it is a social value that binds and obligates potential transactors to each other. It is a way that these people maintain personal identities that reflect as much adherence to a set of moral values about "doing the business" (Hobbs 1989) as they do the desire to maintain personal repute or secure the economic means of survival. And beyond this, the entrepreneurial pose, ever ready to do a deal, helps people identify themselves as "trusted insiders as against the threatening outside" (Mars 1982: 175), and so maintain the distinctive social and cultural identity of the group itself, the boundary between it and the larger world.

More mundane and more pervasive than shady deals struck in pubs in the East End is retail trade, and here I need only recall some of the points I made in Chapter 4. There I described how, well into the twentieth century, many people bought and sold as part of enduring personal relations, and their transactions recreated those relations. These are the types of relationship that underlie the appropriation of Personal Shopping, but as Brett Williams (1988: 83–7) describes for the residents of the Adams-Morgan area of Washington, D.C., they remain less a fantasy and more obligatory for many of the poor (see also Fried 1973: 100–1).

One of the reasons that retail trade is distinctive is that it is the point where different forms of transaction are most likely to intersect, that of the household and that of the firm. This intersection is even more pronounced in forms of direct selling. The neighborhood children who knock on the door to sell Girl Scout cookies, chocolates or Christmas wrap are engaged in retail trade but are carrying it out within the framework of a set of social relationships between seller and customer that already exist. This intersection and overlap appear as well in what the anthropologist John Davis (1973: 167–71) describes as "party selling", perhaps most familiar in the United States as the "Tupperware party". Such selling takes place within a number of social, as distinct from economic, frames. It takes place in a party organized for the purpose; the woman, typically, who organizes the party with the help of a company agent is a "hostess"; the people she invites are friends and neighbors; those invited are urged to buy in order to help the hostess. Here too, then, society pervades economy, and a form of retail trade that supports a number of large corporations does not conform to the cultural understanding of "the economy" and market exchange.

Davis (1973: 166) says that this overlap of economic and social relations is pronounced where different areas of life intersect as they do in retail trade. However, durable personal relationships exist as well at times in the heart of capitalism. Ronald Dore's analysis of relations between large firms, primarily in Japan but also in Britain, addresses this issue. Dore notes that manufacturing firms and their suppliers, for example, often see themselves as bound by durable obligations. A manufacturing firm that faces financial problems may call on its suppliers for relief, expecting them to accept lower prices or deferred payment for a time, and suppliers will expect the same sort of support from their manufacturing customers (Dore 1983: 465; see also Creighton 1991). In other words, these firms are not wholly alienated and independent transactors; rather, they are linked in "social relations . . . [that] take on a moral quality and become regulated by criteria of fairness" (1983: 479). Moreover, evidence of these sorts of relatively durable relationships is not restricted to the level of the firm. Studying relations among agents and employees of various American firms, Mark Granovetter found that "continuing economic relations [between agents of different firms] often become overlaid with social content that carries strong expectations of trust and abstention from opportunism" (Granovetter 1985: 490; see also Gambetta 1988).

Finally, and recalling a point I made in Chapter 2, the relationships among people within firms need not match the impersonality of the world of work, but can have a clear social dimension. For example, much of the New England fishing fleet recruits crew and investment capital among family members, a pattern that has been expanding over the past few decades at the expense of ships organized in terms of commodity relations (Doeringer, Moss and Terkla 1986). As I described in Chapter 2, David Halle (1984: 5–6) found that the American blue-collar chemical workers he studied were frequently linked to their co-workers not just by virtue of common ties to their employer but by kin and affinal ties with one another. Here Halle confirms in the context of American working-class life of the 1970s what Michael Young and Peter

Willmott (1986: 73–6) argued for English working-class life of the 1950s: when there is competition for work, a person on the job can help a relative get into the firm. In such a situation, co-workers are likely to be kin, and social relations are likely to pervade the impersonal relations that are supposed to exist in the firm. Furthermore, as Margaret Grieco (1987: 37–41) argues, this is not a subversion of economic rationality. Rather, in many circumstances firms prefer to recruit the kin of their existing workers for good commercial reasons.

But even to see work relations among strangers as being impersonal relations among autonomous individuals can be misleading. Rather, the older notion of the situated self seems apt. To pursue a point I made in Chapter 7, transactions among co-workers allow little autonomy in any straightforward sense. Sid the maintenance worker does not freely decide to adjust the machinery of Doris the production worker because Doris will give something valuable in return in the manner of a market transaction. Instead, an important basis of Sid's work is that he is the occupant of a position in a structure that defines his relationship with Doris and their obligations toward each other. The fact that Sid and Doris may have decided autonomously to become maintenance and production workers, and the fact that they may have got their jobs through the impersonal labor market, do not mean that their identities and relationships with each other at work resemble the autonomous individuals who are supposed to populate the economic realm.

It is well, however, not to be swept away by the idea that social relations pervade the world of commercial production and circulation. The histories I presented in Chapters 2, 3 and 4 show that these relations are much less important than they used to be. Personal relationships may link many modern workers, as they may link many modern shop clerks and customers. However, these links do little more than pervade a structure determined by employers. Things were quite different before the middle of the eighteenth century, when durable personal relations did not overlay economic relationships, but constituted and shaped them.

In spite of this qualification, it is true that many economic activities, important for people's survival in modern Western countries, depart from the purified rendering of the realm of work and of an economy fully differentiated from society. The social relationships that are part of the economic activities that I described may be shaped by and subordinated to a more powerful and more purely economic structure and logic. However, this is not grounds for dismissing what I have described as trivial either for people's experiences or for the operation of society as a whole. Further, to call the existence of social relations in the economic realm archaic is only to presuppose the validity of the construction of modern Western economy that is at issue. The co-existence, indeed the mutual if unequal penetration and subversion, of social and economic relations means that each is shaped by the other. Even if Western economic systems follow economic logic in the last analysis, elevating that last analysis to an analytical first principle will needlessly and wrongly simplify a complex form of life.

To treat Western economic life in purely economic terms, as the writers of the Scottish Enlightenment and their successors have done, makes sense only on cultural, rather than empirical, grounds. The "economy" of most economists, then, resembles the sociologists' "social exchange" that I described in Chapter 7. Both are little more than common culture writ large, Christmas fantasies taken too seriously (Davis, J. 1992: 18–19). The complex nature of relationships between parents and children, as well as of the relationships between neighbors, kin and friends, makes a nonsense of Adam Ferguson's declaration that personal relationships that are important for people's material survival are "sordid" (in Silver 1990: 1484) and makes a nonsense of his assertion that people see those relationships only in terms of greed and material benefit. Ferguson's assertion does not describe reality as much as it expresses moral outrage at the mixing of cultural categories that need to be kept apart. Such relationships may be dirty, but only in Mary Douglas's (1966) sense of matter out of place.

The belief that the public, economic realm is dominated by autonomous, possessive individuals (Macpherson 1962) is as common among scholars as it is more generally. Indeed, this belief is part of their intellectual inheritance. Many social thinkers of the nineteenth century and the first decades of the twentieth sought to identify the distinguishing genius of the modern West, as did Mauss himself. Though their results are somewhat different, from my perspective they paint pictures that are almost identical. The modern West is the land of *Gesellschaft*, contract, instrumental rationality, organic solidarity, bourgeois individualism. These notions are embedded deeply in social thought, as well as common sense, and it is hard to escape them.

But of course dead intellectual ancestors wrote about many things that living thinkers find boring or even wrong. Granted that these notions form a coherent and impressive theme in Western intellectual patrimony, the question remains, why is that theme accepted and absorbed so readily? More generally, why do people distinguish economy and society, home and work, in such an exaggerated way? In the balance of this chapter I want to suggest some answers to what is really two related questions: Why is the distinction so marked? Why is it drawn in the way it is?

It is true, as I have noted repeatedly, that there have been significant changes in the nature of domestic and economic life. In other words, while the distinction people draw may be ideological, it is by no means pure fancy. But if drawing a distinction is reasonable, why draw it so sharply? This sharp distinction resembles the ways that Pacific Islanders have drawn distinctions between themselves and the encroaching, colonizing Western world. The anthropological research on this topic may help explain what has happened in the West.

Nicholas Thomas suggests that producing a distinctive self-definition that stands opposed to one's definition of others "takes place in a particularly marked and conspicuous fashion in the course of colonial history" (1992b: 65). Crudely put, colonization commonly entails the relatively rapid juxtaposition of two forms of social life that previously were unrelated and mutually unknown. It is, then, not surprising that the colonized would define themselves in opposition to what they perceive of the encroaching colonists. The relatively rapid emergence of capitalist enterprise may have had comparable effects in Britain and the United States. Further, Thomas argues that this process of self-definition exaggerates the difference between the self and the other entity with which it is contrasted. In his discussion of Fiji, Thomas (1992a, 1992b) says islanders came to draw a distinction between what they saw as their own equalitarian "way of the land" and what they saw as the selfish Western "way of money". Thomas is not arguing that these characterizations were accurate descriptions of what Fijians experienced of themselves or the Westerners that they knew. Rather, they are taken to embody essential truths. The analogy seems apt. The Western constructions of home and work are not, as Schneider reminds us, accurate descriptions, but ways of expressing a fundamental distinction. The opposition of the calculating individual to the loving relative identifies in heightened form features that are taken to distinguish home and work in important ways.

This invocation of Pacific anthropology can help explain why the distinction between home and work, economy and society, is drawn so sharply. It does not, however, help answer my second question: Why are these opposed realms given the distinguishing features that they have? There are several reasons that help explain this. John Davis puts forward a relatively simple one in his criticism of assumptions of economistic rationality (1992: ch. 6). There he suggests that the state's need to have visible and hence taxable economic transactions encourages a general stress on monetary calculation in economic activities, at the expense of the recognition of more social and symbolic processes.

Nancy Hartsock suggests an additional reason in her criticism of sociological models of social relations, and especially the predominance of the autonomous actor in these models. To put it most simply, she argues that the autonomous actor is a reasonably accurate reflection of the experience of those in dominant positions in society.[1]

One pertinent dimension on which people can be dominant is that of the market, the home of the autonomous actor. However, Max Weber argued long ago that not all market actors are in a position to act autonomously. The ability to do so is, he said, generally restricted to the dominant, propertied classes, if only because they are not driven to the market by sheer, insistent necessity. The propertyless, however, lack such resources and have no such leisure. They are obliged to transact, and particularly to sell their labor, "in order barely to subsist" (Weber, M. 1946: 182).

Basil Bernstein's studies of working-class families in Bethnal Green around

1960 (especially Bernstein 1971) address more directly the degree to which the autonomous actor reflects the perspective and experience of some classes rather than others. The families that Bernstein studied overwhelmingly were involved in the same sorts of occupation and their social and work lives tended to be restricted to their immediate and very densely populated area in Bethnal Green. The result, reminiscent of Durkheim's description of societies of mechanical solidarity, was a high degree of shared experience, exaggerated in Bethnal Green because people's co-workers were likely to be their neighbors, social companions and even their kin. This complex of factors produced what Bernstein called a "positional orientation", in which people identified themselves and others in terms of their positions in an over-arching and encompassing web of social relations. He distinguished that from what he called a "personal orientation". This, he said, was characteristic of the more mobile and wealthier members of English middle-class families, who identified themselves and each other as independent entities.

Bernstein develops his distinction from the especially homogeneous area of Bethnal Green. However, other scholars have described orientations that echo the ones that he identifies. One such is Alexandra Ouroussoff (1993), in her study of the pseudonymous British corporation, Bion. She found that Bion managers construe themselves as autonomous individuals rationally pursuing their goals. On the other hand, she reports that the firm's workforce commonly saw themselves as defined by their positions in a web of social relationships, a web that determined, among other things, that they would be workers rather than managers.

Those who have Bernstein's personal orientation are more likely to conceive of themselves as having a self that transcends the different areas of their lives. As a corollary, members of the middle class, with their personal orientation, are more likely to make friends among co-workers. Members of the lower class, with their positional orientation, are likely to restrict their sociable relations to specific contexts, though where those contexts overlap, as they did in Bethnal Green, social relations will appear to be more general. Evidence supports this argument. John Goldthorpe and his colleagues studied households in Luton, England, an industrial new town without the integrated and self-contained communities that existed in Bethnal Green. They found that while less than one-fifth of the people that couples identified as friends were also workmates, "white-collar couples draw more heavily on friends made through work" than do blue-collar couples (1969: 90; see also Hunt and Satterlee 1986). Likewise, the British sociologist Graham Allan (1979: 70), drawing on a range of published studies and his own work, suggests that members of the working class tend to "limit their sociable relations [to] particular social contexts and structures". In other words, workmates remain workmates and tend not to become friends; and indeed, the middle-class notion of "friend" may not be very applicable to their social relationships.

Bernstein's argument about the different orientations of the middle and lower classes finds support as well in the study by J. Bussey and his colleagues of the giving of presents by people in Bradford, England. The researchers found that higher-class respondents were more likely to account for the giving by saying it was the spontaneous expression of autonomous sentiment, emotion and affection. On the other hand, lower-class respondents were more likely to explain giving by reference to the expectations of others and the dictates of the situation in which they found themselves (Bussey *et al.* 1967: 61, 67).

The Bethnal Green families that Bernstein studied were of the lower working class, and their experiences were a dimension of their class position. However, in the main the factors that concern Bernstein are part of the broader characteristics of people's experiences of each other and their world. Nancy Hartsock herself illustrates the link between these broader character-istics and the notion of the autonomous self, though she links them to gender. Hartsock says that women generally are compelled to work more than men. Not only do they labor for a wage, the prevailing division of labor by gender in the West means that they also maintain the household and reproduce humanity in their children. In addition to being obliged to work more, the work that women do is different from that of men. Particularly in their domestic labor women are involved in relationships that are more durable, more complex and less discretionary, than the "simple cooperation with others for common goals" (Hartsock 1985: 64) that she says characterizes the work experience of men in the middle classes. As she summarizes her argument, women in their labors experience "a complex, relational world" rather than one of isolated individuals, and their interactions with others are not voluntary: "[T]hose in charge of small children have little choice" (1985: 65, 66). Hartsock is not alone in making this point. For instance, she echoes Nancy Chodorow's (1978) psychoanalytic argument that because sons, but not daughters, must repress their early identification with their mothers, so men more than women come to see themselves as autonomous individuals.

Hartsock's basic point, then, is that the autonomous actor is not a fiction, but predominantly inhabits only particular class and gender locations, locations that are treated deferentially in Western society and taken to define social identity and relationships in academic understandings of social ex-change (see the similar argument in Ouroussoff 1993). Helga Dittmar reviews a mass of studies from social psychology that point to the same conclusion. As Dittmar (1992: 182) says, "a congruence exists between the Western dominant construction of identity as self-determined agency and the reality of belonging to affluent circles."

Hartsock's argument can be extended to include the idea that economic relations exist in a realm that is distinct from social relations. Such an idea is likely to match the experiences of the better-off sections of society that, historically, have been the source of the academics who produce and evaluate such models. The suburban family supported by a single wage may have been a common goal, but for many the goal was elusive, as I argued in Chapter 7. Indeed, in the United States the decay in individual wage levels that has occurred since the 1970s has meant that many households that had achieved the goal lost it again, as the re-emergence of home-working, both as a fact and a topic of academic interest, testifies (e.g. Allen and Wolkowitz 1987; Boris and Daniels 1989).

OPPOSITIONS IN CONTEXT

I have suggested that the dominant, public constructions of home and work are ideological, reflecting the situation of dominant social groups and the ability of those groups to promulgate their own viewpoints as authoritative. The autonomous self and the differentiation of social and economic realms, however, are more than just the experience of those in dominant social locations writ large. In addition, they are part of a broader understanding of modern Western society. This broader understanding emerges from a consideration of the modern West in context. Social thinkers did not, after all, contemplate the West in isolation. Rather, they considered it in context, which meant, either explicitly or implicitly, in relation to non-Western societies and to the West's own past. So, just as home does not seem to exist in people's understandings except in distinction from work, so the modern West of intellectual contemplation does not seem to have existed except in distinction from its opposite.

Mauss's work is useful for illustrating the complexities and consequences of this process, for just as he construed the West in relation to its opposite, so he construed that "opposite" in terms of the West. In *The Gift*, the societies of eastern Melanesia, the Maori, and the people of the Pacific Northwest, with their diversity and complexity, become simplified into unitary and essential categories, "archaic society" and "society of the gift", of which each specific society is only an exemplar. In this, Mauss's work manifests what Edward Said (1978) calls "orientalism", the tendency to reduce the complexity of alien societies to a mirror-image of the West. Mauss's work also, however, manifests an inverse and complementary tendency that Said does not describe, "occidentalism", the tendency to reduce the complexity of Western societies to a mirror image of alien societies (Carrier 1992c).

Taken together, orientalism and occidentalism indicate that scholars like Mauss define the West and alien societies in the way that many Westerners define home and work. These are definitions by dialectical opposition, one that focuses on and heightens distinguishing features, and so exaggerates difference and denies similarity. That Mauss exaggerated is illustrated by the fact that the societies in Melanesia that he describes did in fact have impersonal transactions between autonomous transactors, most notably in local markets where people from different villages traded for each other's produce. Such impersonal markets may well have been less significant in these societies than impersonal markets were in France in the 1920s when Mauss wrote *The Gift*. Mauss's process of dialectical opposition, however, converted a difference of degree into a difference of kind: the West has impersonal markets and autonomous actors, the societies of Melanesia do not.

This twinned orientalism and occidentalism is not restricted to *The Gift*, but is common in the classic attempts to define the modern West that are an important part of the background of modern social thought. I said earlier that the West is construed as the land of *Gesellschaft*, contract, instrumental rationality, organic solidarity, bourgeois individualism. While different writers have used each of these terms and phrases to describe the modern West in slightly different ways, none of these terms or phrases is an only child. Instead, each is part of the same dialectical opposition contained in Mauss's distinction between gifts and commodities. And like Mauss's distinction, each is embedded in an evolutionary frame that evaluates the differences between the here and now of the modern West and the long ago and far away of alien and primitive societies (see Carrier 1992b; Fabian 1983).

Chris Fuller has described this process of dialectical opposition in the work of Louis Dumont. Dumont has tried at length to discover the distinguishing genius of both the modern West and an exemplary non-Western civilization, India, in *Homo Hierarchicus*. As a result, says Fuller (1989: 55), Dumont has "developed and elaborated the contrast between holistic interdependence, said to characterise [India's] jajmani [system], and individualist exclusive rights, characteristic of capitalist market systems". But as Fuller describes, in doing so Dumont has taken the corpus of information on Indian society and selected particular parts as containing the essence of India, while ignoring the rest. Furthermore, Dumont does not derive this essence empirically in terms of its relative weight in the available information. Instead, says Fuller, Dumont derives it dialectically: "[T]he concept of the traditional [Indian] economy has been generated as a negative of the modern by isolating and defining the traits which are *not* characteristic of Western economies" (1989: 56). Though Fuller does not make the point, I would add that Dumont's conception of Western economies, elaborated in *From Mandeville to Marx*, is shaped in turn by its antithesis, his understanding of Indian tradition.

Thus it is that the notions of the autonomous individual and the separation of economy and society rest on a solid cultural foundation. They are not simply generalizations of the experience of dominant Western groups; they are also the West talking to itself about itself and its dominance in the world. These two sorts of dominance are, of course, intertwined in practice, as dominant Western groups can present themselves as embodying and protecting the dominance of the West.

At this point, these rhetorics of dominance can enter into Western political debate, as they did so forcefully in the conservative resurgence in Britain and America in the 1980s. Conservatives in government and out pointed to different Western institutions that did not facilitate what they saw as crucial Western attributes of autonomy and separation, and defined those institutions as archaic, not up to date, and dangerous. These institutions needed to be abolished or brought into the modern world by a healthy injection of market discipline. The same thing happened to those people who do not manifest and espouse autonomy and separation. They are backward and need to be put in a more proper environment that will lead them to develop their autonomous self-reliance.

Autonomy and reliance on the impersonal market, then, are taken to define the genius of the modern West in opposition to societies in other times and places, at the same time that they define the genius of successful Westerners in opposition to the unsuccessful, as they make their dominance legitimate and even valuable. An illustration of this perspective is the rhetoric that sees both the cause and core evil of poverty as dependency. An article by the newspaper columnist William Raspberry (1986), reporting the arguments of a populist academic, John McKnight, shows this linkage. In Raspberry's condensation of McKnight's arguments (see, e.g., Chandler 1985), a key failure of American social policy is that it seeks to identify and fill the needs of the poor, and so leads them to depend passively upon welfare programs for their survival. Such programs, in other words, undercut people's autonomy and encourage them to see as the source of their subsistence their social identity as needy citizens of the polity. (The dependence of the rich on state subsidies and protections escapes scrutiny.)

Raspberry, and through him McKnight, urge an alternative, the "capacity" approach. Here, the poor are to be encouraged to see themselves as autonomous market transactors and to survive by their wages. In the tale that Raspberry relates, poor black women advertised themselves as home health-care workers, and found a ready demand for their labor. In Raspberry's and McKnight's definition of a problem and proposed solution, an injection of autonomy and independence cures the ills of client-hood and moves people from the ranks of failures to the ranks of successes. What makes Raspberry and McKnight particularly interesting is that they frame their argument in the larger rhetoric of the move from alien primitive to modern Western civilization. They do so when they say the dependent poor are like benighted New Guinea villagers, "pitiful 'cargo cultists'" (Raspberry 1986: 11) who tragically, yet foolishly, expect goods to rain down on them from the skies (see generally Lindstrom 1993: ch. 6, who shows the breadth of the uses of the term "cargo cult" in modern America).

The twinned definitions of the modern West and all the rest that I have described have distinct advantages beyond the self-laudatory rhetoric they allow people to produce and believe. Most importantly, they allow people to simplify the complex reality that they confront, and reduce it to manageable proportions. However, these definitions also have costs, for they may make it harder for people to understand the world around them, rather than easier.

A simple example is the nature of capitalist markets, and especially the notion of autonomous and calculating market actors, the vehicles that are supposed to bring about the most efficient allocation of resources. The laudatory self-definition that I have described makes it difficult to see the ways that market rationality is, as Davis argues, a rhetoric (Davis, J. 1992: ch. 6; see also Holy 1992: 234–5). Its connection with real markets and market actors needs to be demonstrated rather than assumed. And, as the contributors to Dilley (1992) show, that demonstration often is difficult. There are more complex instances of the difficulty this powerful self-definition can generate.

In *Sovereign Individuals of Capitalism*, Nicholas Abercrombie, Stephen Hill and Bryan Turner present a prime example. They argue that an important feature of the modern Western understanding of its own success in the world is linked to its understanding of capitalism. Many commentators see capitalism as the most successful motor of power and economic prosperity, and as distinctly marked by autonomous individuals. This historical trajectory, presented by commentators at least from Marx onward, has linked these elements in a developmental process. However, Abercrombie, Hill and Turner point out that the equation is misleading, so that the progressive trajectory implicit in the equation of capitalism and individualism is suspect.

They note (Abercrombie, Hill and Turner 1986: 115–16) that English capitalism through the middle of the nineteenth century flourished by relying on familial structures and resources, as do Leonore Davidoff and Catherine Hall (1987: part 2) at length and in detail. However, their main criticism of the equation and its trajectory rests on their discussion of modern Japan (1986: 121–31). They point out that by any reasonable definition, Japan is a capitalist country. For all its economic success and growing power, however, Japan's capitalism does not entail, much less rest on, autonomous individualism (see also Dore 1992; Rohlen 1973). Indeed, as I described briefly in Chapter 8, the Japanese do not separate the economic and social spheres sharply. Of course, it can be argued that the growth of Japan's economic power since World War II has been accompanied by the decay of Japanese peculiarity. However, the triumph of Western individualism in Japan is distinguished more by its imminence than its arrival, as Millie Creighton's (1991) discussion of recurrent waves of Japanese "internationalism" and the persistence of extended households (Morgan and Hirosima 1983) suggest. The Japanese example suggests that the heady, felicitous trajectory contained in Western twinned orientalism and occidentalism is not so certain as these dialectical constructions imply.

At the other end of the evolutionary scale as well, things do not appear so simple as these models suggest. Summarizing the work of a number of anthropologists in such societies, Maurice Bloch and Jonathan Parry (1989: 23–30) describe the existence of what they call two transactional orders. The existence of these orders indicates that in many simpler societies there is a more purely social sphere that is distinguished from an impersonal and more purely economic sphere. In other words, the differentiation of economy and society does not seem to be limited to modern Western societies.

The more purely social sphere is one in which transactions between people "are concerned with the reproduction of the long-term social or cosmic order" (1989: 24). This can be the household itself, the polity, stable hierarchical orders of various sorts, or the like. What is important is not the particular institution that is involved. Instead, the distinguishing feature of this realm is that people transact to celebrate and recreate a durable structure of relationships of which they are a part. This is what we do at Christmas. At the individual level we celebrate and recreate the family and our particular parts in it; at the collective level we celebrate and recreate the family as a form of social life, one that many people see as the foundation of the social order itself.

Bloch and Parry say the impersonal, more purely economic sphere is one "of short-term transactions concerned with the arena of individual competition" (1989: 24). This is not simply a realm of competitive commerce. It is also the realm of self-indulgence, luxury and individualistic pleasures. Here people exist and deal with each other in relative independence of any enduring relationships with or obligations to each other. Here the goal of their transactions with each other is personal reward, and often people decline to deal with kin in this sphere, for the self-centered acquisitiveness that characterizes such dealings conflicts with the obligations people owe to their relatives.

This model of the two transactional spheres does not simply point out similarities between what Mauss had identified as qualitatively distinct types of society. In addition, it suggests that in societies of these different types people can confront similar problems, among them the transformation of things acquired in the individualistic and short-term sphere into a form suitable for use in the social and long-term sphere. For example, Janet Carsten (1989) describes how Malay fishing families convert the wealth acquired in trade for their catch into a family form through a ritualized cooking. This is the process of appropriation, which I have described at length and which I said was one of the things celebrated in Christmas.

I have described some of the many things that are denied or made difficult to see by the dominant public view of the essence and distinction of the West as calculating, autonomous rationality. I do not claim that there are no differences between modern Western societies and societies of the gift, of Gemeinschaft, of mechanical solidarity, of status and all the rest. There are differences, and they are striking. However, it is too easy to become beguiled by those differences, to elevate them to the level of essential, opposed identities. The allure of absolute difference, of the distinctiveness of the modern West from all the rest, makes it hard to see similarities among different types of society, just as it makes it hard to see differences within a single type.

Much has been written recently of the dangers to anthropologists of essentializing visions of non-Western societies. Less has been written recently of the dangers to people in the West of their essential vision of themselves. If anthropologists err and distort in their academic descriptions of villages in Africa or Latin America, little serious or permanent damage is done. However, if Westerners govern themselves and attempt to impose policies on others on the basis of the rhetoric I have described, they do not just denigrate the reality that many people experience. More importantly, they impose laws and policies that necessarily and knowingly disrupt and damage the lives of those people, justified by the claim that ultimate gain will result (Stirrat 1992). But the gain is suspect, because people are being obliged to conform to an image that is not even valid. Mauss's poignant vision of a West where gift identities and relationships exist and are recognized may help protect us from this fate.

NOTES

INTRODUCTION

1 Obviously there are sociologists and anthropologists whose work on consumption does not fit into either of these two main approaches. Some of the more interesting include the contributors to Silverstone and Hirsch (1992) and to Löfgren (1990b), especially Friedman (1990), Löfgren (1990a) and Miller, D. (1990).

2 Appropriation and possession should interest those who see objects in terms of public structures, for their work presumes that people appropriate objects and their sign values. However, with the exception of Daniel Miller, these writers rarely consider the issue. Those few who do touch on it do so only cursorily (e.g. McCracken 1988: 85–6).

CHAPTER 1

1 In spite of a growing interest in the social meaning of objects, sumptuary laws have attracted little attention. Frances Baldwin is exhaustive on English laws, and some of her comments (esp. 1926: 23) faintly echo my point. A briefer source is Wilfred Hooper (1915), who deals only with Tudor laws.

CHAPTER 2

1 The book has attracted criticism, but generally on theoretical and interpretative, rather than empirical, grounds (e.g. Anderson, M. 1976; Calhoun 1982: 191–6). Michael Anderson (1976: 325) does raise doubts about the ubiquity of the family-based production units that Smelser describes for early spinning factories, which I discuss in the section "Early Factory Production", but he asserts equally that such a pattern was common in a range of industries (1976: 320, 325).

2 Joan Thirsk (1978) suggests the existence of regional, and possibly national, markets in England in the seventeenth century, and doubtless some producers preferred a more standardized and predictable market for their wares. However, the high level of rural English population that cottage production and putting out supported encouraged strong demand for local products (Sabel and Zeitlin 1985: 168). Consequently, much cottage production was for local consumption, bought and sold in regulated local markets in a web of long-standing personal relationships (see Chapter 3). This personal framework for the disposition of goods disappeared with the rise of putting out.

3 This collective control of work did not disappear in the first quarter of the

nineteenth century, as Katherine Stone's (1975) description of the organization of American steel production before the 1890s shows. More strikingly, Graeme Salaman's (1986: 45–54) description of the organization of fire stations in the London Fire Brigade prior to 1981 echoes Rule's description of craft workers. Firemen at a station had a strong common identity: they were self-recruited, they came from a narrow cultural and social background, they spent extended periods of time in each other's company, and they were relatively free of external supervision. In 1981 this cohesive body of autonomous skilled workers came under attack in the pursuit of equity by the Greater London Council, their governing body. The fire service was almost totally white and male, and the Greater London Council issued an Equal Opportunity directive that led to the increased supervision of local stations and the centralized recruitment of new fire-fighters.

CHAPTER 3

1 Localism meant also that people's tastes differed markedly, even over short distances. Gordon Selfridge, the American founder of Selfridges department store in London, noted around 1900 that taste in England was so variable "that what will sell freely in one town will not sell at all in another town only a few miles away" (Darby 1928: 11–12). The strength of local structures, even in urban areas, persisted well into the twentieth century. A study of Glasgow in mid-century showed that 80 percent of households were within 400 yards of a local shopping area, and a further 13 percent were within a half-mile (Chapman 1955: 188).

2 As well, trade could take place at the home of the buyer. People bought from or employed itinerant artisans, like tailors (Mui and Mui 1989: 36), as they bought from the growing number of rural pedlars, hawkers and Scotch drapers. Although legal restrictions on itinerant traders eased around 1700 (Beier 1985: 173), not much is known about pedlars and hawkers in this early period (but see Agnew 1986: 48). However, by the nineteenth century many of them were regular visitors who sold on credit to an established body of customers (Davis, D. 1966: 243–4; Rubin 1986) or who owned or represented shops in near-by market towns and circulated only in local villages (Brown 1986: 51–2). The true passing stranger seems to have been rare.

3 It is worth noting the relationship between this impersonal trade and the "money-back guarantee". Chroniclers of American retail trade in the nineteenth century claim that the appearance of the guarantee marked a strengthening of the relationship of store and customer (e.g. Darby 1928: 133; Hower 1938: 95; Resseguie 1965: 311–12; Walsh, W. 1986: 20), as modern commentators tout it for the same reason (e.g. Hawken 1987: 54). Doubtless they are right in some circumstances. However, the very statement of such a guarantee presupposes the alienation between retailer, object and customer, and the orientation toward an anonymous market, that I describe in this chapter. This is apparent in the description (Mui and Mui 1989: 243) of early guarantees in England in the eighteenth century, associated with impersonal, advertised commodities.

CHAPTER 4

1 It is true, of course, that customers could buy without even entering a shop. "If customers went by their own private transport business was often done outside the shop. As one lady [the daughter of a vicar] recalls, 'I remember driving into Ashford [Kent] in the dog cart and we stopped outside the fishmonger. He would

come out in his striped apron and ask what we wanted. We'd just sit there and he'd go and get it and put it in the cart and we'd go again. That happened in most shops. Practically nobody went into a shop at all. My mother never set foot in a butcher's shop in her life. I didn't until after the war, the last war [World War II]'" (Winstanley 1983: 53). While this practice avoided the physical intimacy of the small shop, it embodies the personal attention that makes the physical intimacy important.

2 This qualifies an argument put forward by Grant McCracken (1988: 26). Drawing on Rosalind Williams's (1982: esp. 92) study of Parisian department stores, he says that department-store credit was an important innovation in the nineteenth century that generated the desire for objects, because it made it easier for people to buy their dreams. Because store credit was disappearing during this period, McCracken's point seems incorrect. If credit were instrumental in encouraging consumption, then the eighteenth century and before would have been the high age of mass consumption. If department stores were part of a credit innovation, it was of impersonal credit of the modern form.

3 Simplification and feminization do not necessarily go hand in hand. In the middle of the nineteenth century, A. T. Stewart "is said to have employed the handsomest men he could obtain because he observed that women liked to converse and even to flirt with male clerks" (Hower 1938: 94).

4 In a modern illustration of indistinguishability, Woolfolk, Castellan and Brooks (1983) found that those who cannot see the label are unlikely to be able to distinguish Coca-Cola and Pepsi Cola. For cost, Morton Salt told retailers early in the twentieth century that the higher price of their brand over bulk salt was necessary to pay for advertising (Strasser 1989: 195). Advertisers tied themselves into some interesting logical knots trying to justify the higher costs that advertising required (Cherington 1913: chs 5, 13).

CHAPTER 5

1 Indeed, it is not even clear that he faithfully reports and summarizes what people think. One anthropologist asked Schneider in a seminar if he could have written *American Kinship* without any of the interviews on which he said he based his analysis. "The reaction was first a long pause. Then he answered, hesitantly, 'The answer is "yes". The ideas did not derive from the project, and I could have written the book without any of the interviews. But I checked every single idea with all the interview data before I finished the book'" (Gullestad 1990: 38). Likewise, though Parsons appears to describe Western societies, the reality often conflicts with his model (see, e.g., Pleck 1976). It may be best to treat him as well as his own best informant.

2 This echoes a passage by Ernest Beaglehole (1932: 142) that makes the same point: "Using a tool or weapon continuously, the savage got to know its peculiarities, whether the arrow must be aimed high or low, whether the bow shot true or the drill bit deep. He became familiar with the tool, he had a lively sense perhaps of the time and trouble required to replace a broken weapon, and thus gradually a sentiment would be built up about the object – familiarity, pride in efficient working, tradition or myth, centred upon a weapon would forge close psychological bonds."

3 Ernest Dichter, mentioned in this passage, appears to have been a guiding force behind *The Hidden Persuaders*, as is evident in the many parallels between Packard's book and what Dichter wrote elsewhere (e.g. Dichter 1947, 1964). Dichter may have been his own main informant (Caplow, pers. comm.), but his

cultural sense rings true. What he says about the importance of cooking for celebrating and recreating family identities and relationships is echoed by others (e.g. the papers in Murcott 1983c).

CHAPTER 6

1 Paul Hawken strongly advocates this personalization of the company in terms of its owners. His *Growing a Business* illustrates this and many of the points I make throughout this book about the cultural construction and opposition of home and work. More immediately, his book illustrates another form of the symbolism of possession. In it he constructs an image of the ideal kind of business that is markedly fetishized, echoing the fetishism of capitalist images of money and commerce that Michael Taussig (1977) describes. For Hawken, a firm is not a set of impersonal relationships between individuals, objects and activities. Instead (Hawken 1987: 61) it has a soul and persona, a genius that derives from its owner. The ideal business is "something that is deep within you, something that can't be stolen because it is uniquely yours . . . . It's not basically different from writing a novel. A good business and a good novel are faithful and uncluttered expressions of yourself."

2 Here Hawken exemplifies what Jean Baudrillard (1981: 53–7) calls the "alibi" of use value. Baudrillard says that the sign value of an object is never enough to justify its existence or acquisition. Instead, this value is mystified and partially hidden by overt attention to use value. (To a degree, this echoes Veblen's observation that the tendency to acquire objects for conspicuous consumption is tempered by the instinct for workmanship, which obliges us to choose suitable and well-made objects.) In effect, Baudrillard says that the symbolism of possession surrounding a commodity is not a sufficient, legitimate reason for buying it. It needs to appeal on other and more utilitarian grounds as well.

CHAPTER 7

1 To recall a point I made briefly in Chapter 1, Emerson's "common gift" resonates with what Francesca Cancian (1986) says is a relatively male and relatively lower-class way of expressing affection, doing instrumental favors and giving instrumental help. This suggests that the radical separation of the sentiment and its vehicle is not a cultural constant. Rather, and to anticipate a point I make later, people appear to vary in systematic ways in the degree to which they adhere to the ideology expressed in "it's the thought that counts".

2 While the type of relationship that concerns me is social, relationships with God, the gods or nature might be pertinent, as Kenneth Burke (1969: esp. 138–46) argues is the case with Spinoza. Burke sees Spinoza as a pivotal historical figure. By stressing the relationship of people and things to a constant God, Spinoza made it possible to eliminate this relationship as invariant and hence unrevealing. What remained were individual sources of being and motive.

3 Campbell's (1987) analysis of cultural changes in the eighteenth and nineteenth centuries also bears on the ideological notion of the disembodied gift. He says that during this time English Romantics created an illusory, imaginative world of symbol and meaning that is distinct from and added on to the physical nature of objects and experiences. Associated with this was an almost Platonist disjunction between the material and ideal worlds. The material world is that of imperfect appearances, false, and hence displeasing in important ways. The ideal world, on

the other hand, is an eternal world of goodness and beauty. Doubtless the way that these Romantics subordinated objects to sentiments helped shape the ideology of the disembodied gift.

4 Silver's rendering of Ferguson may be overdrawn. Hirschman and Duncan Forbes see Ferguson as a more ambivalent character. Of the leading figures of the Scottish Enlightenment, only Ferguson, a Highlander, had direct experience of the clan system that these writers derided. This made him especially aware of the costs of the emerging commercial society and particularly critical of "the negative effects of the division of labor and commerce on the personality and social bonds of the individual citizen" (Hirschman 1977: 120). As Forbes (1966: xxix) put it: "Whereas Smith could only see the external bonds of the clan system . . . and the economic dependence of the clansmen, Ferguson knew the inner bonds".

5 Both were equally happy to support the brutal suppression of those who challenged Polite dominance. This was, after all, the same Polite Society that produced Butcher Cumberland and the battle of Culloden. Indeed, it seems difficult to believe that the writers of the Scottish Enlightenment and the advocates of Polite Society did not occasionally look over their shoulders apprehensively at the Stuart claimants and their supporters among the Highland clans.

CHAPTER 8

1 Russell Belk reports a study of adults in Philadelphia in 1973 that showed a very different pattern: the main recipient was "friend" (33 percent of cases) and there was no difference between "child/child-in-law" and "sibling/sibling-in-law" (12 percent) (Belk 1979: table 2). However, respondents had been asked to describe any three presents they had given over the past year, so the results may represent not typical patterns of giving but presents that were memorable because unusual.

CONCLUSION

1 Michèle Lamont (1992: 180) makes an analogous point about another scholarly model that supposes autonomous actors, rational-choice theory. She says that when theorists using this model posit that "the maximization of self-interest" motivates "all human beings", they "universalize to the population at large the culture of . . . upwardly mobile Americans working in the for-profit sector."

REFERENCES

Abercrombie, Nicholas, Hill, Stephen and Turner, Bryan S. (1986) *Sovereign Individuals of Capitalism*, London: Allen & Unwin.

Adburgham, Alison (1981) *Shops and Shopping 1800–1914*, rev. edn, London: Allen & Unwin.

Agnew, Jean-Christophe (1986) *Worlds Apart: The Market and the Theater in Anglo-American Thought, 1550–1750*, New York: Cambridge University Press.

Alexander, David (1970) *Retailing in England during the Industrial Revolution*, London: Athlone Press.

Alexander, Paul (1992) "What's in a Price? Trading Practices in Peasant (and Other) Markets", in Roy Dilley (ed.) *Contesting Markets: Analyses of Ideology, Discourse and Practice*, Edinburgh: Edinburgh University Press.

Allan, Graham A. (1979) *A Sociology of Friendship and Kinship*, London: Allen & Unwin.

Allen, Sheila and Wolkowitz, Carol (1987) *Homeworking: Myth and Realities*, London: Macmillan.

Anderson, Margaret L. (1988) *Thinking about Women: Sociological Perspectives on Sex and Gender*, second edn, New York: Macmillan.

Anderson, Michael (1976) "Sociological History and the Working-Class Family: Smelser Revisited", *Social History* 1: 317–34.

Anderson, Sarah Jane (1987) "Recent Decisions: *Reed v. Campbell*", *Duquesne Law Review* 25: 329–44.

Appadurai, Arjun (1989) "The Global Ethnoscape: Notes and Queries for a Transnational Anthropology", presented at the Advanced Seminar on Meta-Ethnography, School of American Research, Santa Fe, New Mexico, June 5–9, 1989.

Baldwin, Frances (1926) "Sumptuary Legislation and Personal Regulation in England", *Johns Hopkins University Studies in Historical and Political Sciences* 44, 1: 1–282.

Baldwin, William H. (1929) *The Shopping Book*, New York: Macmillan.

Barger, Harold (1955) *Distribution's Place in the American Economy Since 1869*, Princeton: Princeton University Press.

Barker, Diana L. (1972) "Young People and Their Homes: Spoiling and 'Keeping Close' in a South Wales Town", *Sociological Review* 20: 569–90.

Barnett, Steve and Silverman, Martin (1979) "Separations in Capitalist Societies: Persons, Things, Units and Relations", in *Ideology and Everyday Life*, Ann Arbor: University of Michigan Press.

Baron, James N. and Bielby, William T. (1984) "The Organization of Work in a Segmented Economy", *American Sociological Review* 49: 454–73.

Barthes, Roland (1972) *Mythologies*, St Albans, Herts: Paladin.

212

REFERENCES

Baudrillard, Jean (1981) *For a Critique of the Political Economy of the Sign*, St Louis: Telos Press.

Bauman, Zygmunt (1982) *Memories of Class*, London: Routledge & Kegan Paul.

Beach, Betty A. (1989) "The Family Context of Home Shoe Work", in Eileen Boris and Cynthia R. Daniels (eds) *Homework: Historical and Contemporary Perspectives on Paid Labor at Home*, Urbana: University of Illinois Press.

Beaglehole, Ernest (1932) *Property: A Study in Social Psychology*, London: George Allen & Unwin.

Befu, Harumi (1968) "Gift-Giving in a Modernizing Japan", *Monumenta Nipponica* 23: 445–56.

Beier, A. L. (1985) *Masterless Men: The Vagrancy Problem in England 1560–1640*, London: Methuen.

Belk, Russell W. (1976) "It's the Thought that Counts", *Journal of Consumer Research* 3: 155–62.

—— (1979) "Gift-Giving Behavior", in Jagdish E. Sheth (ed.) *Research in Marketing*, vol. 2, Greenwich, Conn.: JAI Press.

—— (1987) "A Child's Christmas in America: Santa Claus as Deity, Consumption as Religion", *Journal of American Culture* 10, 1: 87–100.

—— (1989) "Materialism and the Modern U.S. Christmas", in Elizabeth C. Hirschman (ed.) *Interpretive Consumer Research*, Provo, Utah: Association for Consumer Research.

Belk, Russell W. and Coon, Gregory S. (1993) "Gift Giving as Agapic Love: An Alternative to the Exchange Paradigm Based on Dating Experiences", *Journal of Consumer Research* 20: 393–417.

Bell, Colin R. (1969) *Middle Class Families*, London: Routledge & Kegan Paul.

Bellah, Robert N., Madsen, Richard, Sullivan, William M., Swidler, Ann and Tipton, Steven M. (1985) *Habits of the Heart: Individualism and Commitment in American Life*, Berkeley: University of California Press.

Bennett, Tony (1981) "Christmas and Ideology", in *Popular Culture: Themes and Issues 1* (The Open University, U203, Popular Culture, Block 1, Units 1/2), Milton Keynes: The Open University Press.

Benney, Mark, Weiss, Robert, Meyersohn, Rolf and Riesman, David (1959) "Christmas in an Apartment Hotel", *American Journal of Sociology* 65: 233–40.

Benson, Susan Porter (1979) "Palaces of Consumption and Machine for Selling: The American Department Store, 1880–1940", *Radical History Review* (Fall): 199–221.

—— (1986) *Counter Cultures: Saleswomen, Managers, and Customers in American Department Stores, 1890–1940*, Urbana: University of Illinois Press.

—— (1989) "Women, Work, and the Family Economy: Industrial Homework in Rhode Island in 1934", in Eileen Boris and Cynthia R. Daniels (eds) *Homework: Historical and Contemporary Perspectives on Paid Labor at Home*, Urbana: University of Illinois Press.

Bernstein, Basil (1971) "A Sociolinguistic Approach to Socialization", in *Class, Codes and Control*, vol. 1, London: Routledge & Kegan Paul.

Biddick, Kathleen (1985) "Medieval English Peasants and Market Involvement", *Journal of Economic History* 45: 823–31.

—— (1989) "The Link that Separates: Consumption of Pastoral Resources on a Feudal Estate", in Henry J. Rutz and Benjamin S. Orlove (eds) *The Social Economy of Consumption*, Lanham, Maryland: University Press of America.

Blackman, Janet (1962) "The Food Supply of an Industrial Town: A Study of Sheffield's Public Markets, 1780–1900", *Business History* 5, 2: 83–97.

—— (1967) "Development of the Retail Grocery Trade in the 19th Century", *Business History* 9: 110–17.

Blanchflower, David G. and Oswald, Andrew J. (1988) "Profit-Related Pay: Prose Rediscovered?" *The Economic Journal* 98: 720–30.

Blau, Peter (1964) *Exchange and Social Power*, New York: John Wiley & Sons.

Blauner, Robert (1964) *Alienation and Freedom: The Factory Worker and His Industry*, Chicago: University of Chicago Press.

Bloch, Maurice and Parry, Jonathan (1989) "Introduction: Money and the Morality of Exchange", in J. Parry and M. Bloch (eds) *Money and the Morality of Exchange*, Cambridge: Cambridge University Press.

Bluestone, Barry, Hanna, Patricia, Kuhn, Sarah and Moore, Laura (1981) *The Retail Revolution: Market Transformation, Investment, and Labor in the Modern Department Store*, Boston: Auburn House Publishing.

Boone, Louis E., Kurtz, David L., Johnson, James C. and Bonna, John A. (1974) "'City Shoppers and Urban Identification' Revisited", *Journal of Marketing* 38: 67–9.

Boris, Eileen and Daniels, Cynthia R. (eds) (1989) *Homework: Historical and Contemporary Perspectives on Paid Labor at Home*, Urbana: University of Illinois Press.

Borsay, Peter (1989) *The English Urban Renaissance: Culture and Society in the Provincial Town, 1660–1770*, Oxford: Clarendon Press.

Bose, Christine (1984) "Household Resources and U.S. Women's Work: Factors Affecting Gainful Employment at the Turn of the Century", *American Sociological Review* 49: 474–90.

Bourdieu, Pierre (1977) *Outline of a Theory of Practice*, Cambridge: Cambridge University Press.

—— (1984) *Distinction: A Social Critique of the Judgement of Taste*, London: Routledge & Kegan Paul.

Braverman, Harry (1974) *Labor and Monopoly Capital: The Degradation of Work in the Twentieth Century*, New York: Monthly Review Press.

Brecher, Jeremy *et al.* (1978) "Uncovering the Hidden History of the American Workplace", *Review of Radical Political Economics* 10, 4: 1–23.

Britton, Edward (1977) *The Community of the Vill*, Toronto: Macmillan of Canada.

Brown, Jonathan (1986) *The English Market Town: A Social and Economic History, 1750–1914*, Marlborough, Wilts: Crowood Press.

Bullock, Roy J. (1933) "The Early History of the Great Atlantic and Pacific Tea Company", *Harvard Business Review* 11: 289–98.

Bulmer, Martin (1986) *Neighbours: The Work of Philip Abrams*, Cambridge: Cambridge University Press.

Burawoy, Michael (1982) *Manufacturing Consent: Changes in the Labor Process under Monopoly Capitalism*, Chicago: University of Chicago Press.

Burke, Kenneth (1969 [1945]) *A Grammar of Motives*, Berkeley: University of California Press.

Bussey, J., Banks, G., Darrington, C., Driscoll, D., Goulding, D., Lowes, B., Phillips, R. and Turner, J. (1967) "Patterns of Gift Giving: Including a Questionnaire Survey of Bradford Households", unpublished B.Sc. (Hons) thesis, University of Bradford.

Calhoun, Craig (1982) *The Question of Class Struggle*, Chicago: University of Chicago Press.

Calkins, Earnest Elmo (1905) "Eliminating the Jobber", *Printer's Ink* (May 31): 8.

Camerer, Colin (1988) "Gifts as Economic Signals and Social Symbols", *American Journal of Sociology* 94 (Supplement: Organizations and Institutions): S180–S214.

Campbell, Colin (1987) *The Romantic Ethic and the Spirit of Modern Consumerism*, Oxford: Basil Blackwell.

Campbell, Joan (1989) *Joy in Work, German Work: The National Debate, 1800–1945*, Princeton: Princeton University Press.

Cancian, Francesca M. (1986) "The Feminization of Love", *Signs* 11: 692–709.

—— (1987) *Love in America: Gender and Self-Development*, New York: Cambridge University Press.

Caplow, Theodore (1982) "Christmas Gifts and Kin Networks", *American Sociological Review* 47: 383–92.

—— (1984) "Rule Enforcement without Visible Means: Christmas Gift Giving in Middletown", *American Journal of Sociology* 89: 1306–23.

Caplow, Theodore, Bahr, Howard M. and Chadwick, Bruce A. (1983) *All Faithful People: Change and Continuity in Middletown's Religion*, Minneapolis: University of Minnesota Press.

Carrier, James G. (1986) "Sociology and Special Education: Differentiation and Allocation in Mass Education", *American Journal of Education* 94: 281–312.

—— (1992a) "The Gift in Theory and Practice in Melanesia: A Note on the Centrality of Gift Exchange", *Ethnology* 31: 186–93.

—— (1992b) "Introduction", in J. G. Carrier (ed.) *History and Tradition in Melanesian Anthropology*, Los Angeles: University of California Press.

—— (1992c) "Occidentalism: The World Turned Upside Down", *American Ethnologist* 19: 195–212.

Carruthers, Bruce G. and Espeland, Wendy Nelson (1991) "Accounting for Rationality: Double Entry Bookkeeping and the Rhetoric of Economic Rationality", *American Journal of Sociology* 97: 31–69.

Carson, Gerald (1954) *The Old Country Store*, New York: Oxford University Press.

Carsten, Janet (1989) "Cooking Money: Gender and the Symbolic Transformation of Means of Exchange in a Malay Fishing Community", in Jonathan Parry and Maurice Bloch (eds) *Money and the Morality of Exchange*, Cambridge: Cambridge University Press.

Carus-Wilson, E. M. (1966 [1941]) "An Industrial Revolution of the Thirteenth Century", in E. M. Carus-Wilson (ed.) *Essays in Economic History*, vol. 1, New York: St Martin's Press.

Chandler, Christopher (1985) "Chicago Interview: John McKnight", *Chicago* 34, 11: 202–7.

Chaney, David (1983) "The Department Store as a Cultural Form", *Theory, Culture and Society* 1, 3: 22–31.

Chapman, Dennis (1955) *The Home and Social Status*, London: Routledge & Kegan Paul.

Chartres, J. A. (1977) *Internal Trade in England, 1500–1700*, London: Macmillan.

Cheal, David J. (1986) "The Social Dimensions of Gift Behaviour", *Journal of Social and Personal Relationships* 3: 423–39.

—— (1987) "'Showing Them You Love Them': Gift Giving and the Dialectic of Intimacy", *Sociological Review* 35: 150–69.

—— (1988) *The Gift Economy*, London: Routledge.

Cherington, Paul Terry (ed.) (1913) *Advertising as a Business Force: A Compilation of Experience Records*, Garden City, New York: Doubleday, Page, for Associated Advertising Clubs of America.

Chitnis, Anand C. (1976) *The Scottish Enlightenment: A Social History*, London: Croom Helm; Totowa, New Jersey: Rowman & Littlefield.

Chodorow, Nancy (1978) *The Reproduction of Mothering*, Berkeley: University of California Press.

Clark, Christopher (1979) "Household Economy, Market Exchange and the Rise of Capitalism in the Connecticut Valley", *Journal of Social History* 13: 169–90.

Comfortably Yours (1988) Untitled catalogue, Maywood, New Jersey: Comfortably Yours.

Corrigan, Peter (1989) "Gender and the Gift: The Case of the Family Clothing Economy", *Sociology* 23: 513–34.

Cowan, Ruth Schwartz (1976) "Two Washes in the Morning and a Bridge Party at Night: The American Housewife between the Wars", *Women's Studies* 3: 147–72.
—— (1983) *More Work for Mother*, New York: Basic Books.
Creighton, Millie R. (1991) "Maintaining Cultural Boundaries in Retailing: How Japanese Department Stores Domesticate 'Things Foreign'", *Modern Asian Studies* 25: 675–709.
Cronk, Lee (1989) "Strings Attached", *The Sciences* (May/June): 2–4.
Crowley, J. E. (1974) *This Sheba, Self: The Conceptualization of Economic Life in Eighteenth Century America*, Baltimore: Johns Hopkins University Press.
Csikszentmihalyi, Mihaly and Rochberg-Halton, Eugene (1981) *The Meaning of Things: Domestic Symbols and the Self*, New York: Cambridge University Press.
Cunningham, Hugh (1980) *Leisure in the Industrial Revolution*, London: Croom Helm.
Daily Progress (1988) "Study: Most People Shop at Last Minute", *The Daily Progress* (Charlottesville, Virginia) (December 4): E4.
—— (1993) "Court Rules to Return Child to Birth Parents", *The Daily Progress* (Charlottesville, Virginia) (July 4): A2.
Darby, William D. (1928) *Story of the Chain Store*, New York: Dry Goods Economist.
Davidoff, Leonore and Hall, Catherine (1987) *Family Fortunes: Men and Women of the English Middle Class, 1780–1850*, Chicago: University of Chicago Press.
Davis, Dorothy (1966) *A History of Shopping*, London: Routledge & Kegan Paul.
Davis, Harry L. (1976) "Decision Making Within the Household", *Journal of Consumer Research* 2: 241–60.
Davis, John (1972) "Gifts and the U.K. Economy", *Man* 7: 408–29.
—— (1973) "Forms and Norms: The Economy of Social Relations", *Man* 18: 159–76.
—— (1992) *Exchange*, Buckingham: Open University Press.
DeBolla, Peter (1989) *The Discourse of the Sublime: Readings in History, Aesthetics and the Subject*, Oxford: Basil Blackwell.
Dichter, Ernest (1947) *The Psychology of Everyday Living*, New York: Barnes & Noble.
—— (1964) *Handbook of Consumer Motivations: The Psychology of the World of Objects*, New York: McGraw-Hill Book Company.
Dickens, Charles (1918 [1843]) *A Christmas Carol*, Philadelphia: Henry Altemus Company.
Dilley, Roy (ed.) (1992) *Contesting Markets: Analyses of Ideology, Discourse and Practice*, Edinburgh: Edinburgh University Press.
DiMaggio, Paul and Powell, Walter (1983) "The Iron Cage Revisited: Institutional Isomorphism and Collective Rationality in Organizational Fields", *American Sociological Review* 48: 147–60.
Dittmar, Helga (1992) *The Social Psychology of Material Possessions: To Have Is To Be*, Hemel Hempstead: Harvester Wheatsheaf.
Doeringer, Peter B., Moss, Philip I. and Terkla, David G. (1986) "Capitalism and Kinship: Do Institutions Matter in the Labor Market?", *Industrial and Labor Relations Review* 40: 48–60.
Donovan, Frances R. (1929) *The Saleslady*, Chicago: University of Chicago Press.
Dore, Ronald (1983) "Goodwill and the Spirit of Market Capitalism", *British Journal of Sociology* 34: 459–82.
—— (1992) "Sovereign Individuals", in John A. Hall and I. C. Jarvie (eds) *Transition to Modernity: Essays on Power, Wealth and Belief*, Cambridge: Cambridge University Press.
Douglas, Mary (1966) *Purity and Danger*, London: Routledge & Kegan Paul.
Douglas, Mary and Isherwood, Baron (1978) *The World of Goods*, Harmondsworth: Penguin.

REFERENCES

Dumont, Louis (1970) *Homo Hierarchicus: The Caste System and its Implications*, London: Weidenfeld & Nicolson.

—— (1977) *From Mandeville to Marx: The Genesis and Triumph of Economic Ideology*, Chicago: University of Chicago Press.

Durkheim, Emile (1951 [1897]) *Suicide: A Study in Sociology*, trans. John A. Spaulding and George Simpson, New York: The Free Press.

Earle, Peter (1989) *The Making of the English Middle Class: Business, Society and Family Life in London, 1660–1730*, Los Angeles: University of California Press.

Economist, The (1983) "Christmas Shopping: Ducks Are Big", *The Economist* 289 (December 17): 22–3.

—— (1990) "To Wal-Mart or not to Wal-Mart. . .", *The Economist* 314 (March 17): 66.

Edwards, Richard (1979) *Contested Terrain: The Transformation of the Workplace in the Twentieth Century*, New York: Basic Books.

Ehrenreich, Barbara and English, Deirdre (1978) *For Her Own Good: 150 Years of the Experts' Advice to Women*, Garden City, New York: Doubleday.

Ellis, Rhian (1983) "The Way to a Man's Heart: Food in the Violent Home", in Anne Murcott (ed.) *The Sociology of Food and Eating*, Aldershot: Gower.

Emerson, Ralph Waldo (1983 [1844]) "Gifts", in Joseph Slater, Alfred R. Ferguson and Jean Ferguson Carr (eds and compilers) *The Collected Works of Ralph Waldo Emerson*, vol. 3, essays: second series, Cambridge, Mass.: Belknap Press.

Emerson, Richard M. (1976) "Social Exchange Theory", *Annual Review of Sociology* 2: 335–62.

Ennew, Judith (1982) "Harris Tweed: Construction, Retention and Representation of a Cottage Industry", in Esther Goody (ed.) *From Craft to Industry: The Ethnography of Proto-Industrial Cloth Production*, Cambridge: Cambridge University Press.

Everitt, Alan (1967) "The Marketing of Agricultural Produce", in Joan Thirsk (ed.) *The Agrarian History of England and Wales, vol. IV, 1500–1640*, Cambridge: Cambridge University Press.

Ewen, Stuart (1976) *Captains of Consciousness*, New York: McGraw-Hill.

Fabian, Johannes (1983) *Time and the Other: How Anthropology Makes its Object*, New York: Columbia University Press.

Fanselow, Frank S. (1990) "The Bazaar Economy: Or How Bizarre Is the Bazaar Really?", *Man* 25: 250–65.

Firth, Raymond (ed.) (1956) *Two Studies of Kinship in London*, London: Athlone Press.

Fisher, F. J. (1966 [1934–5]) "The Development of the London Food Market", in E. M. Carus-Wilson (ed.) *Essays in Economic History*, vol. 1, New York: St Martin's Press.

Forbes, Duncan (1966) "Introduction", in Duncan Forbes (ed.) *Adam Ferguson, An Essay on the History of Civil Society*, Edinburgh: Edinburgh University Press.

Fortune (1956 [1952]) "Salespeople vs. Robots", in John W. Wingate and Arnold Corbin (eds) *Changing Patterns in Retailing*, Homewood, Illinois: Richard D. Irwin. (First published in *Fortune*, November 1952.)

Forty, Adrian (1986) *Objects of Desire*, London: Thames & Hudson.

Foster, John (1974) *Class Struggle and the Industrial Revolution*, London: Weidenfeld & Nicolson.

Foucault, Michel (1979) *Discipline and Punish: The Birth of the Prison*, New York: Random House.

Franklin, Jill (1981) *The Gentleman's Country House and its Plan, 1835–1914*, London: Routledge & Kegan Paul.

Fraser, W. Hamish (1981) *The Coming of the Mass Market, 1850–1914*, London: Macmillan.

French, Cecil L. (1960) "Correlates of Success in Retail Selling", *American Journal of Sociology* 66: 128–34.

Fried, Marc, with Fitzgerald, Ellen, Gleicher, Peggy and Hartman, Chester (1973) *The World of the Urban Working Class*, Cambridge, Mass.: Harvard University Press.

Friedland, Roger and Robertson, A. F. (1990) "Beyond the Marketplace", in R. Friedland and A. F. Robertson (eds) *Beyond the Marketplace: Rethinking Economy and Society*, New York: Aldine de Gruyter.

Friedman, Jonathan (1990) "The Political Economy of Elegance: An African Cult of Beauty", *Culture and History* 7: 101–25.

Fuller, Chris J. (1989) "Misconceiving the Grain Heap: A Critique of the Concept of the Indian Jajmani System", in Jonathan Parry and Maurice Bloch (eds) *Money and the Morality of Exchange*, Cambridge: Cambridge University Press.

Furnas, J. C. (1974) *Great Times: An Informal Social History of the United States, 1914–1929*, New York: G. P. Putnam's Sons.

Gambetta, Diego (ed.) (1988) *Trust: Making and Breaking Cooperative Relationships*, Oxford: Basil Blackwell.

Gardner, Carl and Sheppard, Julie (1989) *Consuming Passion: The Rise of Retail Culture*, London: Unwin Hyman.

Garner, Thesia I. and Wagner, Janet (1988) *Gift-Giving Behavior: An Economic Perspective*, Working Paper 180, Bureau of Labor Statistics, Washington: U.S. Department of Labor.

Geary, Patrick (1986) "Sacred Commodities: The Circulation of Medieval Relics", in Arjun Appadurai (ed.) *The Social Life of Things: Commodities in Cultural Perspective*, New York: Cambridge University Press.

Girouard, Mark (1990) *The English Town*, New Haven: Yale University Press.

Godelier, Maurice (1977) "Salt Money and the Circulation of Commodities among the Baruya of New Guinea", in *Perspectives in Marxist Anthropology*, Cambridge: Cambridge University Press.

Golby, John M. (1981) "A History of Christmas", in *Popular Culture: Themes and Issues 1* (The Open University, U203, Popular Culture, Block 1, Units 1/2), Milton Keynes: The Open University Press.

Golby, John M. and Purdue, A. William (1986) *The Making of Modern Christmas*, Athens: University of Georgia Press.

Goldthorpe, John H., Lockwood, David, Bechhofer, Frank and Platt, Jennifer (1969) *The Affluent Worker in the Class Structure*, Cambridge: Cambridge University Press.

Goody, Esther (1982) "Introduction", in E. Goody (ed.) *From Craft to Industry: The Ethnography of Proto-Industrial Cloth Production*, Cambridge: Cambridge University Press.

Gouldner, Alvin (1960) "The Norm of Reciprocity", *American Sociological Review* 25: 161–78.

Gouldner, Helen and Strong, Mary Symons (1987) *Speaking of Friendship: Middle-Class Women and their Friends*, Westport, Conn.: Greenwood Press.

Graburn, Nelson H. H. (1987) "Material Symbols in Japanese Domestic Tourism", in Daniel W. Ingersoll, Jr, and Gordon Bronitsky (eds) *Mirror and Metaphor: Material and Social Constructions of Reality*, Lanham, Maryland: University Press of America.

Granovetter, Mark (1973) "The Strength of Weak Ties", *American Journal of Sociology* 78: 1360–80.

—— (1985) "Economic Action and Social Structure: The Problem of Embeddedness", *American Journal of Sociology* 91: 481–510.

Gregory, C. A. (1980) "Gifts to Men and Gifts to God: Gift Exchange and Capital Accumulation in Contemporary Papua", *Man* 15: 626–52.

—— (1982) *Gifts and Commodities*, London: Academic Press.

Grenier, Guillermo J. (1988) *Inhuman Relations: Quality Circles and Anti-Unionism in American Industry*, Philadelphia: Temple University Press.

Grieco, Margaret (1987) *Keeping It in the Family: Social Networks and Employment Chance*, London: Tavistock.

Griswold, Wendy (1983) "The Devil's Techniques: Cultural Legitimation and Social Change", *American Sociological Review* 48: 668–80.

Gudeman, Stephen and Rivera, Alberto (1991) *Conversations in Colombia: The Domestic Economy in Life and Text*, New York: Cambridge University Press.

Gullestad, Marianne (1990) "Doing Interpretive Analysis in a Modern Large Scale Society: The Meaning of Peace and Quiet in Norway", *Social Analysis* 29: 38–61.

Hadley, Janet (1986) "Family Planning", *New Statesman* 112 (December 5): 36.

Halle, David (1984) *America's Working Man: Work, Home, and Politics among Blue-Collar Property Owners*, Chicago: University of Chicago Press.

Hareven, Tamara K. (1982) *Family Time and Industrial Time: The Relationship between the Family and Work in a New England Industrial Community*, New York: Cambridge University Press.

Harris, Rosemary (1987) *Power and Powerlessness in Industry: An Analysis of the Social Relations of Production*, London: Tavistock.

Hart, Keith (1986) "Heads or Tails? Two Sides of the Coin", *Man* 21: 637–56.

Hartsock, Nancy C. N. (1985) "Exchange Theory: Critique from a Feminist Standpoint", in S. G. McNall (ed.) *Current Perspectives in Social Theory*, vol. 6, Greenwich, Conn.: JAI Press.

Harvard University Bureau of Business Research (1919) *Management Problems in Retail Grocery Stores*, Bulletin No. 13, Cambridge, Mass.: Harvard University Press.

Hawken, Paul (1987) *Growing a Business*, New York: Simon & Schuster.

Hayden, Delores (1980) "What Would a Non-Sexist City be Like?", *Signs* 5 (Supplement: Women and the American City): S170–S187.

Heeler, Roger, Francis, June, Okechuku, Chike and Reid, Stanley (1979) "Gift versus Personal Use Brand Selection", in William L. Wilkie (ed.) *Advances in Consumer Research*, vol. 6, Ann Arbor: Association for Consumer Research.

Hendrickson, Robert (1978) *The Grand Emporiums*, New York: Stein & Day.

Henry, O. (1917) "The Gift of the Magi", in *The Four Million*, New York: Doubleday, Page & Company for Review of Reviews.

Henry, Stuart (1976) "The Other Side of the Fence", *Sociological Review* 24: 793–806.

Hervey, Thomas K. (1845) *The Book of Christmas*, New York: Wiley & Putnam.

Heyman, Josiah (1994) "The Organizational Logic of Capitalist Consumption on the Mexico–United States Border", *Research in Economic Anthropology* 15: forthcoming.

Hilton, Rodney H. (1985) "Medieval Market Towns and Simple Commodity Production", *Past and Present* 109: 3–23.

Hirsch, Eric (1992) "The Long Term and the Short Term of Domestic Consumption: An Ethnographic Case Study", in Roger Silverstone and Eric Hirsch (eds) *Consuming Technologies: Media and Information in Domestic Spaces*, London: Routledge.

Hirschman, Albert (1977) *The Passions and the Interests*, Princeton: Princeton University Press.

Hobbs, Dick (1989) *Doing the Business: Entrepreneurship, the Working Class, and Detectives in the East End of London*, Oxford: Oxford University Press.

Hochschild, Arlie R. (1983) *The Managed Heart: The Commercialization of Human Feeling*, Berkeley: University of California Press.

Hochschild, Arlie R. (1989) "Reply to Cas Wouter's Review Essay on *The Managed Heart*", *Theory, Culture and Society* 6: 439–45.

Hodges, Richard (1988) *Primitive and Peasant Markets*, Oxford: Basil Blackwell.

Hofferth, Sandra L. (1984) "Kin Networks, Race and Family Structure", *Journal of Marriage and the Family* 46: 791–806.

Holy, Ladislav (1992) "Culture, Market Ideology and Economic Reform in Czechoslovakia", in Roy Dilley (ed.) *Contesting Markets: Analyses of Ideology, Discourse and Practice*, Edinburgh: Edinburgh University Press.

Homans, George C. (1958) "Social Behavior as Exchange", *American Journal of Sociology* 63: 597–606.

Hood, Graham (1991) *The Governor's Palace in Williamsburg: A Cultural Study*, Williamsburg, Virginia: The Colonial Williamsburg Foundation.

Hooper, Wilfred (1915) "The Tudor Sumptuary Laws", *The English Historical Review* 30: 433–49.

Hounshell, David A. (1984) *From the American System to Mass Production, 1800–1932*, Baltimore: Johns Hopkins University Press.

Hower, Ralph M. (1938) "Urban Retailing 100 Years Ago", *Bulletin of the Business Historical Society* 12 (December): 91–101.

Humphries, Jane (1988) "Protective Legislation, the Capitalist State and Working-Class Men: The Case of the 1842 Mines Regulation Act", in R. E. Pahl (ed.) *On Work*, Oxford: Basil Blackwell.

—— (1990) "Enclosures, Common Rights and Women: The Proletarianization of Families in the Late Eighteenth and Early Nineteenth Centuries", *Journal of Economic History* 50: 17–42.

Hunt, Geoffrey and Satterlee, Saundra (1986) "Cohesion and Division: Drinking in an English Village", *Man* 21: 521–37.

Ingold, Tim (1988) "Tools, Minds and Machines: An Excursion in the Philosophy of Technology", *Techniques et Culture* 12: 151–76.

—— (1990) "Society, Nature and the Concept of Technology", *Archaeological Review from Cambridge* 9, 1: 5–17.

Jackson, Tom (1978) *Guerilla Tactics in the Job Market*, New York: Bantam Books.

Jacoby, Sanford M. (1985) *Employing Bureaucracy: Managers, Unions, and the Transformation of Work in American Industry, 1900–1945*, New York: Columbia University Press.

James, Mervyn (1974) *Family, Lineage and Civil Society*, Oxford: Clarendon Press.

James, William (1890) *The Principles of Psychology*, vol. 1, New York: Henry Holt & Company.

Jefferys, James B. (1954) *Retail Trading in Britain: 1850–1950*, Cambridge: Cambridge University Press.

Jhering, Rudolph von (1915) *The Struggle for Law*, second edn, Chicago: Callaghan & Company.

Johnson, Paul (1985) *Saving and Spending*, Oxford: Clarendon.

Jolibert, Alain J. P. and Fernandez-Moreno, Carlos (1982) "A Comparison of French and Mexican Gift Giving Practices", in Richard P. Bagozzi and Alice M. Tybout (eds) *Advances in Consumer Research*, vol. 10, Ann Arbor: Association for Consumer Research.

Jones, Charles W. (1978) *Saint Nicholas of Myra, Bari, and Manhattan*, Chicago: University of Chicago Press.

Jones, Gareth Stedman (1971) *Outcast London*, Oxford: Clarendon.

Josephides, Lisette (1985) *The Production of Inequality: Gender and Exchange among the Kewa*, London: Tavistock.

Kalman, H. (1972) "The Architecture of Mercantilism: Commercial Buildings by

George Dance the Younger", in Paul Fritz and David Williams (eds) *The Triumph of Culture: 18th Century Perspectives*, Toronto: A. M. Hakkert, Ltd.

Kanter, Rosabeth Moss (1977) *Men and Women of the Corporation*, New York: Basic Books.

Katz, Jack (1988) *Seductions of Crime*, New York: Basic Books.

Kelley, Maryellen R. and Harrison, Bennett (1991) "Unions, Technology, and Labor–Management Cooperation", in Lawrence Mishel and Paula Voos (eds) *Unions and Economic Competitiveness*, New York: M. E. Sharpe.

Kelly, John D. (1992) "Fiji Indians and the 'Commoditization of Labor'", *American Ethnologist* 19: 97–120.

Kerr, Marion and Charles, Nicola (1986) "Servers and Providers: The Distribution of Food within the Family", *Sociological Review* 34: 115–57.

Komarovsky, Mirra (1987 [1964]) *Blue-Collar Marriage*, second edn, New Haven: Yale University Press.

Kopytoff, Igor (1986) "The Cultural Biography of Things: Commoditization as Process", in Arjun Appadurai (ed.) *The Social Life of Things: Commodities in Cultural Perspective*, New York: Cambridge University Press.

Kowinski, William Severini (1985) *The Malling of America: An Inside Look at the Great Consumer Paradise*, New York: William Morrow & Company.

Kula, Witold (1976) *An Economic Theory of the Feudal System*, London: New Left Books.

Kumar, Krishan (1988) "From Work to Employment and Unemployment: The English Experience", in R. E. Pahl (ed.) *On Work*, Oxford: Basic Blackwell.

Lamont, Michèle (1992) *Money, Morals, and Manners: The Culture of the French and the American Upper-Middle Class*, Chicago: University of Chicago Press.

Lancaster, Osbert (1953) *All Done from Memory*, London: John Murray.

Lanchester, H. V. (1913) "The Design and Architectural Treatment of the Shop", *Journal of the Royal Society of Arts* 61: 577–89.

Lands' End (1988) Untitled catalogue, Dodgeville, Wisconsin: Lands' End, Inc.

Lathrop, Richard (1977) *Who's Hiring Who*, Berkeley: Ten Speed Press.

Lea, Stephen E. G., Walker, Catherine M. and Webley, Paul (1992) "An Interview Study on the Origins of Problem Debt", presented at the conference of the Society for the Advancement of Socio-Economics, Irvine, California, March, 1992.

Lears, T. J. Jackson (1983) "From Salvation to Self-Realization: Advertising and the Therapeutic Roots of the Consumer Culture, 1880–1930", in Richard Wightman Fox and T. J. J. Lears (eds) *The Culture of Consumption: Critical Essays in American History, 1880–1980*, New York: Pantheon Books.

Leiss, William, Kline, Stephen and Jhally, Sut (1986) *Social Communication in Advertising*, London: Methuen.

Leonini, Luisa (1984) "The Quest for Identity: The Role of Objects in Contemporary Everyday Life", unpublished Ph.D. thesis, Edinburgh University.

Lévi-Strauss, Claude (1966) "The Culinary Triangle", *New Society* (December 22): 937–40.

—— (1969a) *The Elementary Structures of Kinship*, Boston: Beacon Press.

—— (1969b) *Totemism*, Harmondsworth: Penguin.

Levine, David (1985) "Industrialization and the Proletarian Family in England", *Past and Present* 107: 168–203.

Lindstrom, Lamont (1993) *Cargo Cult! Strange Stories of Desire from New Guinea and Beyond*, Honolulu: University of Hawaii Press.

Livingstone, Sonia M. (1992) "The Meaning of Domestic Technologies: A Personal Construct Analysis of Familial Gender Relations", in Roger Silverstone and Eric Hirsch (eds) *Consuming Technologies: Media and Information in Domestic Spaces*, London: Routledge.

Löfgren, Orvar (1990a) "Consuming Interests", *Culture and History* 7: 7–36.

—— (ed.) (1990b) "Consumption", *Culture and History* 7 (special issue).

Loudon, J. B. (1961) "Kinship and Crisis in South Wales", *British Journal of Sociology* 12: 333–50.

Lowes, Bryan, Turner, John and Wills, Gordon (1968) "Patterns of Gift Giving and their Marketing Implications", *British Journal of Marketing* 2 (Autumn): 217–29.

Lubasz, Heinz (1992) "Adam Smith and the Invisible Hand – of the Market?", in Roy Dilley (ed.) *Contesting Markets: Analyses of Ideology, Discourse and Practice*, Edinburgh: Edinburgh University Press.

Macaulay, Stewart (1963) "Non-Contractual Relations in Business: A Preliminary Study", *American Sociological Review* 28: 55–67.

McClelland, W. G. (1962) "The Supermarket and Society", *Sociological Review* 10: 133–44.

McCracken, Grant (1988) *Culture and Consumption: New Approaches to the Symbolic Character of Consumer Goods and Activities*, Bloomington: Indiana University Press.

Macfarlane, Alan (1978) *The Origins of English Individualism*, Oxford: Basil Blackwell.

McGrory, Mary (1987) "The Hafts' Hunger", *The Washington Post* (December 31): A2.

MacKeith, Margaret (1986) *The History and Conservation of Shopping Arcades*, London: Mansell Publishing.

McKendrick, Neil (1974) "Home Demand and Economic Growth: A New View of the Role of Women and Children in the Industrial Revolution", in N. McKendrick (ed.) *Historical Perspectives: Studies in English Thought and Society*, London: Europa Publications.

McKendrick, Neil, Brewer, John and Plumb, J. H. (1982) *The Birth of a Consumer Society*, Bloomington: Indiana University Press.

MacLean, Annie M. (1899) "Two Weeks in Department Stores", *American Journal of Sociology* 4: 721–41.

Macpherson, C. B. (1962) *The Political Theory of Possessive Individualism: Hobbes to Locke*, Oxford: Clarendon Press.

—— (1979) "Property as Means or End", in Anthony Parel and Thomas Flanagan (eds) *Theories of Property: Aristotle to the Present*, Waterloo, Ont.: Wilfred Laurier University Press.

Malinowski, Bronislaw (1922) *Argonauts of the Western Pacific*, London: Routledge & Kegan Paul.

Mansfield, Penny and Collard, Jean (1988) *The Beginning of the Rest of Your Life?*, Basingstoke: Macmillan.

Marglin, Stephen A. (1974) "What Do Bosses Do? The Origins and Functions of Hierarchy in Capitalist Production", *Review of Radical Political Economics* 6: 33–60.

Mars, Gerald (1982) *Cheats at Work: An Anthropology of Workplace Crime*, London: George Allen & Unwin.

Martin, Judith (1988) "Miss Manners: After the Gifts Are Given", *The Washington Post* (July 6): D5.

Mathias, Peter (1967) *Retailing Revolution: A History of Multiple Retailing in the Food Trades Based upon the Allied Suppliers Group of Companies*, London: Longman.

Matthews, Glenna (1987) *Just a Housewife: The Rise and Fall of Domesticity in the United States 1830–1963*, New York: Oxford University Press.

Mauro, Frédéric (1990) "Merchant Communities, 1350–1750", in J. D. Tracy (ed.)

The Rise of Merchant Empires: Long-Distance Trade in the Early Modern World, 1350–1750, Cambridge: Cambridge University Press.

Mauss, Marcel (1985 [1938]) "A Category of the Human Mind: The Notion of Person; the Notion of Self", in Michael Carrithers, Steven Collins and Steven Lukes (eds) *The Category of the Person*, Cambridge: Cambridge University Press.

—— (1990 [1925]) *The Gift: The Form and Reason for Exchange in Archaic Societies*, trans. W. D. Halls, London: Routledge.

Mayer, Caroline (1987) "Retailers Worry as Holiday Shopping Begins", *The Washington Post* (November 27): C1, C3.

Maynard, H. H. (1951) "Developments of Science in Selling and Sales Management", in Hugh G. Wales (ed.) *Changing Perspectives in Marketing*, Urbana: University of Illinois Press.

Maza, Sarah C. (1981) "An Anatomy of Paternalism: Masters and Servants in Eighteenth-Century French Households", *Eighteenth Century Life* 7, 1: 1–24.

Medick, Hans (1976) "The Proto-Industrial Family Economy: The Structural Function of Household and Family during the Transition from Peasant Society to Industrial Capitalism", *Social History* 1: 291–315.

Medick, Hans and Sabean, David Warren (eds) (1984) *Interest and Emotion: Essays in the Study of Family and Kinship*, Cambridge: Cambridge University Press.

Miller, Daniel (1987) *Material Culture and Mass Consumption*, Oxford: Basil Blackwell.

—— (1988) "Appropriating the State on the Council Estate", *Man* 23: 353–72.

—— (1990) "Fashion and Ontology in Trinidad", *Culture and History* 7: 49–77.

Miller, Michael B. (1981) *The Bon Marché*, Princeton: Princeton University Press.

Millman, Marcia (1991) *Warm Hearts and Cold Cash: The Intimate Dynamics of Families and Money*, New York: Free Press.

Mitchell, S. I. (1981) "Retailing in Eighteenth and Early Nineteenth Century Cheshire", *Transactions of the Historical Society of Lancashire and Cheshire* 130: 37–60.

Modell, John (1979) "Changing Risks, Changing Adaptations: American Families in the Nineteenth and Twentieth Centuries", in Allan J. Lichtman and Joan R. Challinor (eds) *Kin and Communities*, Washington: Smithsonian Institute Press.

Modell, Judith (1986) "In Search: The Purported Biological Basis of Parenthood", *American Ethnologist* 13: 646–61.

Moeran, Brian (1984) "Individual, Group and *Seishin*: Japan's Internal Cultural Debate", *Man* 19: 252–66.

Morgan, S. Philip and Hirosima, Kiyosi (1983) "The Persistence of Extended Family Residence in Japan: Anachronism or Alternative Strategy?", *American Sociological Review* 48: 269–81.

Morris, Lydia (1990) *The Workings of the Household: A US–UK Comparison*, Cambridge: Polity Press.

Morrison, Blake (1988) "Importing the *droit moral*", *The Times Literary Supplement* (July 8–14): 754.

Mui, Lorna and Mui, Hoh–cheung (1989) *Shops and Shopkeeping in Eighteenth Century England*, London: Routledge.

Murcott, Anne (1983a) "Cooking and the Cooked", in A. Murcott (ed.) *The Sociology of Food and Eating*, Aldershot: Gower.

—— (1983b) "It's a Pleasure to Cook for Him", in Eva Gamarnikov, David H. J. Morgan, June Purvis and Daphne Taylorson (eds) *The Public and the Private*, London: Heinemann.

—— (1983c) (ed.) *The Sociology of Food and Eating*, Aldershot: Gower.

Myers, Milton L. (1983) *The Soul of Modern Economic Man: Ideas of Self-Interest, Thomas Hobbes to Adam Smith*, Chicago: University of Chicago.

223

Myles, John (1990) "States, Labor Markets, and Life Cycles", in Roger Friedland and A. F. Robertson (eds) *Beyond the Marketplace: Rethinking Economy and Society*, New York: Aldine de Gruyter.

Nakane, Chie (1986) "Criteria of Group Formation", in Takie Sugiyama Lebra and William P. Lebra (eds) *Japanese Culture and Behavior*, rev. edn, Honolulu: University of Hawaii Press.

New York Times News Service (1988) "Returning Unwanted Gifts Takes Much Tact", *The Daily Progress* (Charlottesville, Virginia) (December 18): F10.

Nichols, Theo and Beynon, Huw (1977) *Living with Capitalism: Class Relations in the Modern Factory*, London: Routledge & Kegan Paul.

Noonan, John T. (1984) *Bribes*, Berkeley: University of California Press.

Nystrom, Paul H. (1925) "An Estimate of the Volume of Retail Business in the United States", *Harvard Business Review* 3: 150–9.

—— (1930) *Economics of Retailing*, vol. 1, New York: Ronald Press.

O'Toole, James (1985) *Vanguard Management: Redesigning the Corporate Future*, Garden City, New York: Doubleday & Company.

Oldham, J. Thomas and Caudill, David S. (1984) "A Reconnaissance of Public Policy Restrictions upon Enforcement of Contracts between Cohabitants", *Family Law Quarterly* 18: 93–141.

Orlove, Benjamin S. and Rutz, Henry J. (1989) "Thinking about Consumption: A Social Economy Approach", in H. J. Rutz and B. S. Orlove (eds) *The Social Economy of Consumption*, Lanham, Maryland: University Press of America.

Oschinsky, Dorothea (1971) *Walter of Henley and other Treatises on Estate Management and Accounting*, Oxford: Clarendon Press.

Ouroussoff, Alexandra (1993) "Illusions of Rationality: False Premises of the Liberal Tradition", *Man* 28: 281–98.

Packard, Vance (1957) *The Hidden Persuaders*, New York: David McKay Company.

Pahl, R. E. (1984) *Divisions of Labour*, Oxford: Basil Blackwell.

Parry, Jonathan (1986) "*The Gift*, the Indian Gift and the 'Indian Gift'", *Man* 21: 453–73.

Parry, Jonathan and Bloch, Maurice (eds) (1989) *Money and the Morality of Exchange*, Cambridge: Cambridge University Press.

Parsons, Talcott (1959) "The Social Structure of the Family", in Ruth Nanda Anshen (ed.) *The Family*, New York: Harper & Row.

Pasdermadjian, Hrant (1954) *The Department Store: Its Origins, Evolution, and Economics*, London: Newman. (1976, New York: Arno Press, repr.)

Penn, Roger (1985) *Skilled Workers in the Class Structure*, Cambridge: Cambridge University Press.

Pennington, Shelley and Westover, Belinda (1989) *A Hidden Workforce: Home-workers in England, 1850–1985*, Basingstoke: Macmillan.

Perin, Constance (1977) *Everything in Its Place: Social Order and Land Use in America*, Princeton: Princeton University Press.

Peters, Thomas J. and Waterman, Jr, Robert H. (1982) *In Search of Excellence: Lessons from America's Best-Run Companies*, New York: Harper & Row.

Pimlott, J. A. R. (1978) *The Englishman's Christmas: A Social History*, Hassocks: Harvester.

Piot, Charles D. (1991) "Of Persons and Things: Some Reflections on African Spheres of Exchange", *Man* 26: 405–24.

Piotrkowski, Chaya (1979) *Work and the Family System*, New York: The Free Press.

Pleck, Elizabeth H. (1976) "Two Worlds in One: Work and Family", *Journal of Social History* 10: 178–95.

Pocock, John G. A. (1975) *The Machiavellian Moment*, Princeton: Princeton University Press.

REFERENCES

—— (1979) "The Mobility of Property and the Rise of Eighteenth Century Sociology", in Anthony Parel and Thomas Flanagan (eds) *Theories of Property: Aristotle to the Present*, Waterloo, Ont.: Wilfred Laurier University Press.

Polanyi, Karl (1957) *The Great Transformation: The Political and Economic Origins of Our Time*, Boston: Beacon Press.

Post, Elizabeth (1969) *Emily Post's Etiquette*, twelfth edn, New York: Funk & Wagnall's.

Post, Emily (1927) *Etiquette in Society, in Business, in Politics and at Home*, seventeenth edn, New York: Funk & Wagnall's Company.

Postan, M. M. (1966 [1928]) "Credit in Medieval Trade", in E. M. Carus-Wilson (ed.) *Essays in Economic History*, vol. 1, New York: St Martin's Press.

Postles, David (1986) "The Perception of Profit before the Leasing of Demesnes", *Agricultural History Review* 34: 12–28.

Price, Richard (1983) "The Labour Process and Labour History", *Social History* 8: 57–75.

Pruitt, Bettye Hobbs (1984) "Self-Sufficiency and the Agricultural Economy of Eighteenth-Century Massachusetts", *The William and Mary Quarterly* 41: 333–64.

Prus, Robert (1986) "It's on 'Sale!': An Examination of Vendor Perspectives, Activities, and Dilemmas", *Canadian Review of Sociology and Anthropology* 23: 72–96.

—— (1987) "Developing Loyalty: Fostering Purchasing Relationships in the Marketplace", *Urban Life* 15: 331–66.

Raspberry, William (1986) "Tapping the Poor's Capacity to Produce", *Tulsa World* (January 7): 11.

—— (1988) "Christmas Run Amok: Our Gift-Giving Has Gotten Out of Hand", *The Washington Post* (January 4): A13.

Reliable (1988) *Reliable, The Office Supply People, 1988 Edition*, Chicago: Reliable.

Resseguie, Harry E. (1965) "Alexander Turney Stewart and the Development of the Department Store, 1823–1876", *Business History Review* 39: 301–22.

Richards, Katherine Lambert (1971 [1934]) *How Christmas Came to the Sunday Schools*, Ann Arbor: Gryphon. (New York: Dodd, Mead.)

Robins, Lee N. and Tomanec, Miroda (1962) "Closeness to Blood Relatives Outside the Immediate Family", *Marriage and Family Living* 24: 340–6.

Robinson, Joe (1977) *The Life and Times of Francie Nichol of South Shields*, London: Allen & Unwin.

Robinson, Robert V. and Briggs, Carl M. (1991) "The Rise of Factories in Nineteenth-Century Indianapolis", *American Journal of Sociology* 97: 622–56.

Rochberg-Halton, Eugene (1986) *Meaning and Modernity*, Chicago: University of Chicago Press.

Rohlen, Thomas P. (1973) "'Spiritual Education' in a Japanese Bank", *American Anthropologist* 75: 1542–62.

Ronco, William and Peattie, Lisa (1988) "Making Work: A Perspective from Social Science", in R. E. Pahl (ed.) *On Work*, Oxford: Basil Blackwell.

de Roover, Raymond Adrien (1974) *Business, Banking, and Economic Thought in Late Medieval and Early Modern Europe: Selected Studies of Raymond de Roover*, ed. Julius Kirshner, Chicago: University of Chicago Press.

Roy, D. F. (1960) "Banana Time: Job Satisfaction and Informal Interaction", *Human Organization* 18: 158–68.

Rubin, Gerry (1986) "From Packmen, Tallymen and Perambulating Scotchmen to Credit Drapers' Associations, c. 1840–1914", *Business History* 28: 206–25.

Rule, John (1987) "The Property of Skill in the Period of Manufacture", in Patrick Joyce (ed.) *The Historical Meanings of Work*, Cambridge: Cambridge University Press.

Ryans, Adrian (1977) "Consumer Gift Buying Behavior: An Exploratory Analysis", in Barnett A. Greenberg and Danny N. Bellenger (eds) *Contemporary Marketing Thought, 1977 Educators' Proceedings*, Chicago: American Marketing Association.

Rybczynski, Witold (1988) *Home: A Short History of an Idea*, London: Heinemann.

Sabean, David Warren (1990) *Property, Production, and Family in Neckarhausen, 1700–1870*, Cambridge: Cambridge University Press.

Sabel, Charles and Zeitlin, Jonathan (1985) "Historical Alternatives to Mass Production: Politics, Markets and Technology in Nineteenth-Century Industrialization", *Past and Present* 108: 133–76.

Sahlins, Marshall (1974a) "On the Sociology of Primitive Exchange", in *Stone Age Economics*, London: Tavistock.

—— (1974b) *Stone Age Economics*, London: Tavistock.

—— (1976) *Culture and Practical Reason*, Chicago: University of Chicago Press.

Said, Edward (1978) *Orientalism*, Harmondsworth: Penguin.

Salaman, Graeme (1986) *Working*, London: Tavistock.

Sampson, Henry (1875) *A History of Advertising from the Earliest Times: Illustrated by Anecdotes, Curious Specimens, and Biographical Notes*, London: Chatto & Windus.

Sanders, Claire (1993) "Listening for the Soft Voices", *The Times Higher Education Supplement* (June 4): 44.

Sayer, Derek (1992) "A Notable Administration: English State Formation and the Rise of Capitalism", *American Journal of Sociology* 97: 1382–415.

Schiltz, Marc (1987) "War, Peace, and the Exercise of Power: Perspectives on Society, Gender and the State in the New Guinea Highlands", *Social Analysis* 21: 3–19.

Schneider, David (1979) "Kinship, Community, and Locality in American Culture", in Allan Lichtman and Joan Challinor (eds) *Kin and Communities: Families in America*, Washington: Smithsonian Institution Press.

—— (1980) *American Kinship: A Cultural Account*, second edn, Chicago: University of Chicago Press.

—— (1984) *A Critique of the Study of Kinship*, Ann Arbor: University of Michigan Press.

Schneider, Jane (1978) "Peacocks and Penguins: The Political Economy of European Cloth and Colors", *American Ethnologist* 5: 413–47.

Schudson, Michael (1984) *Advertising, The Uneasy Persuasion*, New York: Basic Books.

Schwartz, Barry (1967) "The Social Psychology of the Gift", *American Journal of Sociology* 73: 1–11.

Schwimmer, Erik (1973) *Exchange in the Social Structure of the Orokaiva*, London: C. Hurst & Company.

Scott, Alison MacEwen (ed.) (1986) "Rethinking Petty Commodity Production", *Social Analysis* 20 (special issue).

Scull, Penrose (1967) *From Peddlers to Merchant Princes: A History of Selling in America*, Chicago: Follett Publishing.

Segalen, Martine (1983) *Love and Power in the Peasant Family*, Oxford: Basil Blackwell.

Sennett, Richard (1976) *The Fall of Public Man*, New York: Vintage Books.

Shammas, Carole (1982) "Consumer Behavior in Colonial America", *Social Science History* 6: 67–86.

Shaw, Arch W. (1912) "Some Problems in Market Distribution", *Quarterly Journal of Economics* 26: 703–65.

Shaw, Gareth (1985) "Changes in Consumer Demand and Food Supply in Nineteenth-Century British Cities", *Journal of Historical Geography* 11: 280–96.

Shurmer, Pamela (1971) "The Gift Game", *New Society* (December 23): 1242–4.

Sickel, H. S. J. (1940) *Thanksgiving: Its Source, Philosophy and History*, Philadelphia: International Printing Company.

Silver, Allan (1990) "Friendship in Commercial Society: Eighteenth-Century Social Theory and Modern Sociology", *American Journal of Sociology* 95: 1474–504.

Silverstone, Roger and Hirsch, Eric (eds) (1992) *Consuming Technologies: Media and Information in Domestic Spaces*, London: Routledge.

Silverstone, Roger, Hirsch, Eric and Morley, David (1992) "Information and Communication Technologies and the Moral Economy of the Household", in Roger Silverstone and Eric Hirsch (eds) *Consuming Technologies: Media and Information in Domestic Spaces*, London: Routledge.

Simmel, Georg (1950) "Faithfulness and Gratitude", in Kurt Wolff (ed.) *The Sociology of George Simmel*, Glencoe: Free Press.

Sinclair, Upton (1906) *The Jungle*, New York: Doubleday, Page.

Smelser, Neil (1959) *Social Change in the Industrial Revolution*, Chicago: University of Chicago Press.

Smith & Hawken (1988) *Smith & Hawken Catalog for Gardeners, Spring 1988*, Mill Valley, Cal.: Smith & Hawken.

Smith, Charles W. (1988) *Auctions: The Social Construction of Value*, New York: Free Press.

Smith, Paul (1988) "Visiting the Banana Republic", in Andrew Ross (ed.) *Universal Abandon? The Politics of Post-Modernism*, Minneapolis: University of Minnesota Press.

Smuts, Robert W. (1971) *Women and Work in America*, New York: Schocken Books.

Snyder, Phillip V. (1985) *December 25th: The Joys of Christmas Past*, New York: Dodd, Mead.

Sofer, Cyril (1965) "Buying and Selling: A Study in the Sociology of Distribution", *Sociological Review* 13: 183–209.

Spooner, Brian (1986) "Weavers and Dealers: The Authenticity of an Oriental Carpet", in Arjun Appadurai (ed.) *The Social Life of Things: Commodities in Cultural Perspective*, New York: Cambridge University Press.

Staples, William G. (1987) "Technology, Control, and the Social Organization of Work at a British Hardware Firm, 1791–1891", *American Journal of Sociology* 93: 62–88.

Stepan-Norris, Judith and Zeitlin, Maurice (1991) "'Red' Unions and 'Bourgeois' Contracts?", *American Journal of Sociology* 96: 1151–200.

Stirrat, R. L. (1992) "'Good Government' and 'the Market'", in Roy Dilley (ed.) *Contesting Markets: Analyses of Ideology, Discourse and Practice*, Edinburgh: Edinburgh University Press.

Stone, Gregory P. (1954) "City Shoppers and Urban Identification: Observations of the Social Psychology of City Life", *American Journal of Sociology* 60: 36–45.

Stone, Katherine (1975) "The Origins of Job Structures in the Steel Industry", in Richard C. Edwards, Michael Reich and David Gordon (eds) *Labor Market Segmentation*, Lexington, Mass.: D. C. Heath.

Strasser, Susan (1989) *Satisfaction Guaranteed: The Making of the American Mass Market*, New York: Pantheon.

Strathern, Marilyn (1988) *The Gender of the Gift: Problems with Women and Problems with Society in Melanesia*, Berkeley: University of California Press.

Streitfeld, David (1987) "Tip o' the Season", *The Washington Post* (December 11): C5.

Sugarman, Carol (1987) "When the Tough Go Shopping: The Supermarket Strategies of Three Budget-Conscious Consumers", *The Washington Post* (September 23): E1, E14.

Sutherland, John (1990) "Authors' Rights and Transatlantic Differences", *The Times Literary Supplement* (May 25–31): 554.

Swanson, Heather (1989) *Medieval Artisans: An Urban Class in Late Medieval England*, Oxford: Basil Blackwell.

Taussig, Michael (1977) "The Genesis of Capitalism amongst a South American Peasantry: Devil's Labor and the Baptism of Money", *Comparative Studies in Society and History* 19: 130–55.

Tentler, Leslie Woodcock (1979) *Wage-Earning Women: Industrial Work and Family Life in the United States, 1900–1930*, New York: Oxford University Press.

Thirsk, Joan (1978) *Economic Policy and Projects: The Development of a Consumer Society in Early Modern England*, Oxford: Clarendon Press.

Thomas, Nicholas (1991) *Entangled Objects: Exchange, Material Culture and Colonialism in the Pacific*, Cambridge, Mass.: Harvard University Press.

—— (1992a) "The Inversion of Tradition", *American Ethnologist* 19: 213–32.

—— (1992b) "Substantivization and Anthropological Discourse: The Transformation of Practices into Institutions in Neotraditional Pacific Societies", in James G. Carrier (ed.) *History and Tradition in Melanesian Anthropology*, Berkeley: University of California Press.

Thompson, E. P. (1967) "Time, Work Discipline and Industrial Capitalism", *Past and Present* 38: 56–98.

—— (1971) "The Moral Economy of the English Crowd in the Eighteenth Century", *Past and Present* 50: 76–136.

Tilly, Louise A. (1984) "Linen Was Their Life: Family Survival Strategies and Parent–Child Relations in Nineteenth-Century France", in Hans Medick and David Warren Sabean (eds) *Interest and Emotion: Essays on the Study of Family and Kinship*, Cambridge: Cambridge University Press.

Trigilia, Carlo (1990) "Work and Politics in the Third Italy's Industrial Districts", in Frank Pyke, Giacomo Becattini and Werner Sengenberger (eds) *Industrial Districts and Inter-Firm Co-operation in Italy*, Geneva: International Institute for Labor Studies.

Trilling, Lionel (1972) *Sincerity and Authenticity*, Cambridge, Mass.: Harvard University Press.

Tucker, Robert C. (ed.) (1978) *The Marx–Engels Reader*, second edn, New York: W. W. Norton.

Turner, Ralph (1976) "The Real Self: From Institution to Impulse", *American Journal of Sociology* 81: 989–1016.

Uehara, Edwina (1990) "Dual Exchange Theory, Social Networks and Informal Social Support", *American Journal of Sociology* 96: 521–57.

Ulrich, Laurel Thatcher (1990) *A Midwife's Tale: The Life of Martha Ballard, Based on Her Diary, 1785–1812*, New York: Random House.

Valadez, Joseph and Clignet, Rémi (1984) "Household Work as an Ordeal: Culture of Standards versus Standardization of Culture", *American Journal of Sociology* 89: 812–35.

Vanek, Joann (1974) "Time Spent in Housework", *Scientific American* 231, 5: 116–20.

Veblen, Thorstein (1927) *The Theory of the Leisure Class*, New York: Vanguard Press.

Walsh, Lorena S. (1983) "Urban Amenities and Rural Sufficiency: Living Standards and Consumer Behavior in the Colonial Chesapeake", *The Journal of Economic History* 43: 109–17.

Walsh, William I. (1986) *The Rise and Decline of the Great Atlantic & Pacific Tea Company*, Secaucus, New Jersey: Lyle Stuart, Inc.

Walton, Penelope (1991) "Textiles", in John W. Blair and Nigel Ramsay (eds) *English Medieval Industries: Craftsmen, Techniques, Products*, London: Hambledon.

Wannamaker, Annette (1989) "Thwarted! Woman Foils Would-be Flag Burner", *The Daily Progress* (Charlottesville, Virginia) (July 5): A1, A14.

Warde, Alan (1990) "Introduction to the Sociology of Consumption", *The Sociology of Consumption*, *Sociology* 24 (special issue): 1–4.

Weatherill, Lorna (1988) *Consumer Behaviour and Material Culture in Britain 1660–1760*, London: Routledge.

Weber, Eugen (1976) *Peasants into Frenchmen: The Modernization of Rural France 1870–1914*, Stanford: Stanford University Press.

Weber, Max (1946 [1922]) "Class, Status, Party", in Hans Gerth and C. Wright Mills (eds) *From Max Weber*, New York: Oxford University Press.

—— (1958 [1904–5]) *The Protestant Ethic and the Spirit of Capitalism*, New York: Charles Scribner's Sons.

Webley, Paul, Lea, Stephen E. G. and Portalska, Renata (1983) "The Unacceptability of Money as a Gift", *Journal of Economic Psychology* 4: 223–38.

Weiner, Annette (1992) *Inalienable Possessions: The Paradox of Keeping-While-Giving*, Los Angeles: University of California Press.

Weiss, E. B. (1956 [1952]) "Sales People Can't Be Trained – And Shouldn't Be", in John W. Wingate and Arnold Corbin (eds) *Changing Patterns in Retailing*, Homewood, Illinois: Richard D. Irwin. (First published in *Fortune*, November, 1952.)

Wellman, Barry and Wortley, Scot (1990) "Different Strokes from Different Folks: Community Ties and Social Support", *American Journal of Sociology* 96: 558–88.

Werbner, Pnina (1990) *The Migration Process: Capital, Gifts and Offerings among British Pakistanis*, Oxford: Berg.

Westerfield, R. B. (1915) "Middlemen in English Business 1660–1760", *Transactions of the Connecticut Academy of Arts and Sciences* 19.

van de Wetering, M. (1984) "The Popular Concept of 'Home' in Nineteenth-Century America", *Journal of American Studies* 18, 1: 5–28.

Whyte, William H. (1956) *The Organization Man*, New York: Simon & Schuster.

Willan, T. S. (1967) *The English Coasting Trade, 1600–1750*, Manchester: Manchester University Press.

—— (1976) *The Inland Trade*, Manchester: Manchester University Press.

Williams, Brett (1988) *Upscaling Downtown: Stalled Gentrification in Washington, D.C.*, Ithaca: Cornell University Press.

Williams, Rosalind H. (1982) *Dream Worlds: Mass Consumption in Late Nineteenth-Century France*, Berkeley: University of California Press.

Willmott, Peter and Young, Michael (1960) *Family and Class in a London Suburb*, London: Routledge & Kegan Paul.

Wills, Garry (1978) *Inventing America: Jefferson's Declaration of Independence*, Garden City, New York: Doubleday.

Winship, Janice (1983) "'Options – For the Way you Want to Live Now', or a Magazine for Superwoman", *Theory, Culture and Society* 1, 3: 44–65.

Winstanley, Michael J. (1983) *The Shopkeeper's World, 1830–1914*, Manchester: Manchester University Press.

Woolfolk, Mary E., Castellan, William and Brooks, Charles I. (1983) "Pepsi versus Coke: Labels, not Tastes, Prevail", *Psychological Reports* 52: 185–6.

Woolworth, F. W., Company (1954) *Woolworth's First 75 Years*, New York: F. W. Woolworth Company.

Yamey, Basil S. (1954) "The Evolution of Shopkeeping", *Lloyds Bank Review* 31 (January): 31–44.

Young, Michael and Willmott, Peter (1986 [1957]) *Family and Kinship in East London*, rev. edn, London: Routledge & Kegan Paul.

Zelizer, Viviana A. (1989) "The Social Meaning of Money: 'Special Monies'", *American Journal of Sociology* 95: 342–77.

Zetka, James R., Jr (1992) "Work Organization and Wildcat Strikes in the U.S. Automobile Industry, 1946 to 1963", *American Sociological Review* 57: 214–26.

Zimmerman, Max M. (1937) *Super Market, Spectacular Exponent of Mass Distribution*, New York: Super Market Publishing Company.

Zukin, Sharon (1990) "Socio-Spatial Prototypes of a New Organization of Consumption: The Role of Real Cultural Capital", *Sociology* 24: 37–56.

INDEX